THE FILM PHOTOGRAPHER'S HANDBOOK

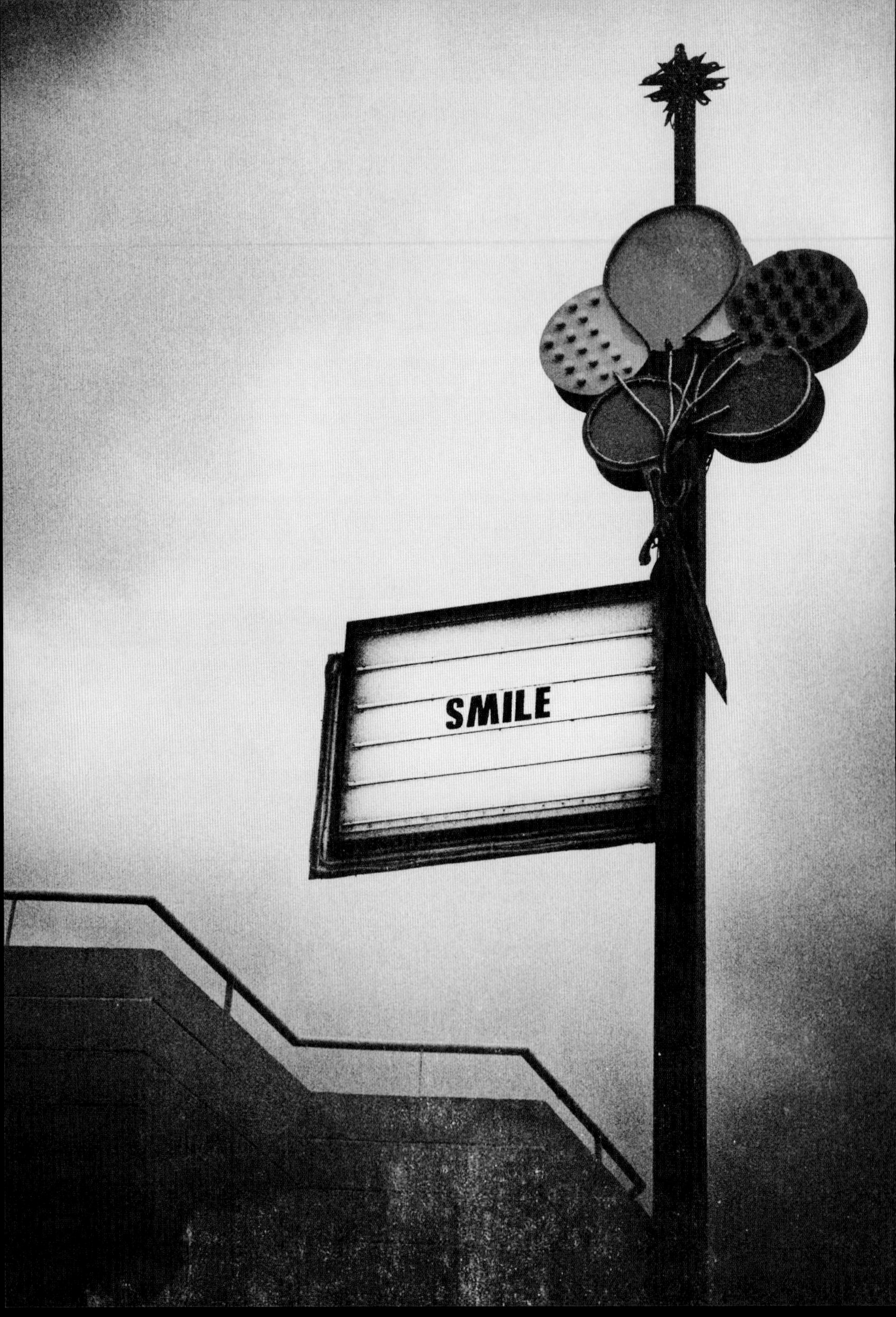
SMILE

THE FILM PHOTOGRAPHER'S HANDBOOK

COMPOSE • DEVELOP • PRINT

STEVE BAVISTER

CHRIS GATCUM

DAVID & CHARLES
— PUBLISHING —

www.davidandcharles.com

CONTENTS

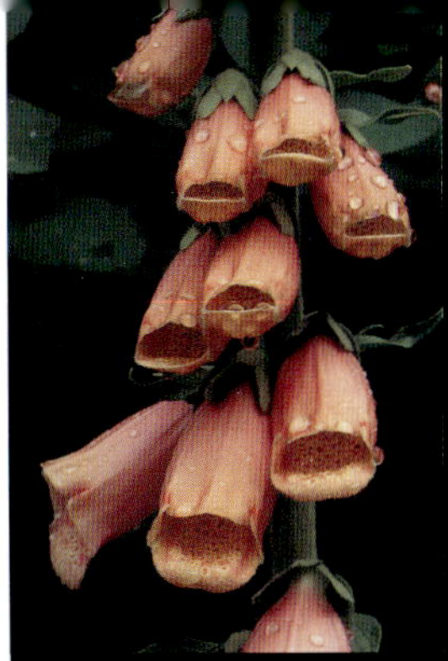

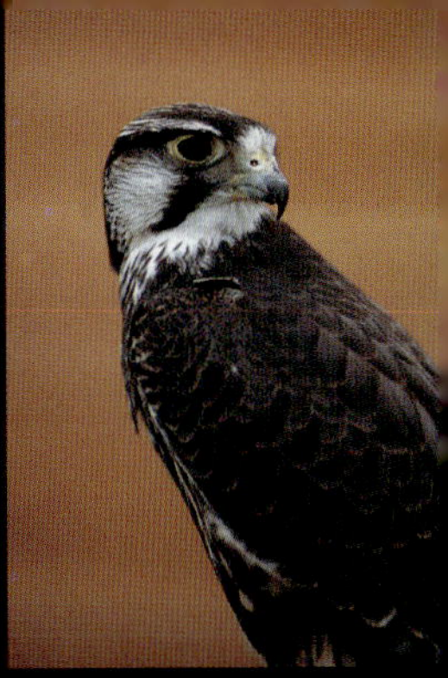

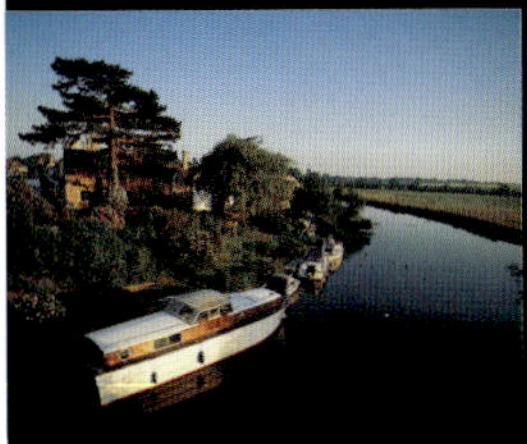

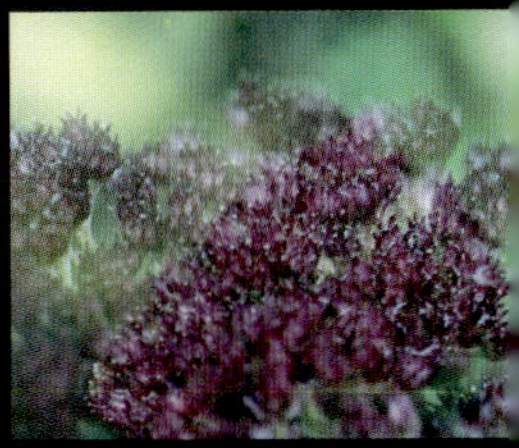

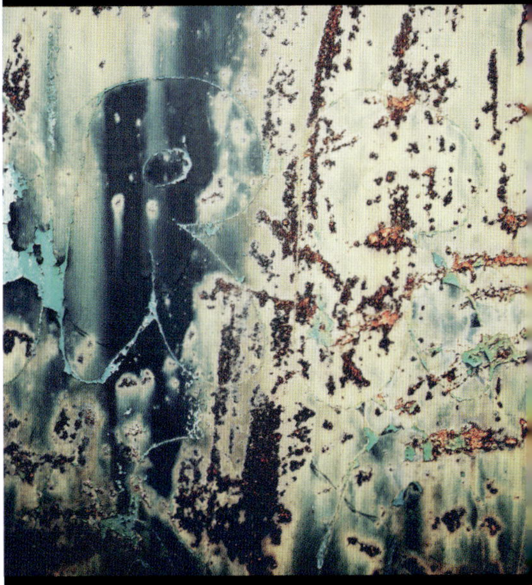

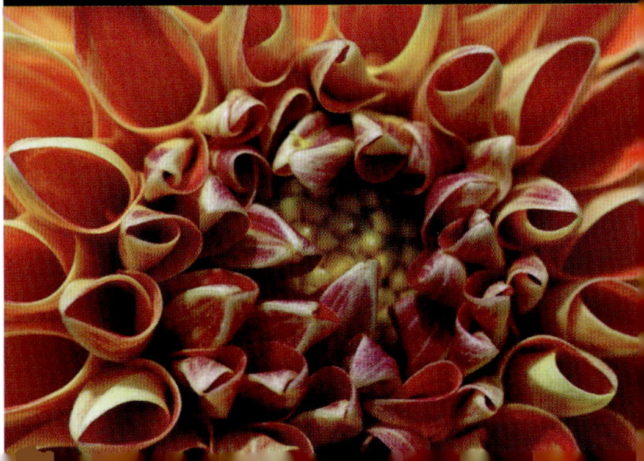

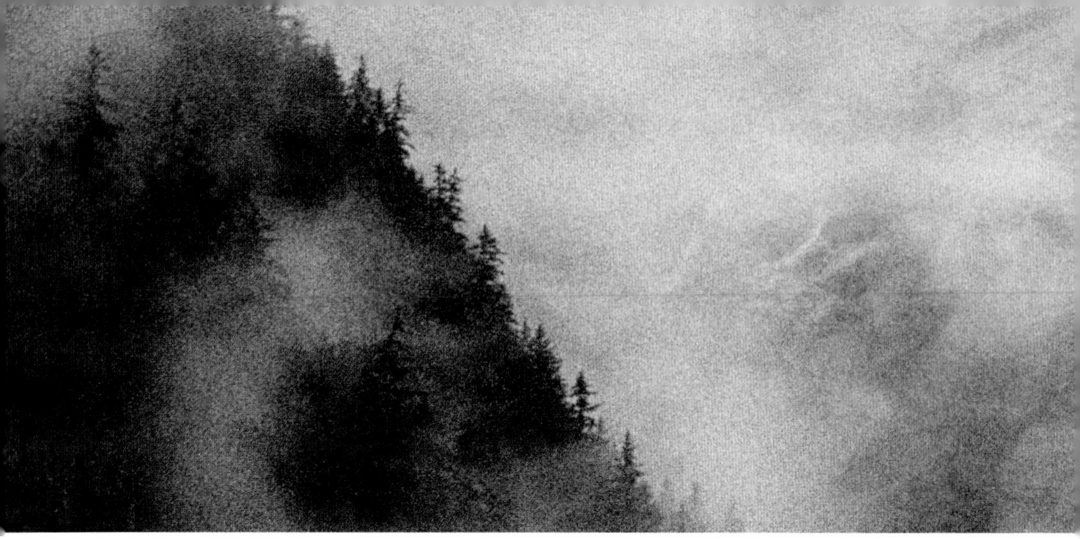

INTRODUCTION

In an era defined by rapid technological change, it's remarkable how long film has endured as a creative and practical medium. Since the early 20th century, film photography has evolved through numerous formats, camera designs, and manufacturing philosophies – yet its appeal has remained surprisingly constant.

Film's early years were dominated by large, heavy plate and roll-film cameras that required patience and skill. Although they produced impressive image quality, their bulk limited spontaneity, so manufacturers sought ways to make cameras more portable and accessible.

By the 1920s and 30s, smaller roll-film and early 'miniature' formats started to appear, offering an alternative to traditional equipment. The cameras that used them were mechanically simple. Photographers had to manually judge exposure, wind their own film, and often compose their images through a separate viewfinder. Yet these limitations encouraged skill and experimentation, and their simplicity made the cameras reliable in challenging conditions, especially as interchangeable lenses became more common.

Perhaps one of the greatest developments in film photography was the refinement of the single-lens reflex (SLR) design. Although the concept originated in the 19th century, practical SLRs did not emerge until the mid-20th century. By allowing photographers to look directly through the taking lens, SLRs merged accuracy, flexibility, and intuitive handling. Over subsequent decades, manufacturers added features that reshaped photography, such as integrated light meters, automatic exposure modes, fast and precise autofocus systems, motorised film winding, and eventually, advanced electronics that made cameras increasingly intelligent.

Automation played a key role in photography's widespread adoption, as techniques that once required specialist knowledge became automatic or selectable through simple controls. Microprocessor-driven cameras offered multiple exposure modes, sophisticated metering patterns, and customisable flash control. Even compact point-and-shoot cameras evolved from basic boxes into capable devices with zoom lenses and reliable autofocus.

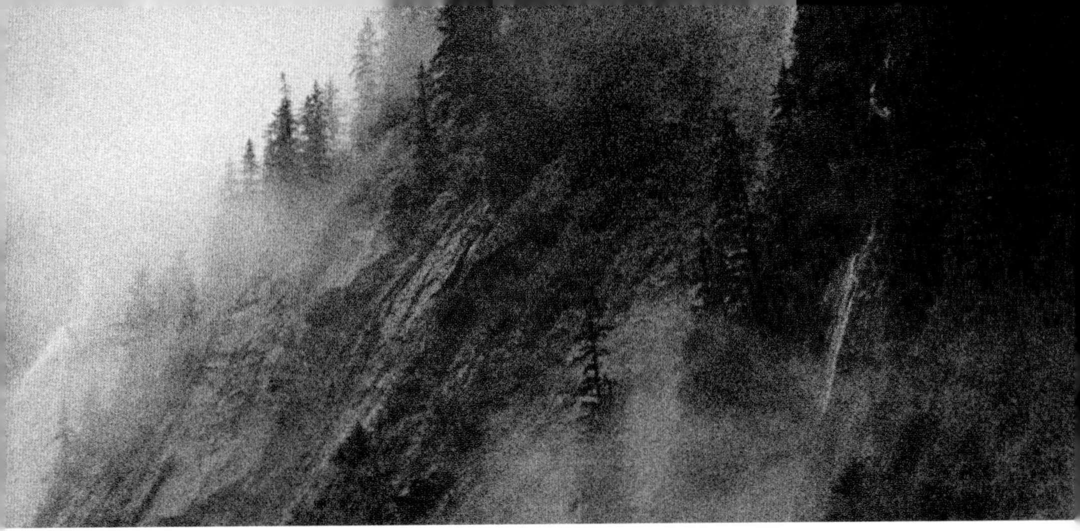

Film technology also advanced. While early emulsions produced grainy black-and-white images with low sensitivity, over time they became finer-grained, sharper, and available in a range of speeds – and colour. The result was that regardless of skill level, anyone could achieve sharp, well-exposed images at the touch of a button, and the anxiety of wondering whether a photo would 'come out' gradually disappeared.

These sophisticated analogue cameras paved the way for digital capture, at which point photography got fast. Perhaps too fast. Now, before you've even taken your finger off a digital camera's shutter button or your phone screen, your picture's in front of you, waiting to be prodded and poked into submission. That speed is undeniably handy, but it's also a bit... well, exhausting.

Maybe that's why you're here. Maybe this is why film – this old-fashioned, allegedly out-of-date medium – is starting to look tempting. Certainly, part of the appeal of film photography today lies in the creative experience it offers; in the backwards step it forces you to take in order to produce a well-exposed photograph. There is something appealing about a process that doesn't sprint ahead of you; that asks you to slow down just enough to notice what you're doing.

A process that lets you breathe.

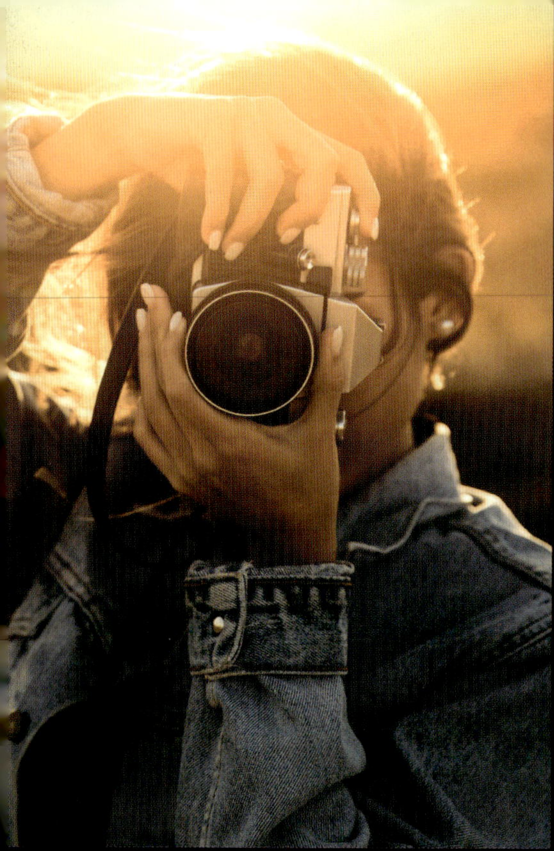

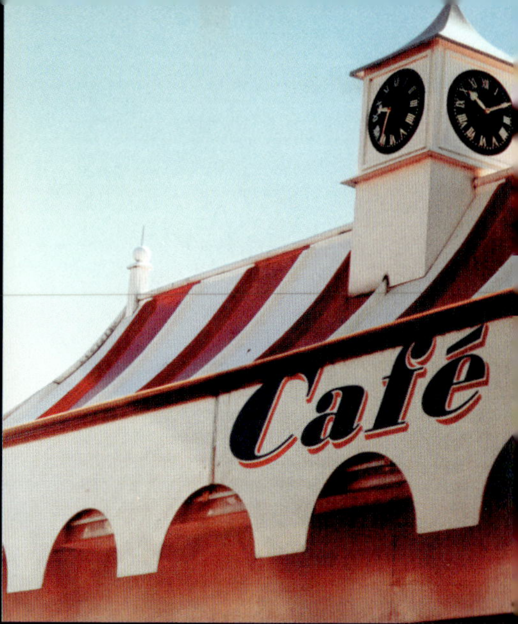
Café

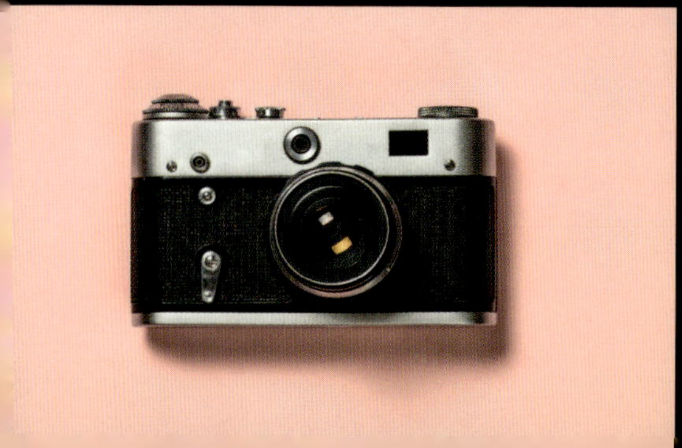

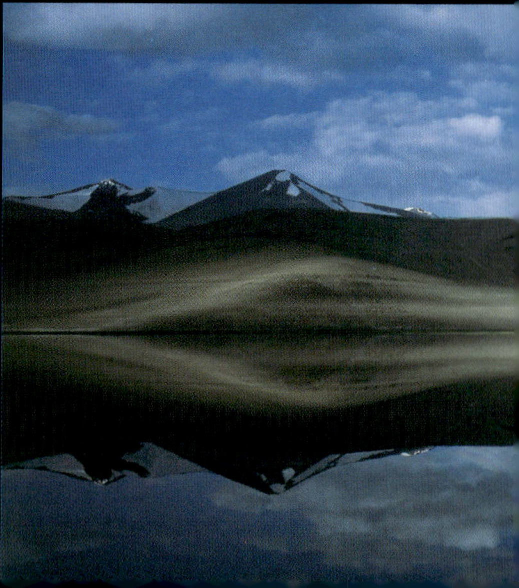

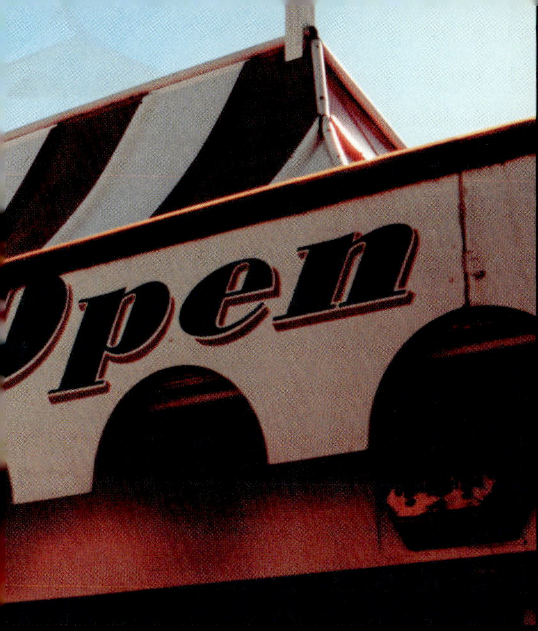
Open

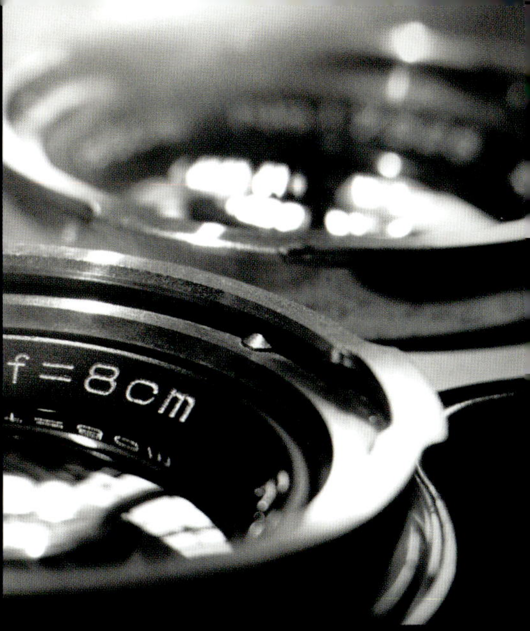
f=8cm

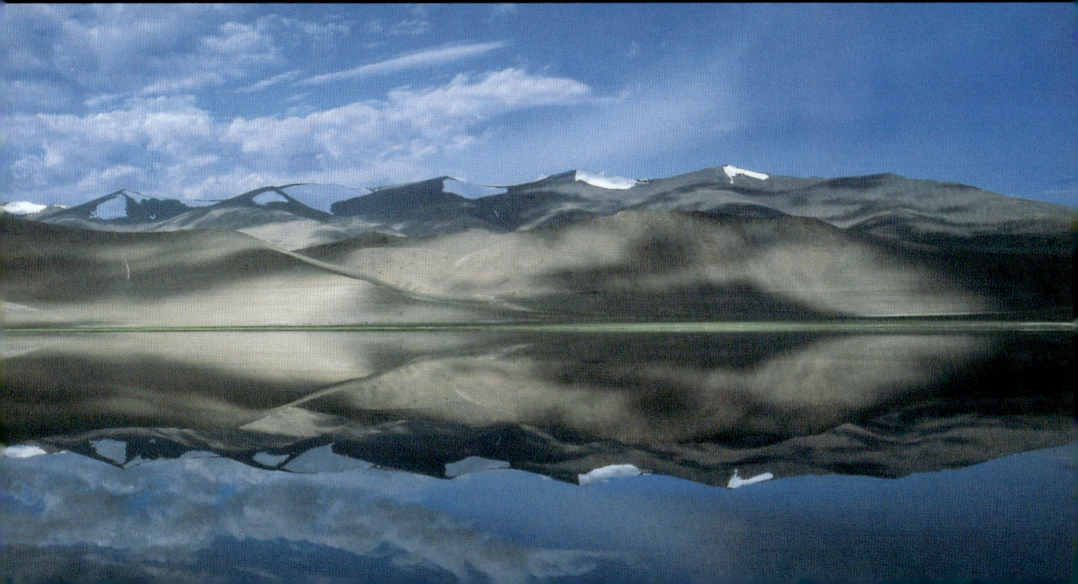

THE 35MM SLR

Single lens reflex cameras, or SLRs as they're more commonly known, are the perfect choice for anyone who is serious about photography. The unparalleled control and versatility you get with an SLR makes it possible to tackle virtually any subject and achieve almost any effect you can imagine.

SLRs generally fall into two categories: sophisticated electronic models bursting with advanced technological features, and mechanical models that keep things simple. Whichever you opt for, a key SLR advantage is its reflex viewing system, (see below). This provides a WYSIWYG (What You See Is What You Get) viewing system that enables you to compose your pictures with great accuracy (although some viewfinders show fractionally less of the scene than will actually appear in the finished picture).

What this means is that as you switch from one lens to another, the viewfinder shows exactly what each lens is 'seeing'. The same is true of anything else you fit in the optical path, from filters to close-up accessories, which allows you to make adjustments until you get the effect you want.

On SLRs that have a depth-of-field preview option, you can also get a visual idea of what will appear sharp and what will be out of focus in the finished picture.

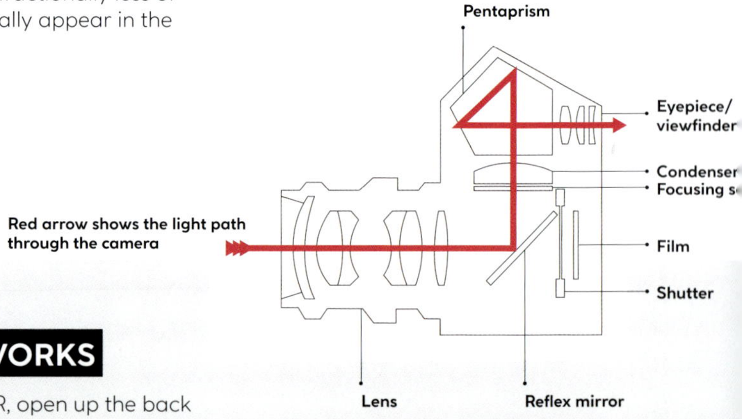

HOW AN SLR WORKS

Take the lens off an SLR, open up the back (check there's no film in it first), and you'll get some idea of how an SLR works. The image seen through the lens is reflected upwards by a mirror at 45°. It then passes through a pentaprism – a block of glass with five sides. This shows an image in the viewfinder that is the right way up, and not laterally reversed, which is what you would see if the pentaprism was not there.

When you take a photograph, the mirror flips up, and the shutter opens to let the light that forms your image pass through to the film. Once the exposure time is complete, the shutter closes and the mirror flips back down. This procedure happens every time you take a picture.

EXTENDIBILITY

An SLR camera body is only the beginning. It is the foundation upon which an entire camera 'system' can be built, and as you get more involved in photography you can extend your system to allow you to do more with your SLR.

What you buy will be determined by the subjects you like to shoot and the kinds of pictures you want to take, but one of the key ways to expand your options is to invest in additional lenses. Most electronic SLRs come with a standard zoom lens (from 28mm or 35mm up to 70, 80, 90, or 105mm). Manual cameras typically come with a 50mm prime lens. While this is great for general picture-taking, and it will handle many of your requirements, sooner or later you will most likely want to add more lenses.

Fitting a lens with a wider angle of view, for example, will allow you to include more in the frame and open up perspective for a more dramatic image. The ultimate wide-angle lens is a fisheye lens, which captures a full 180°, including – if you're not careful – your toes and the tips of your fingers.

Conversely, a long telephoto lens will allow you to pull in distant subjects, such as Formula 1 action or birds on the wing. They will also enable you to isolate a subject in sharp focus against a heavily blurred background.

Between these extremes lies a plethora of lenses that can take your photography in a myriad of directions. You can also extend your system with accessories that allow you to take close-up photographs, illuminate large areas by using an add-on flash, or creatively modify images by fitting different filters over the lens. With an SLR, the options are almost limitless!

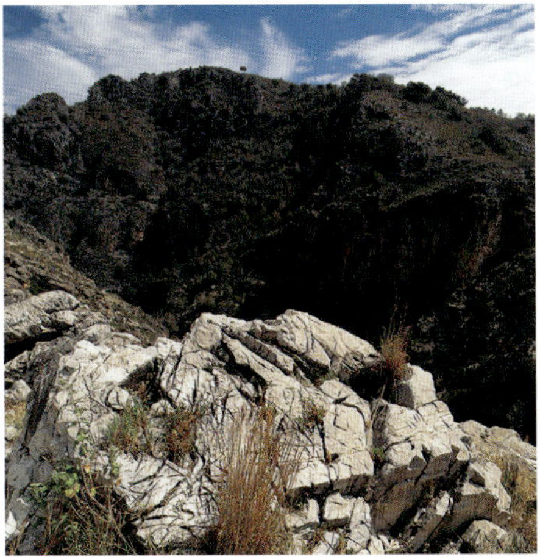

LANDSCAPES

If you enjoy landscape photography, a wide-angle lens will probably be an early addition to your camera system. Here, a 24mm lens was used, but even wider focal lengths are available.

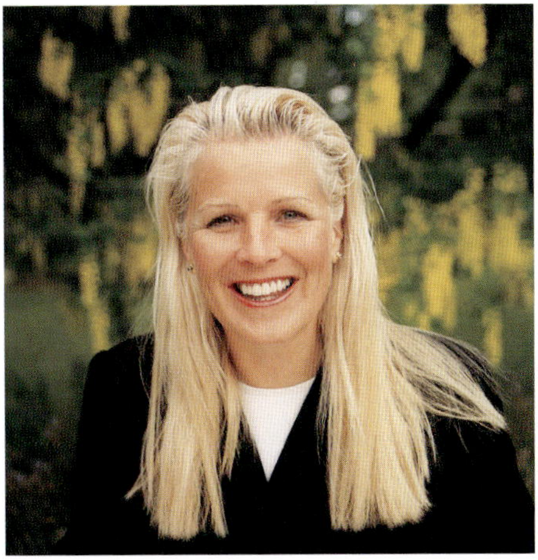

PORTRAITS

Telephoto lenses are widely used in portrait photography to help isolate the subject. Most camera systems offer plenty of telephoto options, covering focal lengths of 90–1000mm or more.

ELECTRONIC SLRS

Electronic SLR cameras are the direct predecessors to modern digital SLRs and, by extension, today's mirrorless digital cameras (albeit with a different viewing system). Consequently, they will be familiar to anyone who has used a DSLR or mirrorless camera.

Like their digital counterparts, SLRs typically have a wide range of exposure metering options that allow you to fine-tune your exposure. They offer a range of shooting modes that make it easy to select the optimum combination of shutter speed and aperture. Their autofocus systems help to ensure the right part of the scene is sharply focused. And a built-in flash provides controlled light whenever you need it – and much more.

Generally speaking, these sophisticated SLRs will let you take as little or as much control as you want. The majority of them can be used as 'point-and-shoot' cameras if you choose, so that as you press the shutter release, all the technicalities are handled for you automatically: the light is measured and the exposure set, the lens is accurately focused, and the built-in flash is activated if necessary and primed ready to fire. Then, when the picture has been taken, the film is automatically wound on ready for the next shot. Combined with automatic film loading, this makes life incredibly easy, and you're almost guaranteed decent results.

Typical features on an electronic SLR

1. **Viewfinder** Typically showing 92–95 per cent of the actual picture area, it is surrounded by exposure, focusing, and other information. This means you don't have to take your eye away from it when making adjustments.
2. **Exposure compensation** Systems for fine-tuning exposure include AE-lock, exposure compensation, and sometimes auto-exposure bracketing.
3. **Custom functions** Some advanced SLRs allow you to tailor operation to your own preferences – such as by leaving the film leader out or winding it in when rewinding.
4. **Rewind button** Most electronic cameras rewind the film automatically when it reaches the end, but this button lets you rewind it mid-roll if you need to.

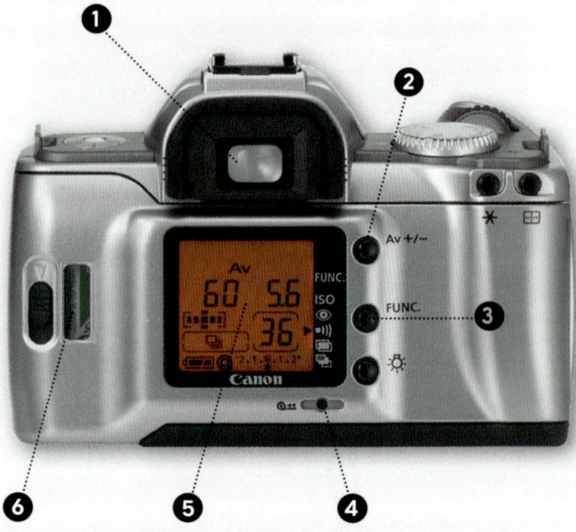

5. **LCD (liquid crystal display) panel** Provides information about shutter speed, aperture, and other aspects of operation.

6. **Film window** Lets you see what film is loaded. On most electronic cameras the film speed (ISO) is set automatically via a DX coding system, but some provide an override to allow the film to be 'pushed' or 'pulled'.

7. **Zoom lens** Most electronic SLRs come with a standard zoom lens that is ideal for general picture-taking.

8. **Focal length** Zoom lenses tell you the longest and shortest focal length available, along with a number of common intermediate settings, such as the 50mm standard focal length.

9. **Shutter release** Gentle pressure activates metering, firmer pressure takes the picture. The shutter release often acts as a focus lock, too.

10. **Input dial** Used to make changes to the aperture, shutter speed, and other settings, depending on the mode the camera is set to.

11. **Exposure mode selector** To some extent, the more exposure modes the better. There are usually four creative modes and a number of subject-based modes, often selected via a mode dial.

12. **Accessory hotshoe** To accommodate a more powerful flash.

13. **Motorised film advance** Most electronic SLRs have automated film loading and advance, with a choice of taking a single shot or a continuous burst of images when the shutter release is held down.

14. **Lens release** Allows the lens to be removed and swapped for other optics.

15. **Built-in flash** This usually has a guide number of 12m/ISO 100, sufficient for shots up to around 3–4m (10–13ft).

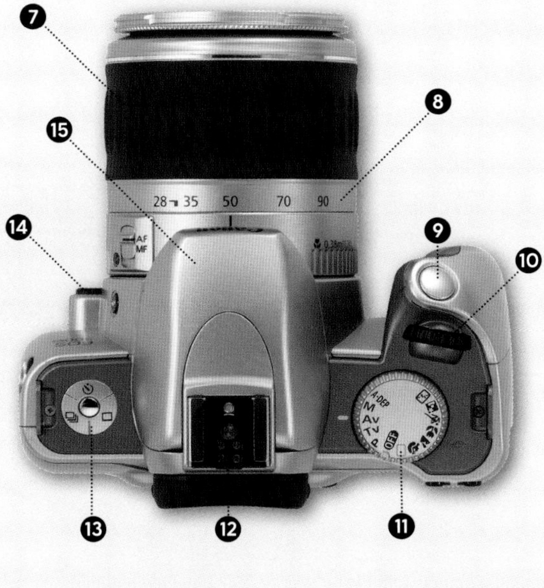

MECHANICAL SLRS

For many photographers, the whole point of using an SLR is to decide the settings themselves, so that their images turn out exactly as they like. One of the most important ways of taking control is by selecting the shutter speed and aperture, which determines not only the exposure, but also the way in which movement is recorded and how much of the subject appears sharp in the photograph.

Although most fully featured electronic SLRs have a manual shooting mode that lets you take control when you want to, mechanical or semi-mechanical SLR models offer less automation (some offer none). The exposure metering systems tend to be less sophisticated than those in fully electronic cameras, and may only have one or two different shooting modes. The focus also has to be set manually.

This places greater emphasis on the photographer, because the camera simply doesn't have an electronic 'brain' to help you out. This may sound daunting, but it will encourage you to think about what you are doing, and help to develop and improve your skills to become a better photographer – there's no 'lazy' option to fall back on.

Typical features on a mechanical SLR

1. **Viewfinder** Most mechanical cameras have a viewfinder screen with a simple split microprism focus aid on it. Some advanced models let you change the focusing screen so you can use a choice of focusing aids.
2. **Film reminder** A simple frame that holds the printed card from the end of a film box, providing you with a reminder of the film that's loaded.
3. **Flash sync socket (behind cover)** Also known as a PC (Prontor-Compur) socket. Used to attach a flash via a PC sync cable.
4. **Lens** Most mechanical cameras come with a 50mm prime lens, otherwise known as a standard lens; this camera has a 28mm wide-angle lens fitted.
5. **Aperture** A ring around the lens lets you set the aperture.

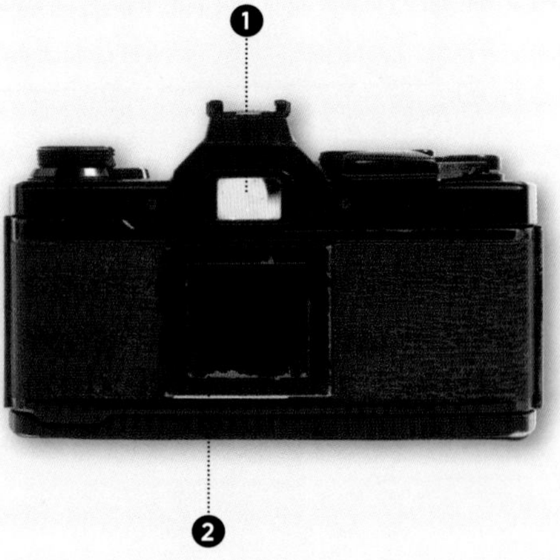

6. **Focusing scale** Indicates the distance the lens is focused at.
7. **Shutter speed** The shutter speed is often set using a dial on top of the camera, but the Olympus OM camera (shown here) uses a ring around the lens dial instead. The range of shutter speed varies depending on the camera model. Here, the range runs from B (Bulb) to 1/1000 sec.
8. **Exposure compensation** Allows you to adjust the exposure (here by +2 stops).
9. **Film speed setting** Sets the ISO rating of the film so the camera's exposure meter knows how sensitive it is.
10. **Shutter release button** Pressed to make an exposure. On mechanical cameras, most shutter release buttons are threaded to accept a mechanical cable release (as opposed to an electronic cable release).
11. **Frame counter** Lets you know how many frames you've shot, and therefore how many are left on the roll of film.
12. **Film advance crank** Also known as the 'wind-on lever'; used to wind the film on to the next frame, once a photograph has been taken.
13. **Rewind button** Releases the winding mechanism so the film can be rewound manually.
14. **Accessory hotshoe** For attaching a more powerful flash unit, or accessories such as a hotshoe bubble level.
15. **Mode selector** Allows you to switch between the camera's shooting modes, such as Auto, Manual, and Program. Depending on the camera, this may be a dial or a selection lever (as here), or it may not appear at all if the camera is a manual model.
16. **Rewind crank** For rewinding film back into the cassette when you reach the end of the roll.

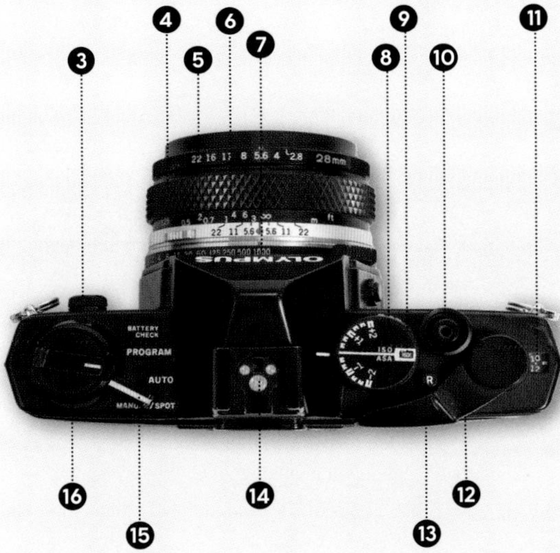

BUYING AN SLR

The first 35mm SLR was launched almost 100 years ago, and since then a wide range of SLRs from competing manufacturers have appeared on the market. These largely fall into two categories – electronic and mechanical – with the former being the most recent and the latter being older – sometimes considerably so. Between the two lies an array of cameras with modest electronic functionality, primarily in terms of exposure metering options. With so many different features available, choosing the right model can be confusing, but here are some factors to consider.

Brand

From around the 1970s to the early 2000s, there were five main Japanese players in the SLR film camera market: Canon, Nikon, Minolta, Olympus, and Pentax. Between them, they launched numerous 35mm camera bodies, lenses, and accessories, and most of these are still available today on the second-hand market.

The popularity of these camera systems meant that a host of third-party manufacturers added their own lenses and accessories, so when it comes to building a comprehensive camera 'system' for your area of interest, it isn't difficult.

However, these weren't the only companies making 35mm SLRs, and there are countless cameras (and lenses) from less mainstream manufacturers. Some have a proprietary lens mount, as is the case with some Praktica models, while others utilised existing lens mounts; later Soviet Zenits use the Pentax K mount, for example.

Whatever your preference, do your homework before you decide. There's plenty of information online about the various brand and camera model differences.

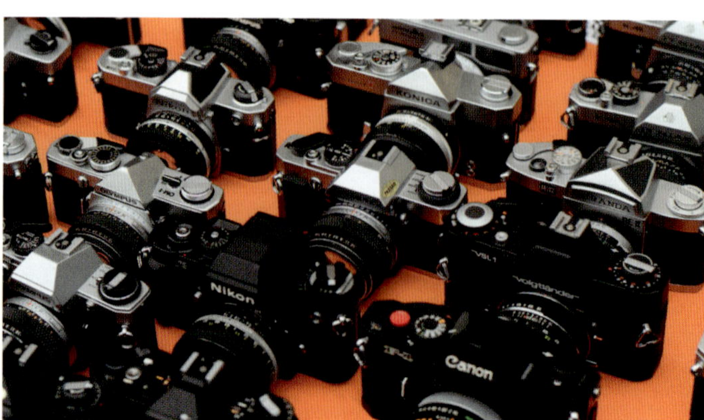

HUGE CHOICE

Countless companies made manual 35mm SLRs and lenses in the heyday of film photography. Many were interchangeable with the cameras and lenses from the 'big five' Japanese manufacturers.

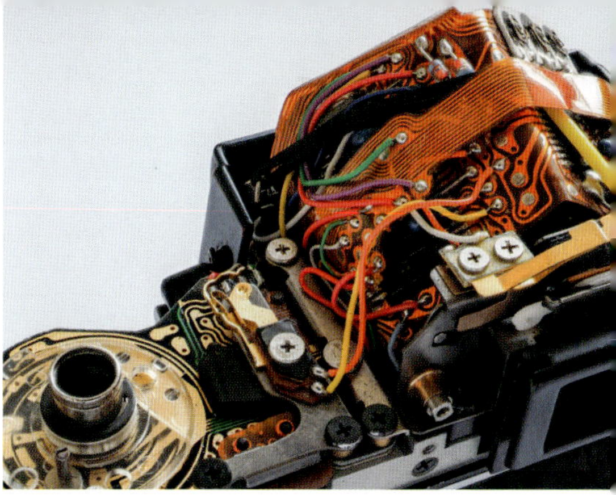

DETERIORATION

Flexible printed circuits (FPCs) can deteriorate over time, leading to intermittent faults or even complete camera failure.

Automation

As SLR technology evolved, cameras gained increasingly sophisticated electronic controls. By the early 2000s, even the cheapest entry level cameras had multiple exposure modes, multi-point autofocus systems, and intelligent flash control. Combined with zoom lenses, these cameras were easy to use and incredibly popular.

However, fast-forward 25–30 years, and what once made these cameras so desirable is now their Achilles heel. In some instances, the batteries are simply no longer available, and if they are, they are both specialist and expensive. The electronics, too, can be a weakness, as spare parts are no longer made and there is a dwindling supply of 'spares' – cameras that can be plundered for them. There are also fewer people who are capable of repairing these cameras. The upshot is that one minor knock can turn what was once a high-end electronic SLR into a camera-shaped paperweight.

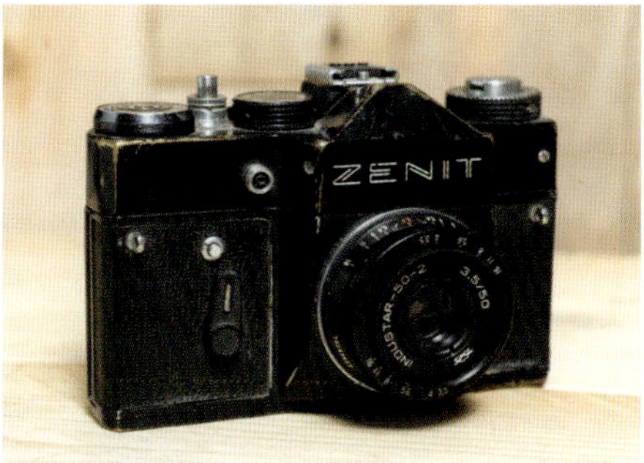

MECHANICAL

This battered Soviet Zenit SLR was unearthed in a charity shop for about the same price as a large coffee. Despite its poor cosmetics, it works just fine, mainly because there are no fancy exposure modes or automated systems, so very little to go wrong.

While slightly older, manual-focus cameras have fewer electronic systems inside them, they are not immune to the ageing process. The flexible printed circuits (FPCs) that are typically used in the exposure metering circuitry can become brittle over time and eventually deteriorate, no matter how well a camera is looked after. Depending on the model, this can lead to minor issues that don't necessarily affect the camera's basic functionality, through to complete failure.

By comparison, fully mechanical cameras are much simpler tools with far less to go wrong. They may not offer the same level of automation, but it's far easier to repair a mechanism that relies on springs and cogs than one that relies on complex circuitry – something that is definitely worth bearing in mind when you're choosing a camera.

Camera checks

Regardless of the camera you ultimately decide on, there are a few simple checks you should make to ensure it's working. Obviously, if you're buying online, it isn't possible to 'try before you buy', but any reputable retailer will provide a warranty of some sort, and most online marketplaces have strict rules about mis-selling items and returns. If in doubt, use a credit card for your purchase to give an added layer of buyer protection.

In other instances – at a car boot sale, charity shop, or a private sale – you can get 'hands on' with the camera before you buy, in which case the following list is easier to run through:

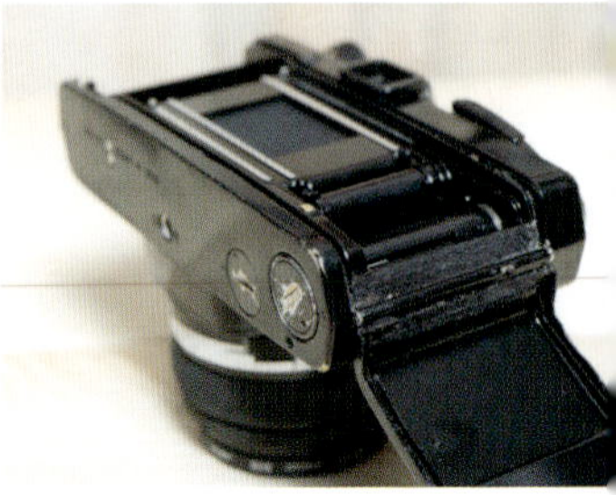

LEAKING?

The hinge on the camera back is prone to leaking light, so be sure to check the light seals. This one needs replacing.

- **What does it look like?** The condition of a camera can give you an idea of the life it's had; whether it's been nestled in a padded camera bag most of its life or carries the dents of hard use.
- **Does the shutter fire?** Press the shutter release button and see if the mirror flips up and back down again. If it does, that's a good sign; if it doesn't, it could simply be that the battery needs changing. If a fresh battery doesn't fix it, the camera may have a serious issue.
- **Test the shutter speeds:** If the shutter is working, try it out at different speeds. If you adjust the shutter speed in 2-stop increments you should be able to hear a difference when you fire the camera, especially at slower speeds.
- **Check the meter:** Aim the camera towards and then away from a light source, and see if the exposure indicated in the viewfinder changes. Adjust the aperture and shutter speed to see if that makes a difference as well. Every adjustment should alter the exposure.
- **Check the rest:** Check all the other buttons, dials, and knobs are working as they should. If a camera's sat around for a while, things may have tightened up, but should loosen with use (or a clean).
- **Look inside:** Open the camera back and check the light seals (also known as light traps). On a mechanical camera, these are likely to be made from black foam or velvet, and typically run around the film door and hinge, creating a light-tight seal. Perished light seals will need replacing before you can use the camera, unless you want light to leak in and fog your film. Replacing light seals is something you can do yourself for minimal cost. Note that electronic SLRs may not have light seals, and might rely on moulded channels in the polycarbonate camera body to prevent light leaks.

Lens checks

Whether you're buying an SLR with a lens, or purchasing an additional lens, a few preliminary checks will let you know if it's working as it should be.

- **Physical condition:** As with a camera, the first thing is to take in the general condition of the lens. Are the rubber zoom and focusing rings heavily worn, indicating heavy use? Or clean, with a crisp grip, suggesting lighter use? Has the lens been dropped at any point? A dent in the filter ring at the front is a sure-fire indicator the lens has had a knock, and may prevent you from using filters.
- **Is the glass clean?** Check the surface of the front and rear lens elements for scratches and marks that can't be removed. Then hold the lens up to a light and look through it. A few specks of dust inside the lens are unlikely to be a major problem, but lens fungus, which can appear as wispy white spots or webs, is a more serious problem that will require expensive professional intervention.
- **Is the focus/zoom ring smooth?** Turn the focus ring from end to end a few times. It should be smooth, without any noticeable tight spots or sudden loose spots. If it's a zoom lens, the zoom should be equally smooth throughout its range.
- **Check the aperture:** Open the back of the camera, select a slow shutter speed (say 1/4 sec), and take a series of shots at different aperture settings. Aim the camera towards a window or light and look through the back of the camera as you shoot. You should see the aperture close down when an exposure is made, and then open again. Check that the aperture not only changes at different settings, but also snaps back open again after each shot. If it's slow to open, the lens may need lubricating (and servicing). If the aperture is stuck at a single setting, the mechanism may be broken and the whole lens require repair.

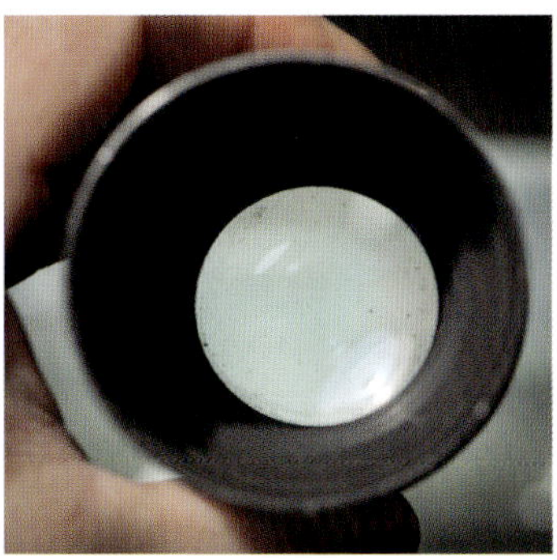

THROUGH THE LENS

If you open a lens to its widest aperture setting and hold it up to the light you will be able to see any defects. This lens has a lot of grime trapped inside!

COSMETICS

The cosmetic condition of a camera and lens will give you an idea of whether it's been looked after or not. This Praktica kit looks like it's had a hard life, but the camera still works.

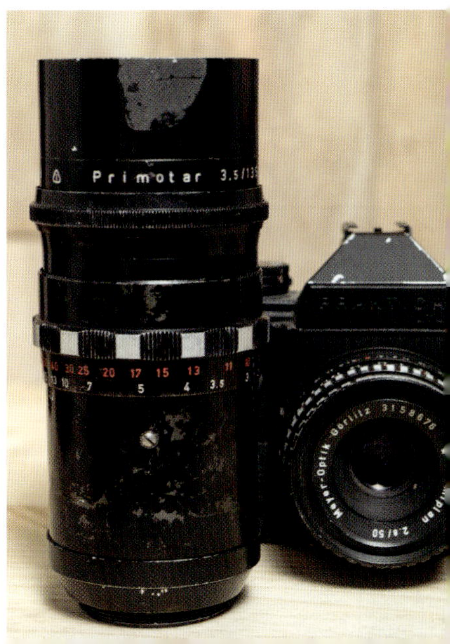

THE 35MM RANGEFINDER

The majority of 35mm cameras bought and used today are SLRs, but for some photographers there are more specialist cameras that will be the perfect tool.

You might have thought that with the advent of 35mm SLRs and compacts, traditional rangefinder designs would have faded away. However, they're still extremely popular, despite their high prices and the limited number of models on the market. They are particularly favoured by reportage and documentary photographers because, with no mirror to flip up and down, the shutter is far quieter than on a reflex camera.

Like an SLR, rangefinder cameras have interchangeable lenses, although the range of focal lengths is usually more limited, particularly when it comes to telephoto options. Rangefinder cameras are much smaller than an SLR, but more versatile than a compact camera (see over the page). In many ways they are an ideal compromise between the two.

The rangefinder focusing system is very different to the reflex viewing on an SLR. Instead of having a single image, a rangefinder system presents you with two images that you have to coincide to bring the lens to focus. This can take some getting used to, but it is quick and easy once you've got the hang of it.

As well as classic designs from Leica, which are the epitome of high-quality rangefinder cameras, there are also superb systems from Contax and Voigtländer at a more modest cost. Soviet FED and Zorki cameras offer a low-cost path into rangefinder ownership for the budget-conscious buyer, but their build quality and reliability tends to match their price. Some Soviet rangefinders are deliberately styled as Leica copies, complete with Leica logos and fake serial numbers (but most definitely *not* Leica performance). While most of these are marketed as 'copies' – and priced accordingly – fake Leicas with premium price tags are also in circulation.

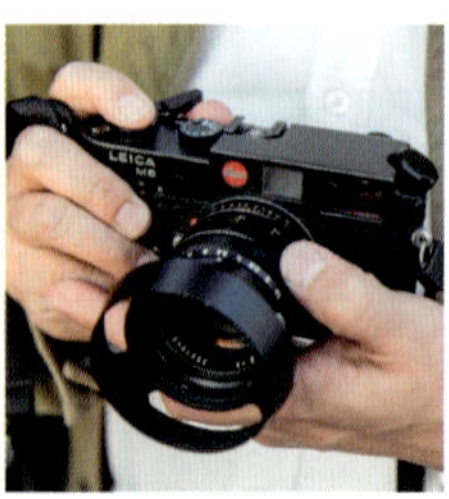

LEICA

The Leica name is synonymous with high-quality rangefinder cameras and outstanding lenses.

FAKING IT

Failing shutters and light leaks are common in Soviet cameras. This image was taken on a faux Luftwaffe Leica (in reality a vintage Soviet FED camera with Leica branding).

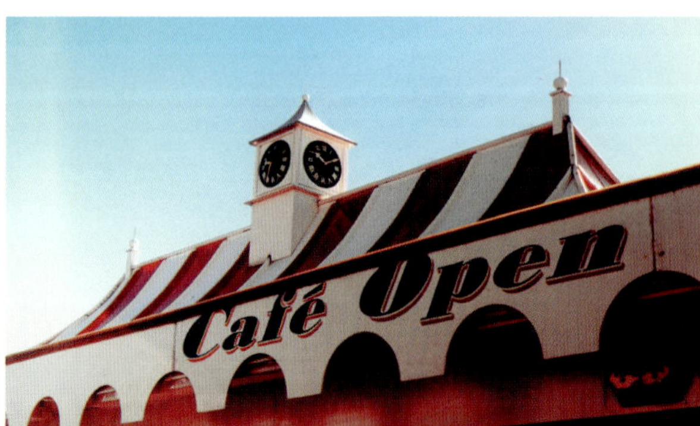

HASSELBLAD XPAN

While it is possible to produce long, thin panoramic prints from standard 35mm negatives, either by printing conventionally or cropping on a computer, the quality isn't good because a large part of the picture area is lost from the top and bottom of the image. But if the idea of taking pictures of this kind appeals, there's a better (though considerably more expensive) option.

The Hasselblad XPan is a panoramic rangefinder camera that was produced in conjunction with Fujifilm (in Japan it is known as the Fujifilm TX-1). It uses standard 35mm film, but produces a negative size of 24 x 65mm, which is almost twice as wide as a standard 35mm frame.

The XPan is a beautiful piece of equipment, built to the highest standards. It has a comprehensive specification, including aperture priority and manual operation, shutter speeds from 8–1/1000 sec, exposure compensations and auto-bracketing, and integral film winder. Most importantly, there's a choice of three interchangeable lenses: 30mm, 45mm, and 90mm.

As well as being able to shoot panoramic compositions (giving you 21 panoramic shots on a 36-exposure roll of film), you can also take standard 35mm full-frame images, which allows you to use it more like a regular rangefinder camera. This makes the XPan (or TX-1) extremely versatile, and a great buy if you can afford it.

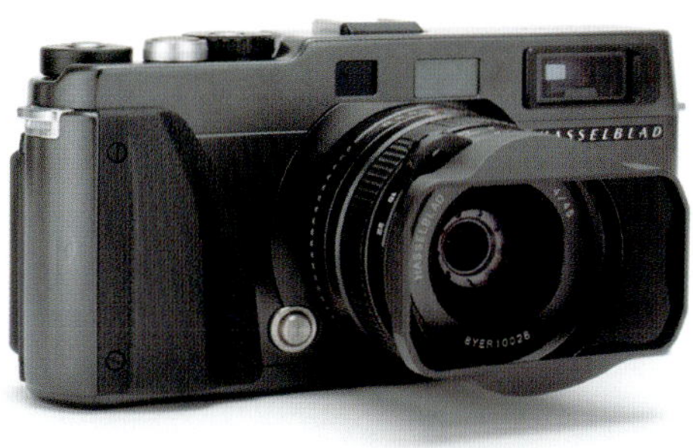

XPAN

The Hasselblad XPan allows you to take panoramic images using standard 35mm film.

LANDSCAPES

Panoramic compositions are ideal for landscape photography, especially when you want to give a sense of the scale of a place.

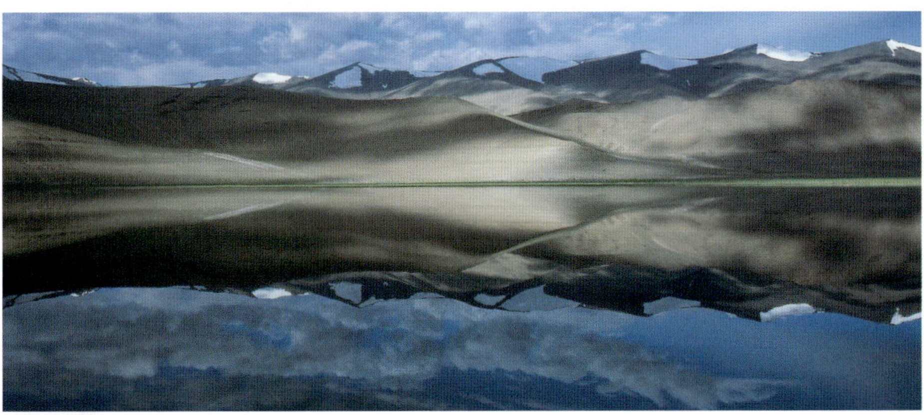

THE 35MM COMPACT

There was a time when it used to be easy choosing between a compact camera and an SLR. Compacts were simple, automated cameras with a basic exposure system, mediocre optics, and a limited range of features, and were really only suitable for taking snaps. However, as film camera technology evolved, so did compact cameras, with mid- and high-end models appearing that offered advanced features, greater control, and high-quality lenses. SLRs may be more flexible and versatile, but it's possible to use a compact for serious photography – and many people do.

PORTABILITY

One reason compacts are so popular is their size – or their lack of it. A typical zoom compact will slip easily into a coat pocket or handbag. Even compacts that go all the way up to 140mm or 200mm are still highly portable, while models without a zoom lens can look like miniature jewellery.

As compact cameras are designed to be pretty much all-inclusive, everything is built-in, from the flash to the zoom lens. In fact, the only accessories you could buy to enhance a compact are a tripod to guard against camera shake, filters – which on most models you have to hold in front of the lens yourself – and a case to keep it in.

WALKABOUT CAMERA

The compact camera can be thought of as the film photography equivalent of a mobile phone – small, portable, and on hand to photograph anything that catches your eye. Their main appeal is their point-and-shoot simplicity, although some models have an aperture priority mode that lets you control the depth of field for creative effect.

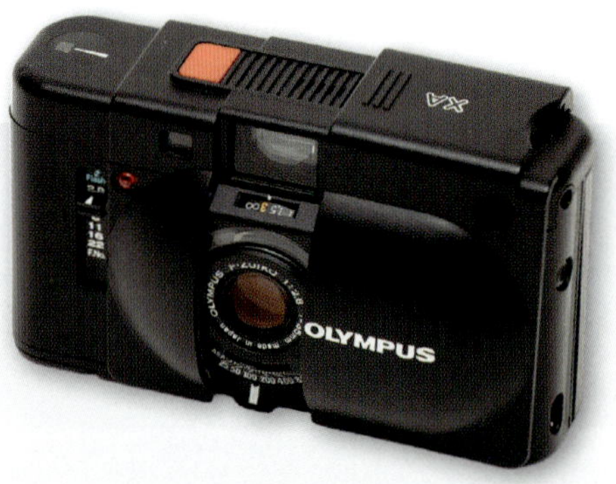

VINTAGE COMPACT

Olympus XA cameras may be tiny, but they are well-made and capable of fantastic results, making them a popular compact option.

While there's no denying the benefit of being able to swap lenses, as you can on an SLR or rangefinder, you can tackle many popular subjects using a compact – it just comes down to choosing a suitable model.

If you expect to shoot groups, interiors, and landscapes, for example, then you may want a camera with a wide-angle lens. In this case, Ricoh's GR high-end series is hard to beat, with its GR1 offering a 28mm lens and the GR21 housing a 21mm ultra-wide angle lens, along with aperture priority and programmed shooting modes.

If, on the other hand, it's action, candid shots, and natural history that interest you, then a model with greater telephoto coverage – up to 160mm or even 200mm – would be more suitable.

POINT AND SHOOT

Most 35mm compacts feature autofocus and 'programmed' operation, so you press the shutter and the camera does the rest. This can be considered good or bad, depending on how creative you want to be. It makes a compact quick and easy to use, but leaves little room for input from the user.

However, some compacts offer a range of subject and technique-based modes, such as landscape, sport, close-up, and night, which allow you to influence the bias of the shutter speed and aperture (landscape tends to set a small aperture, for example, while sport leans towards fast shutter speeds). There are also high-end compacts that add aperture priority to the mix, for even greater control.

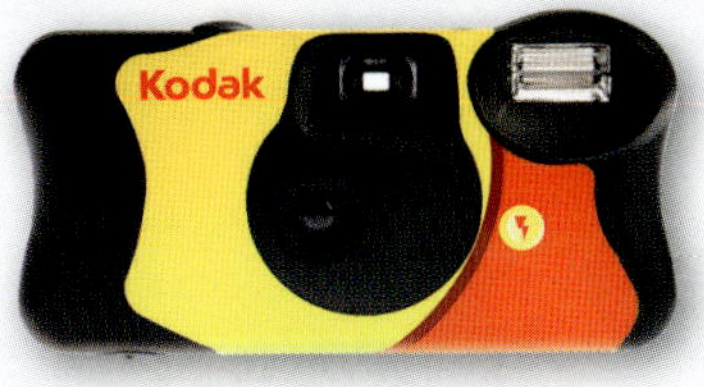

SINGLE-USE 35MM CAMERAS

The simplest compact cameras are pre-loaded with 35mm film and are designed to be used once (they are usually discarded by the lab when the film is removed for processing). With the ubiquity of mobile phones, 'disposable' cameras aren't used nearly as widely as they once were, but they can have their uses. Waterproof single-use cameras can take pictures in situations where you wouldn't want to risk your phone – surfing shots in the ocean, perhaps – while cameras pre-loaded with black-and-white film are popular at weddings, where they can be handed out or left on tables for guests to take shots of the day that would otherwise go unseen. In either case, the results can be surprisingly good given the camera's limitations.

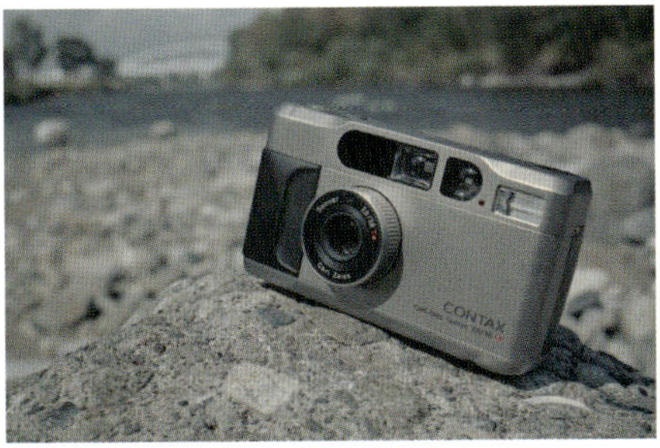

HIGH END

The Contax T2 is one of a number of high-end compact cameras that are now sought after for their superb image quality.

THE BIGGER PICTURE

Although 35mm film was – and still is – the most popular film format, it is not the only option for your analogue image-making. Medium-format film is still available, giving photographers a physically larger negative (or slide) that can be enlarged to a greater degree without losing sharpness or appearing too grainy.

It was these traits that made them the go-to for professional photographers working in fashion, advertising, and fine-art landscapes. Of course, professional photographers demand professional tools, so medium-format cameras and lenses tended to be well made and capable of producing high-quality images. They were also priced for a professional audience that would earn their money back, which could easily put them out of financial reach for casual photographers.

However, as photography shifted into the digital arena, a lot of this high-end kit entered the second-hand market, where the supply of medium-format equipment quickly started to outstrip the demand.

The result? Prices have dropped. That's not to say that medium-format photography is cheap. Cameras and lenses are still more expensive than their 35mm counterparts, and the cost per frame in terms of buying and processing the film is higher.

CAMERAS

Just like their 35mm counterparts, medium-format cameras come in a variety of styles, including SLR, rangefinder, and TLR (Twin Lens Reflex), and each has its advantages.

SLRs fall into two camps: models, such as the Pentax 67, which look like oversized mechanical 35mm SLRs (and handle in much the same way), and the 'modular' box-like cameras from Bronica, Hasselblad, and Mamiya. The latter type is typically used with a waist-level viewfinder and features interchangeable film backs that let you change the film quickly (you simply swap one back for another when the film runs out). But in many cases, this also allows you to switch formats.

There are also rangefinder models – from older bellows cameras by Zeiss Ikon, to the modern Mamiya 7 system with interchangeable lenses. Like their 35mm counterparts, these cameras tend to be lighter and quieter than an SLR, making them well-suited to street photography, reportage, and other subjects where hand-holding the camera is preferred.

MEDIUM-FORMAT OPTIONS

Medium-format cameras come in a variety of shapes and sizes.

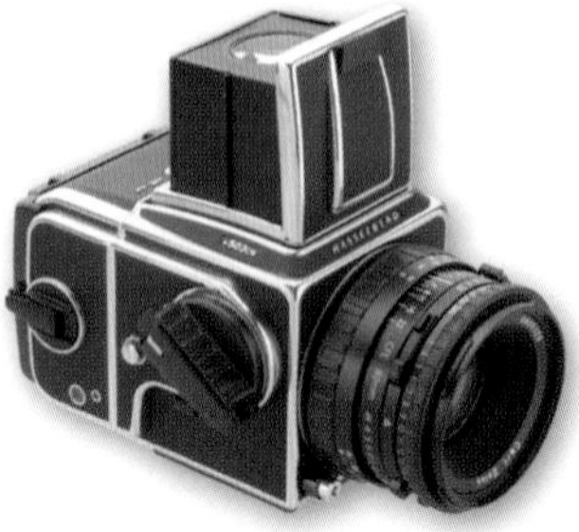

HASSELBLAD 500-SERIES SLR

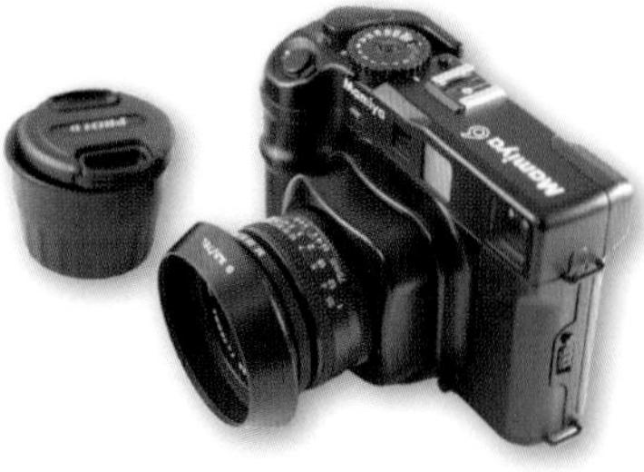

MAMIYA 6 RANGEFINDER

The final option is the TLR, or Twin Lens Reflex. Epitomised by German manufacturer, Rollei, this camera design typically has a waist-level viewfinder and two fixed lenses – one for viewing the image and the other for taking the picture. Although a fixed lens might seem restrictive, the pay-off is the phenomenal sharpness of some of these cameras, which made them exceptionally popular with studio portrait photographers in the 1960s.

FORMATS

While a standard 35mm frame measures 36 x 24mm, medium format doesn't have a fixed size. Instead, frame sizes range from 6 x 4.5cm up to a panoramic 6 x 17cm.

The most popular sizes and shapes are the 6 x 6cm square, as delivered by Hasselblads and Rolleiflex, and 6 x 7cm, which is common in Mamiya cameras (the RB67 and RZ67 SLRs and Mamiya 7 rangefinder, for example), as well as the Pentax 67.

Other regular formats include 6 x 4.5cm, 6 x 8cm, and 6 x 9cm. The more specialist 6 x 12cm and 6 x 17cm is used in panoramic photography. Each of these frame sizes uses the same film (120 roll film). The only difference is the number of shots on a roll; 16 if you're shooting 6 x 4.5cm images, 10 for 6 x 7cm, and 4 for 6 x 17cm.

Which format you choose will largely be determined by the camera and your preferred subject, but the simple rule is: the bigger the original, the less enlargement it needs to reach a given print size.

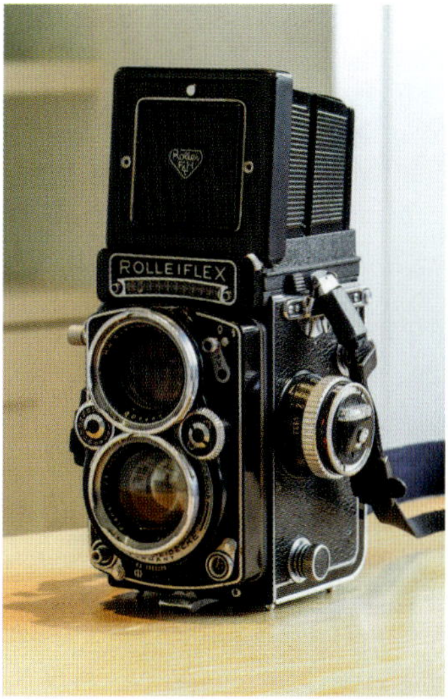

ROLLEIFLEX TLR

LARGE FORMAT

If medium format isn't big enough, you can always try your hand at large-format photography instead. Reminiscent of the very earliest cameras, the most common film formats still in use today are 5 x 4 and 10 x 8, but these are measured in *inches*, not centimetres. Large-format negatives can be contact-printed to give a decent print size with phenomenal image quality. Large-format photography is challenging, though. The cameras are fully manual and very different to an SLR in the way they work, not least because they use single sheets of (expensive) film loaded in dedicated film holders. For the truly adventurous, the film can be replaced with glass plates for an even more 'retro' experience.

OTHER OPTIONS

Compared to the uniformity of today's digital cameras, film photography lets you enter a veritable playground of film formats, quirky cameras, and alternative technologies. So let's take a brief look beyond the 'vanilla' world of SLRs, rangefinders, and compacts.

SUBMINIATURE CAMERAS

Historically, 35mm cameras were also referred to as 'miniature' cameras, as they were far smaller than their predecessors and took (comparatively) 'miniature' 35mm film. However, the so-called 'subminiature' formats are smaller still:

- **Half frame:** Cameras use regular 35mm film, but they produce images measuring 24 x 18mm (half the size of a 35mm frame, hence the name). This gives twice as many shots on a roll of film.
- **110:** This cartridge film is still being made, as are the cameras that take it. It produces a 17 x 13mm negative that is perfect for grainy, atmospheric enlargements.
- **16mm:** The classic 'spy camera' format uses 16mm motion picture film loaded into cassettes, both of which are still available. Some gorgeous-looking spy cameras were produced in the 1950s and 60s, but they are generally more collectible than usable.

TOY CAMERAS

'Toy camera' is something of a catch-all term used to describe a hotch-potch of primarily plastic cameras with low-tech lenses. Essentially, they are the antithesis of digital photography, with most providing a single fixed aperture and shutter speed and delivering a 'lo-fi' look that celebrates analogue photography through light leaks and lens flare.

Ironically, toy camera lenses are now available for digital photographers looking to achieve a similar result, although that kind of misses the point.

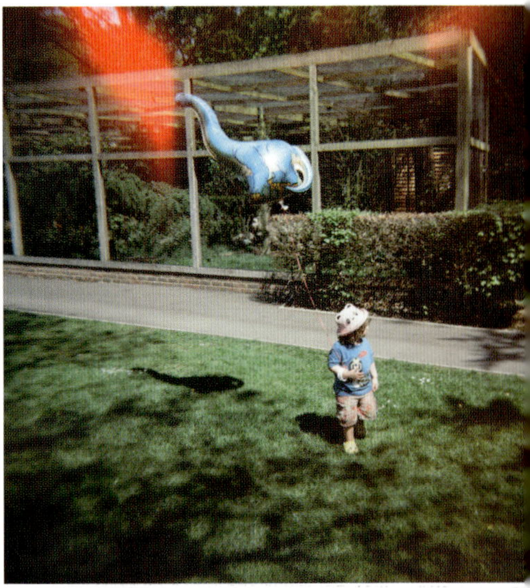

PLASTIC CAMERAS

Light leaks and vignetting (dark corners) are common with toy cameras. This photograph was taken on a medium format Holga 120 – a classic toy camera model.

PINHOLE CAMERAS

Pinhole cameras are about as simple as a camera can get. Most are essentially a light-tight box with a tiny hole (the 'pinhole') instead of a more conventional lens. Exposures are made by uncovering the pinhole, so exposing the film (or photographic paper) you are using. As the aperture of a pinhole lens can typically be in the region of f/200, exposure times are often measured in minutes, rather than seconds, creating ethereal images. Both pinhole cameras and lenses are available commercially, but this is one area where you can easily make your own. Pinhole lens plates can be made from empty drinks cans and the camera simply needs to be a light-tight box that will hold your photographic film or paper somehow.

STEREO CAMERAS

Stereo photography was incredibly popular during the late 19th century, when amateur photographers would use a camera with a pair of lenses to produce two slightly offset images of the same scene. When the 'stereo pair' was subsequently viewed in a special viewer, the images would come together to create the illusion of three dimensions – essentially mimicking human vision.

Although stereo photography is no longer popular (and hasn't been for a long time), stereo cameras still appear second-hand. Many of them use 35mm or 120 roll film, which means they can still be used if you want to take your film photography into the third dimension.

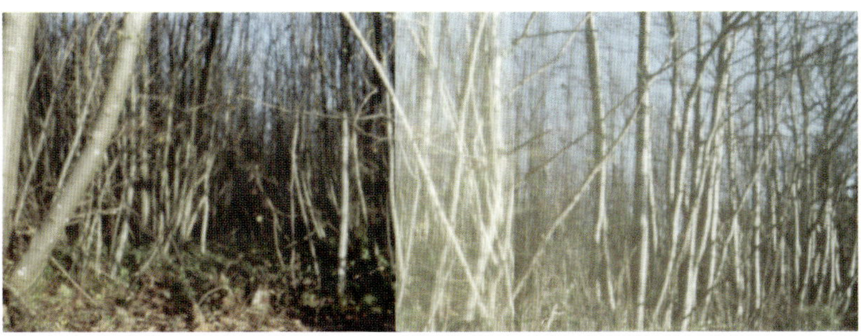

DIY PINHOLE

This photograph was taken with a homemade pinhole camera that uses medium format film. Here, two overlapping frames have created a panoramic image.

SEEING DOUBLE

Stereo cameras use two lenses to take a pair of images that mimic human vision. When viewed in a special viewer, the photographs give the impression of a 3D image.

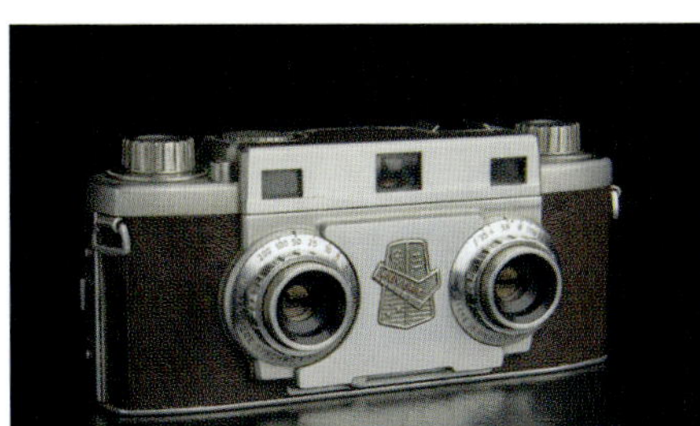

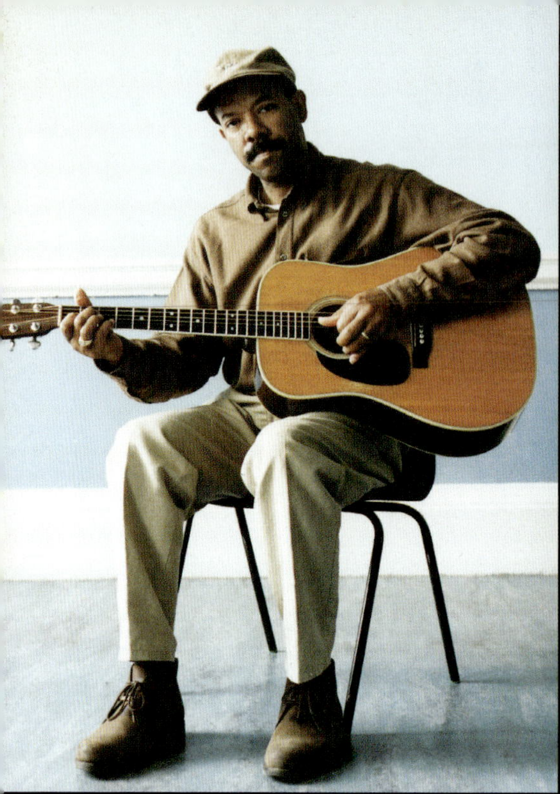

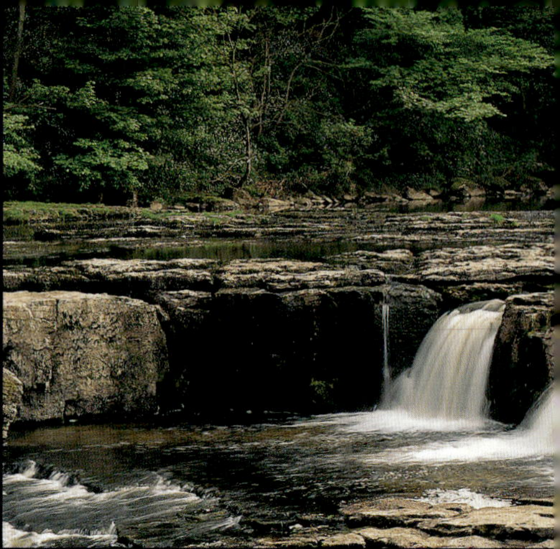

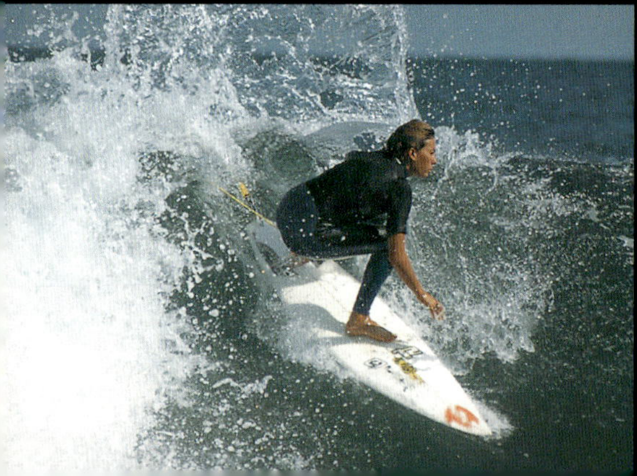

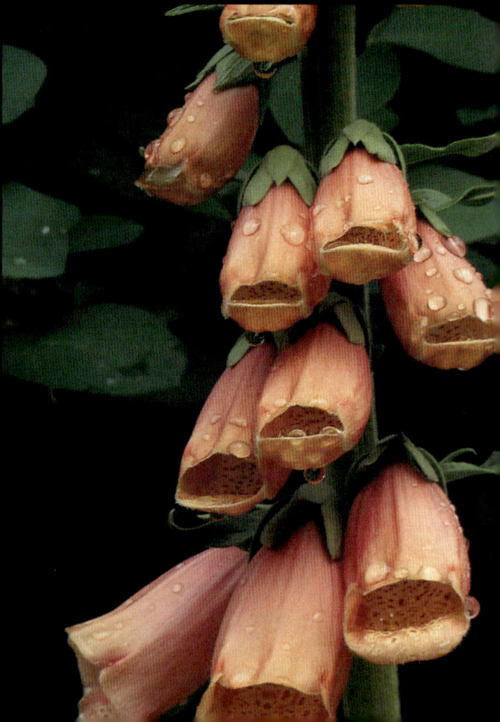

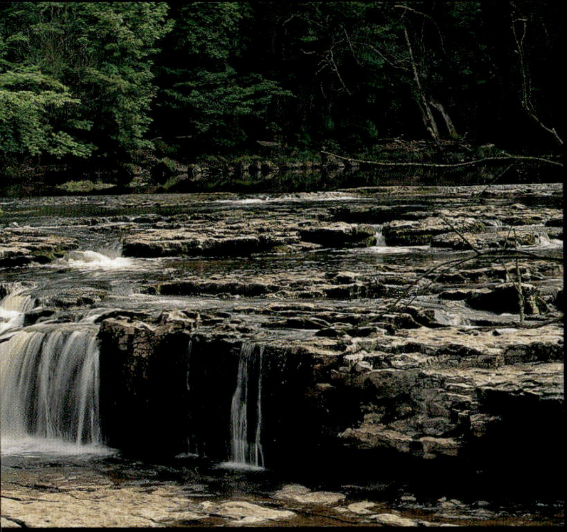

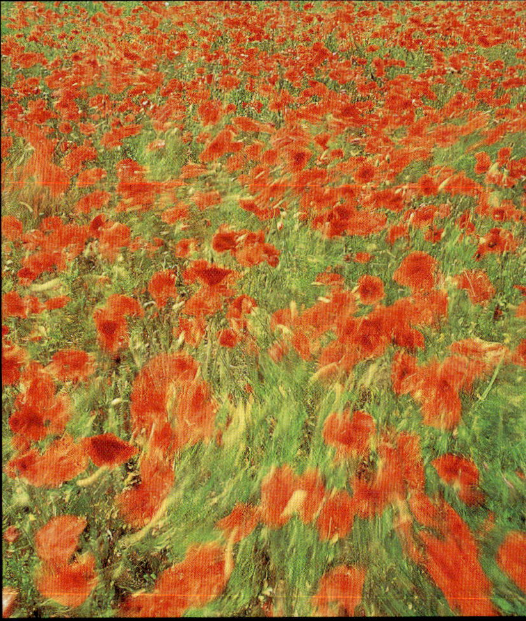

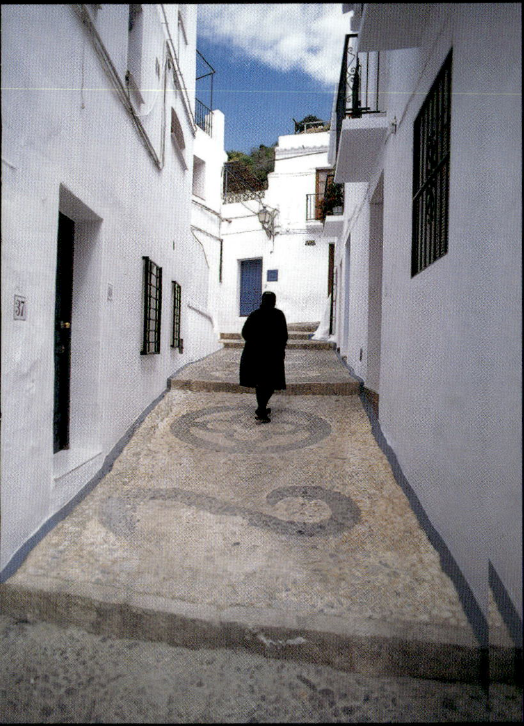

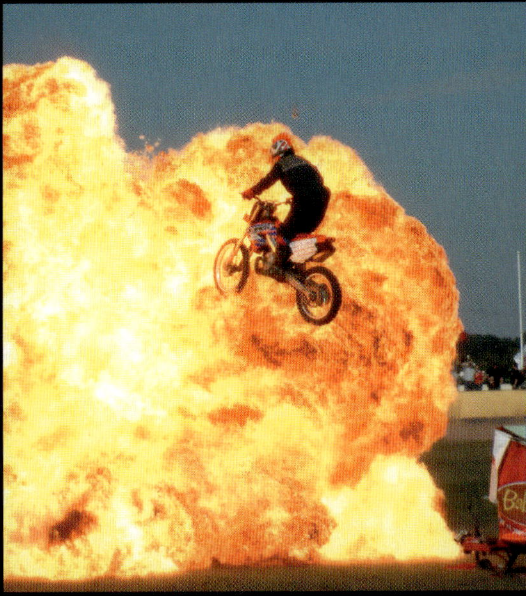

USING A 35MM CAMERA

FOCUSING

The majority of 35mm cameras sold today, both SLR and compact, have autofocus, though some manual-focus models are still produced, and a great many more are in use and widely available at attractive prices on the second-hand market.

The reasons autofocus has proved so popular are not hard to find. Focusing, along with setting exposure, was something many users of SLRs found tricky to do manually. When the option of an automated focusing system became available in 1985, it was an instant success, and as it became more affordable, an increasing number of photographers made the switch.

Autofocusing is a boon. It has also made cameras a lot more responsive. Today, it's possible to see a photogenic subject, pick up an SLR, and take a pin-sharp picture in less than a second. That was never possible with manual focusing, even for those skilled in its use. You can even take a shot of a subject a metre in front of you and another at infinity without catching breath.

Advances in autofocusing technology mean that it is now possible to photograph a moving subject. As the camera tracks its movement, it can predict exactly where the subject will be when the picture is taken.

USING AUTOFOCUS

For all their advantages, autofocus SLRs are not foolproof – they need to be used with intelligence to get the best from them.

The key thing to watch out for is that the focusing envelope in the viewfinder falls over the part of the subject you want to be in focus. This is also true if you have an autofocus 35mm compact. One of the classic errors occurs when you're photographing two people and the sensor goes between their heads and focuses on the background. You need to place the envelope over one of the faces, lock the focus position by holding first pressure on the shutter release, and then reframe the shot. The same procedure should be followed when photographing scenes where the subject is off-centre. When you first use the focus lock, you have to think what you're doing, but after a few times the technique becomes automatic, and can be carried out quickly and easily without slowing down the picture-taking process.

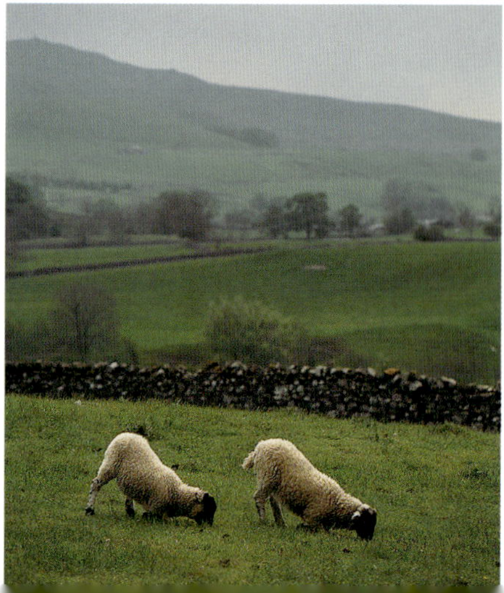

MULTI-POINT FOCUSING

Advanced SLRs with multi-point focusing will handle off-centre compositions like this easily, but users with a standard system need to use the focus lock or switch to manual.

Some of the latest cameras have more advanced focusing systems to minimise the problems caused by subjects that are not in the centre of the frame. If your SLR has a wide-area focusing envelope, which covers a greater proportion of the picture area, your subject has to be much nearer the edge of the frame for it to be missed.

The most sophisticated focusing systems have been pioneered by Canon, and an increasing number of their cameras feature multi-point autofocusing. With a much larger number of sensors ranged across the viewfinder, and advanced software controlling it, the system is capable of astonishing accuracy, even with the most difficult of subjects.

The most technologically advanced systems are even capable of being controlled by the user's eye movements. This may sound like science fiction, but they really work. Once calibrated – and this takes only a couple of minutes – they can detect which of the sensors you're looking at, and the camera is focused accordingly.

FOCUSING MODES

Many autofocus (AF) cameras offer a choice of focusing modes, and you need to make sure you're using the right one.

Single shot AF

As its name suggests, this is intended to allow you to take just one shot at a time, and is for general picture-taking. The aim is to eliminate out-of-focus pictures by locking the shutter until the lens is focused. A first pressure on the shutter release activates the autofocusing system, which focuses the lens and then locks the focus so it doesn't change until the pressure is released, allowing you to frame the shot. Increasing the pressure takes the picture. Single shot autofocus is best for general photography, where the subject is either static or slow-moving.

Servo AF

This is best reserved for moving subjects. It enables the autofocusing system to refocus the lens continually to keep a moving subject sharp. Once the lens has been focused, it remains locked unless the subject moves, in which case it refocuses automatically. All you have to do in this mode is keep your finger pressed halfway down on the shutter release.

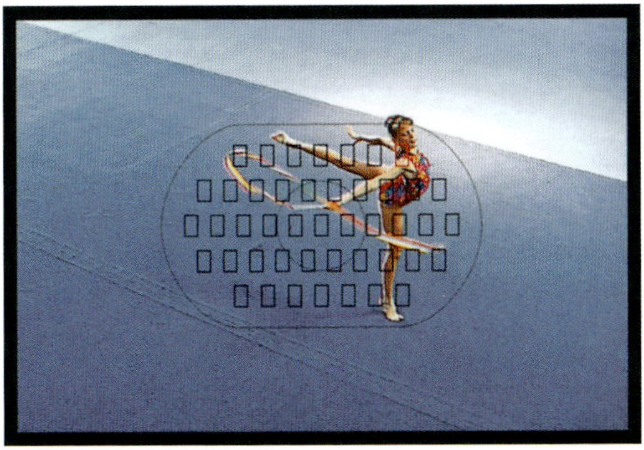

CANON'S 45-POINT AUTOFOCUS SYSTEM

One of the most advanced 35mm AF systems features 45 individual focusing points across a wide area of the screen.

Predictive AF

On advanced SLRs, this system kicks in automatically when it detects the subject moving at a certain speed. It tracks its speed and direction and then adjusts the focusing accordingly. Also called focus tracking, predictive autofocus anticipates where moving subjects will be at the moment the shutter is opened, and sets the focusing in order to give a sharp result.

MANUAL FOCUSING

Even the best autofocus cameras will struggle in some situations – such as where there's very little contrast or light levels are low – and you may need to switch to manual focusing. Of course, you may be using a manual focus camera and, if so, there's no need to feel like a second-class citizen. Despite the undoubted charms of autofocus, many photographers still prefer to focus manually. It may take a fraction of a second longer, but it makes them feel more in touch with the picture-taking process.

Focusing manually is just a matter of rotating the focusing ring on the lens until the picture looks sharp. Often there is a micro-prism/split-image focusing aid in the centre of the viewfinder to act as a guide, or some models have a focusing confirmation light, which is illuminated when the focusing is correct.

FOCUS TRACKING

The 'predictive' focusing found on most modern SLRs anticipates the position where moving subjects will be at the moment the picture is taken, and sets the lens position automatically.

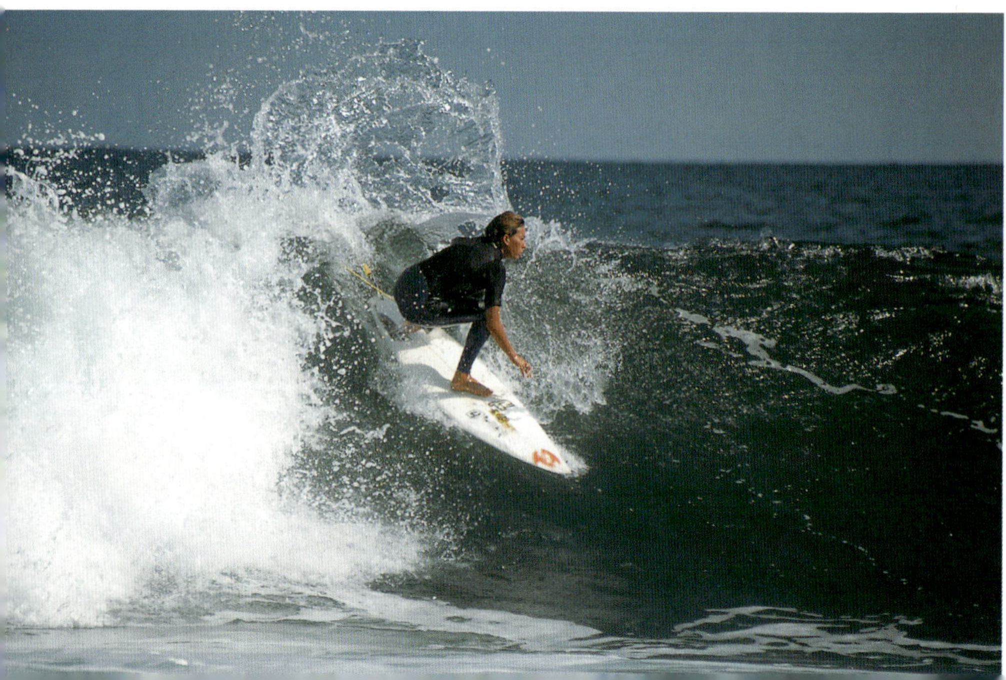

FOCUSING TECHNIQUES

Follow focusing

This useful technique involves continually refocusing to follow a moving subject. It can be done either manually or using autofocus, and it works well when the subject is relatively slow-moving, but it is more difficult as speeds increase. Then you need to resort to pre-focusing, where you focus on a spot ahead of the subject that it will pass, and fire the shutter as it does so. At an event with a pre-determined route this is easy. Otherwise you need to be alert and anticipate which way the action will move. Timing is critical; fire the shutter a fraction of a second too soon or too late, and the subject will be out of focus.

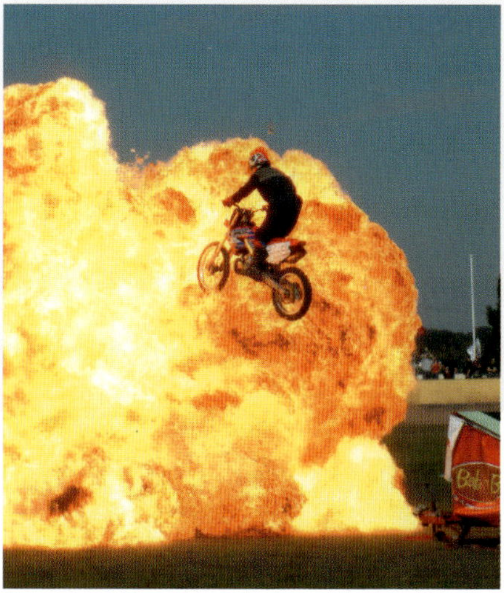

TRACKING SHOT

To make sure this motorcycle was sharp at the decisive moment, the photographer tracked its movement as it approached the jump.

Tracking

This technique involves shooting a moving subject from a moving camera. The theory is simple: if the subject and the vehicle carrying the photographer are moving at the same speed they do not move in relation to each other. Autofocus will be quick and accurate, or you can pre-focus on manual and let depth of field give the sharpness required. However, the subject and the camera are moving in relation to the background, which will streak dramatically. The degree of streaking depends on three main factors:

- The speed of the vehicles: the faster they're going, the more blurred the background will be.
- The shutter speed: the longer it is, the more pronounced the streaking.
- The focal length of the lens: the wider the angle of view, the more background will be included, enhancing the movement. As a starting point for your own tests, use a 35mm or 28mm lens, 1/125 sec, and travel at around 80kph (50mph). A vehicle with an open back, such as a Jeep, pick-up truck, or convertible, offers a safe platform.

EXPOSURE BASICS

The great advantage of modern cameras is that because they're so automated, almost anyone can pick one up and start taking decent shots immediately. But in the same way that you'll probably get the best from your car if you have some idea of what's under the bonnet, so you'll make the most of your camera if you understand a little about how it works.

This is particularly true of exposure. Have you ever had pictures back from processing and wondered where you went wrong? Do you find yourself asking why this one came out too dark or that one too light? If so, you need to learn the basics of exposure.

EXPOSURE CONTROL

Modern cameras may be packed with exposure goodies, with numerous modes and metering patterns, but if you don't know how they work and what they're trying to achieve, you'll never make the most of the potential they offer. The first thing an exposure meter aims to do is to put the right amount of light on the film to give a good picture. To do this, it reads the light that is reflected back to the camera from the subject and analyses it using a metering pattern. This establishes the correct exposure level for the shot.

There are two controls that regulate the amount of light that reaches the film. One determines the aperture – the hole behind the lens that can be varied in size. The control is marked with a series of numbers (f/32, f/22, f/16, f/11, f/8, /5.6, f/4, f/2.8, f/2) that express the aperture size. Each setting lets in either twice as much or half as much light as its neighbour.

The other control is the shutter speed, which is the length of time the shutter is open to take the photograph. Shutter speed is measured in fractions of a second: 1/1000, 1/500, 1/250, 1/125, 1/60, 1/30, 1/15, 1/8, and so on. Each setting lets in either twice as much or half as much light as its neighbour.

In any situation, there are different ways in which aperture and shutter speed can be combined to expose the film to the right amount of light. As the aperture increases, a faster shutter speed is needed to give the same exposure. On a sunny day, for instance, when using ISO 100 film, you could choose any of the following combinations:

Aperture	Shutter speed
f/32	1/15 sec
f/22	1/30 sec
f/16	1/60 sec
f/11	1/125 sec
f/8	1/250 sec
f/5.6	1/500 sec
f/4	1/1000 sec
f/2.8	1/2000 sec

However, although the exposure level might remain constant at all these pairs of settings, the photographic effects would be very different. That's because both aperture and shutter speed are also important creative controls.

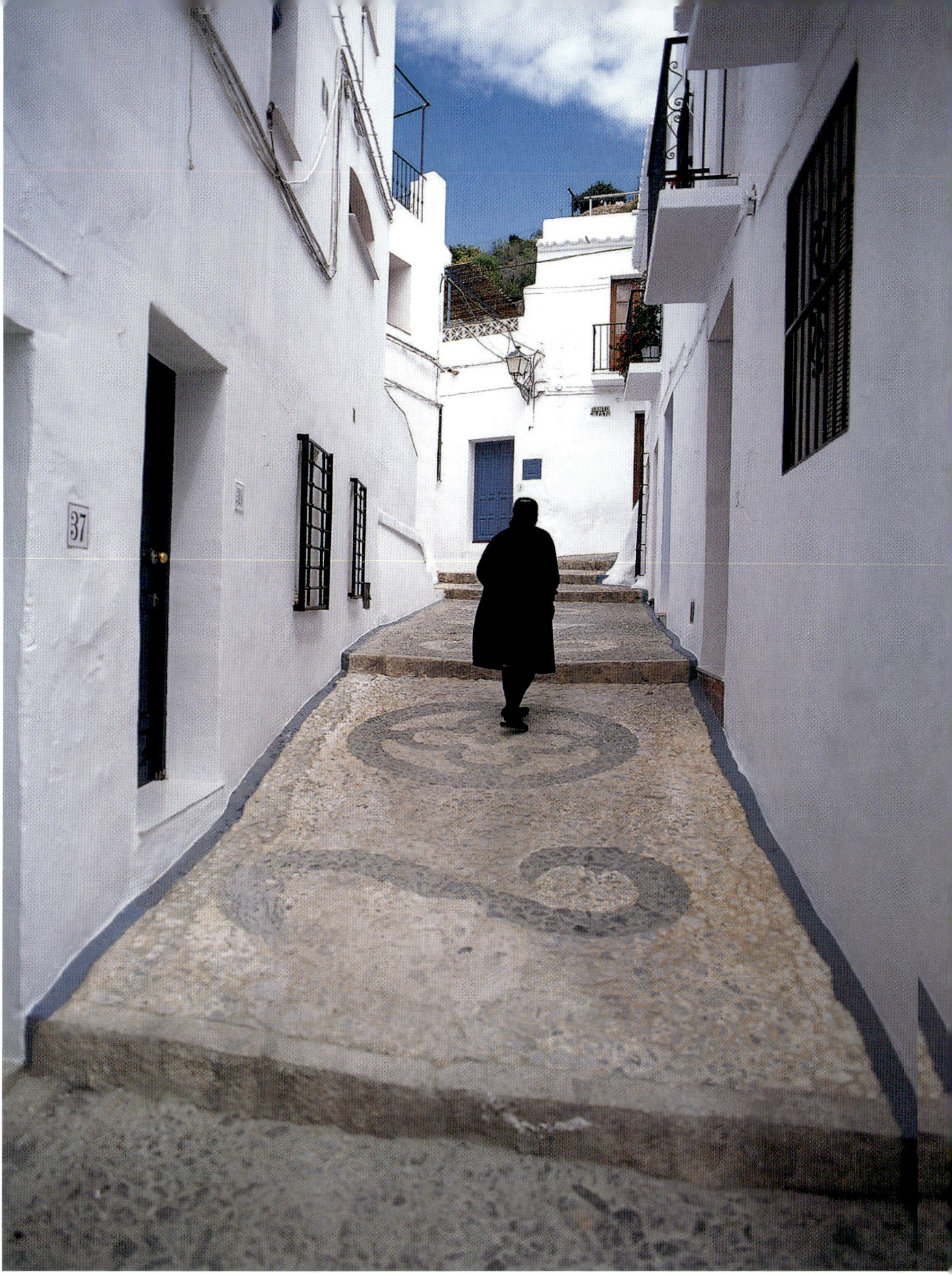

EXPOSURE

Put simply, exposure is all about getting the correct amount of light to reach the film, to create a photograph that is neither too light, nor too dark. Achieving this involves balancing the lens aperture, the shutter speed, and the sensitivity (ISO) of the film.

SHUTTER SPEED

The shutter is one of the key picture-taking controls on a camera, opening up as you take the picture to let in light, which exposes the film. On simple cameras, including some 35mm compacts, the shutter opens only for a fixed time, often 1/125 sec, but on modern SLRs there's usually a wide range of shutter speeds – from at least 1 sec to 1/1000 sec. Some cameras can be set at speeds as brief as 1/12,000 sec, or as long as 30 sec.

There are two main reasons for this wide range. The first is that shutter speeds control the amount of light falling on the film. Fast shutter speeds limit the amount of light admitted – which is useful in bright conditions or when working with fast film – while long shutter speeds make it possible to continue taking pictures when light levels fall, even if slow film is being used. The second reason is that the choice of shutter speed plays an important part in determining how the finished picture looks, especially when it involves movement. Within the limits imposed by the amount of light in the scene, the speed of the film you're using, and the maximum aperture of the lens, you can select whatever speed you want.

On traditional manual focus cameras there's usually a dial on the top plate, marked with the speeds, which allows you to control the shutter speed. Simply rotate the dial to select the speed required. More recent cameras, especially autofocus models, feature advanced electronics that allow you to select your shutter speed by means of push buttons and input dials. Such cameras often have a large number of exposure modes that give you even more control over the shutter speed, either directly through shutter priority mode, or indirectly by one of the other modes.

LOW LIGHT
Having a wide range of shutter speeds lets you take photographs in an equally wide range of situations, from the brightest sunny day to vivid night-time scenes.

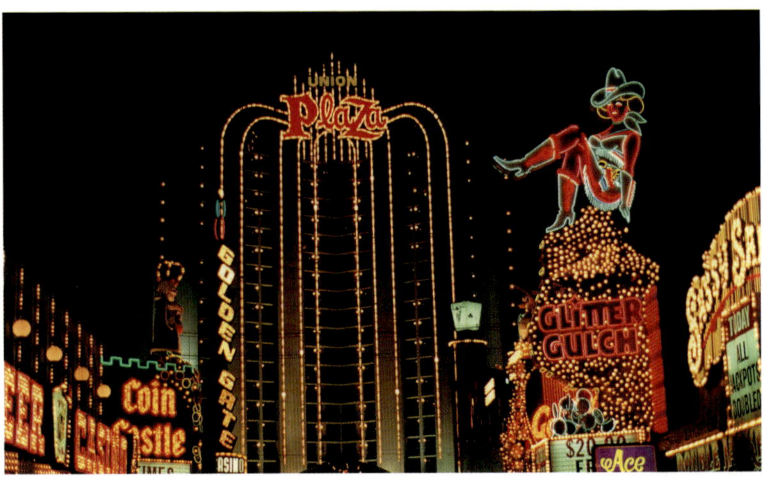

IF YOU HAVE A 35MM COMPACT...

... you won't have any direct control over shutter speed. Along with the aperture, it will be set automatically by the camera's exposure system. However, there are a few things you can do to bias the meter towards long or short shutter speeds.

To achieve a shorter shutter speed:

- Shoot in bright sunlight.
- Load up with more sensitive film, with a higher ISO number.
- If you have a zoom compact, set the lens to its shortest focal length, which will have the largest maximum aperture.

To achieve a longer shutter speed:

- Shoot in overcast weather.
- Load up with less sensitive film, with a lower ISO number.
- If you have a zoom compact, set the lens to its longest focal length, which will have the smallest maximum aperture.

MOVING WATER

Allowing water to blur in a landscape image will create a sense of movement in an otherwise static scene. Simply attach your camera to a tripod to avoid camera shake and set a shutter speed of between 1 sec and 1/8 sec – the slower the shutter speed, the more blurred the water will be.

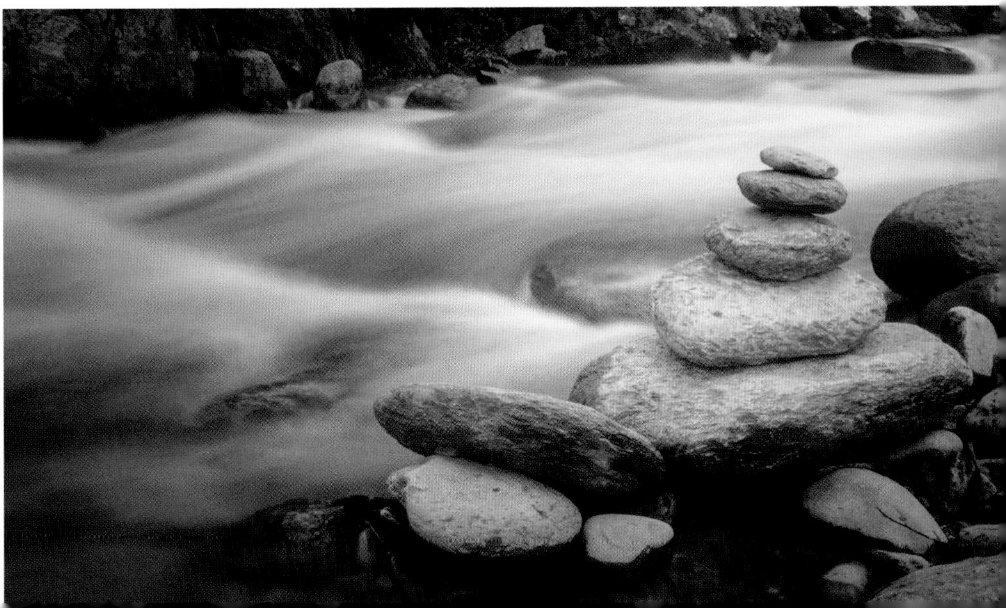

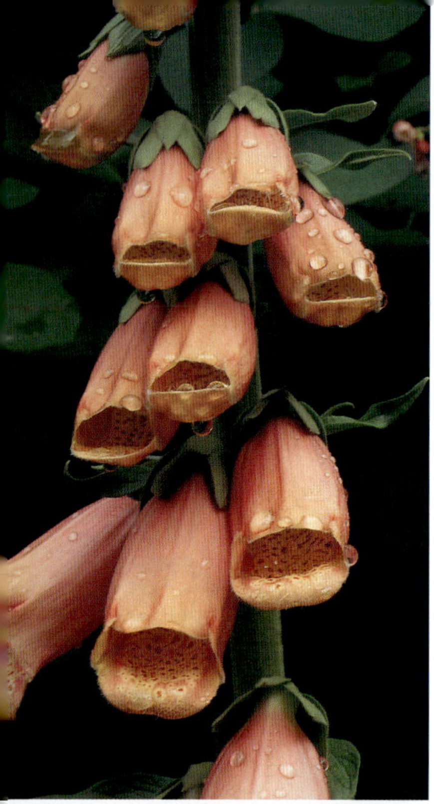

AVOIDING CAMERA SHAKE

Control of shutter speed is an important weapon in the battle against camera shake. Even the slightest movement of the camera at the moment of exposure can lead to unsharp results when you're hand-holding – but the faster the shutter speed you set, the less likely you are to get blurred images. However, that doesn't mean you need to take all your pictures at 1/1000 sec. The lens you're using is also relevant; the longer its focal length the faster the shutter speed needs to be. As a rule of thumb, a safe speed is one that is the reciprocal of the focal length in use. With a zoom, it's the actual setting used that's important, not the range of the lens.

Here's a guide to the minimum speeds to use with a variety of lenses:

Focal length	Shutter speed
90/100mm	1/125 sec
135/200mm	1/250 sec
300/400/500mm	1/500 sec
600/800mm	1/1000 sec

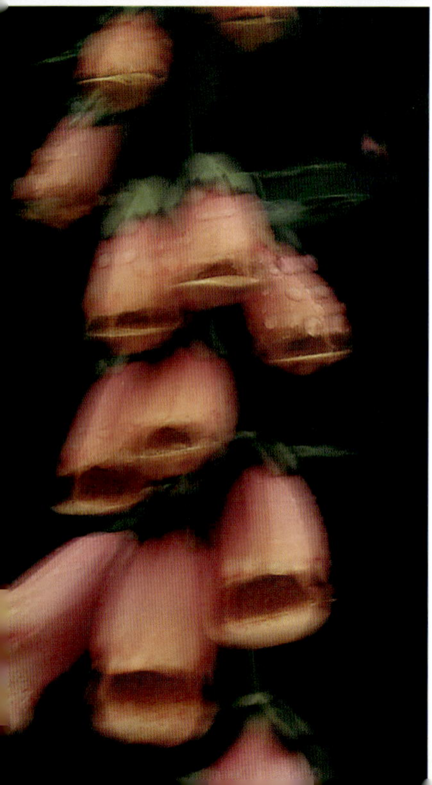

CAMERA SHAKE

Many people overestimate their ability to hand-hold without camera shake being apparent – and the difference shutter speed makes can be dramatic. A speed of 1/60 sec with a telephoto zoom results in a surprisingly blurred image (left), while switching to 1/500 sec renders the subject pin-sharp (top).

FREEZING OR BLURRING

If there's no movement in the picture, the shutter speed makes little creative difference and the choice of aperture may be more important because of its effect on the depth of field. Most everyday pictures are taken using shutter speeds in the range 1/60–1/500 sec.

When there's some kind of action, such as someone running or a speeding car, you need to decide whether you want to freeze or blur the movement. If you use a brief shutter speed – 1/1000 sec or faster – there will be so little movement while the shutter is open that it will look as if the subject is standing still – producing a frozen image that is perfectly sharp. But if you use a longer speed, say 1/30 or 1/15 sec, the subject's movement during the period the shutter is open will result in an image in which the subject is blurred.

CREATIVE BLURRING

Movement doesn't have to be fast to provide the potential for interesting results. Setting a shutter speed of 1/8 sec has created an impressionistic image of these poppies blowing in the wind.

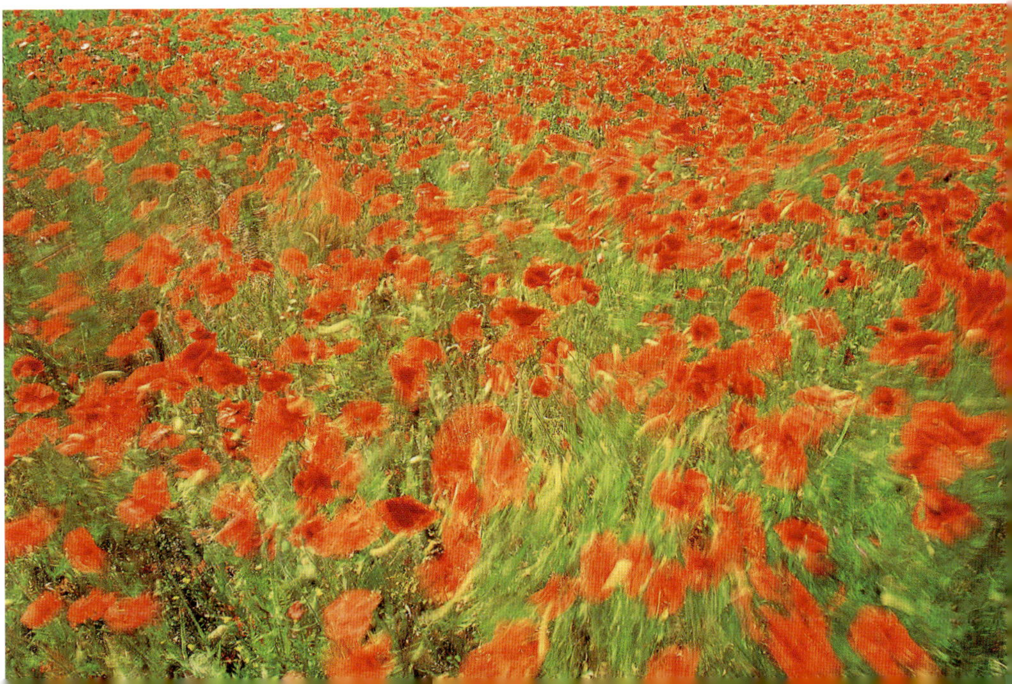

APERTURE

In simple terms, the aperture is a hole through which light passes to reach the film. Its size is varied by means of a series of thin, curved iris blades within the lens, which open up to let more light through and close down to reduce it. On manual focus cameras, it is generally controlled by an aperture ring on the lens that is turned by hand, and clicks into position against a range of aperture numbers. On electronic cameras, the aperture is controlled by push-button controls and the setting is usually displayed on an LCD screen.

The standard numbering sequence for apertures is: f/1.4, f/2, f/2.8, f/4, f/5.6, f/8, f/11, f/16, f/22, and f/32. Each number is known as an f-stop. The values are calculated by dividing the focal length of the lens by the diameter of the hole created by the iris. In practice, the important part is that each step along the scale represents a doubling or halving of the light transmitted. For example, f/8 lets in twice as much light as f/11, but only half as much as f/5.6.

'Small' apertures are those in which the hole produced by the iris blades is physically small; large apertures are those in which the hole is physically large. Confusingly, small apertures have *high* numbers, such as f/11, f/16, and f/22, while large apertures have low numbers, such as f/2.8, f/4, and f/5.6. The distinction between 'small' and 'large' is important here, because the size of the aperture determines the depth of field in the finished picture.

For greater control over exposures, most cameras let you set the aperture in 1/2-stop increments, with some pro-spec cameras allowing you to adjust it in 1/3 stop. This becomes especially important with transparency film, but is of less benefit if you're shooting colour negative film.

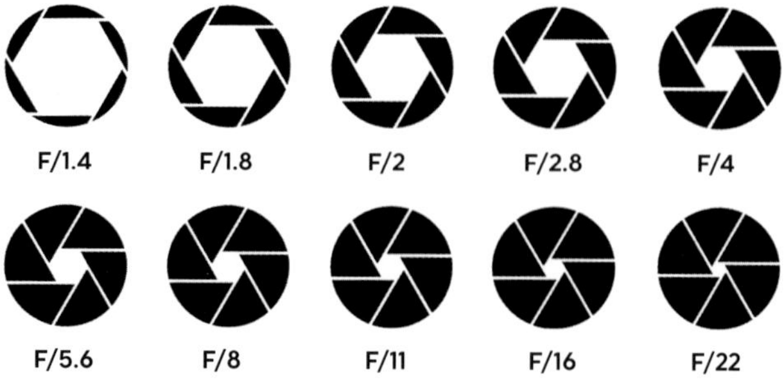

APERTURE RANGE

Most of the confusion about aperture settings is because a small f-stop number refers to a large aperture; remember that and you're well on your way to mastering exposure.

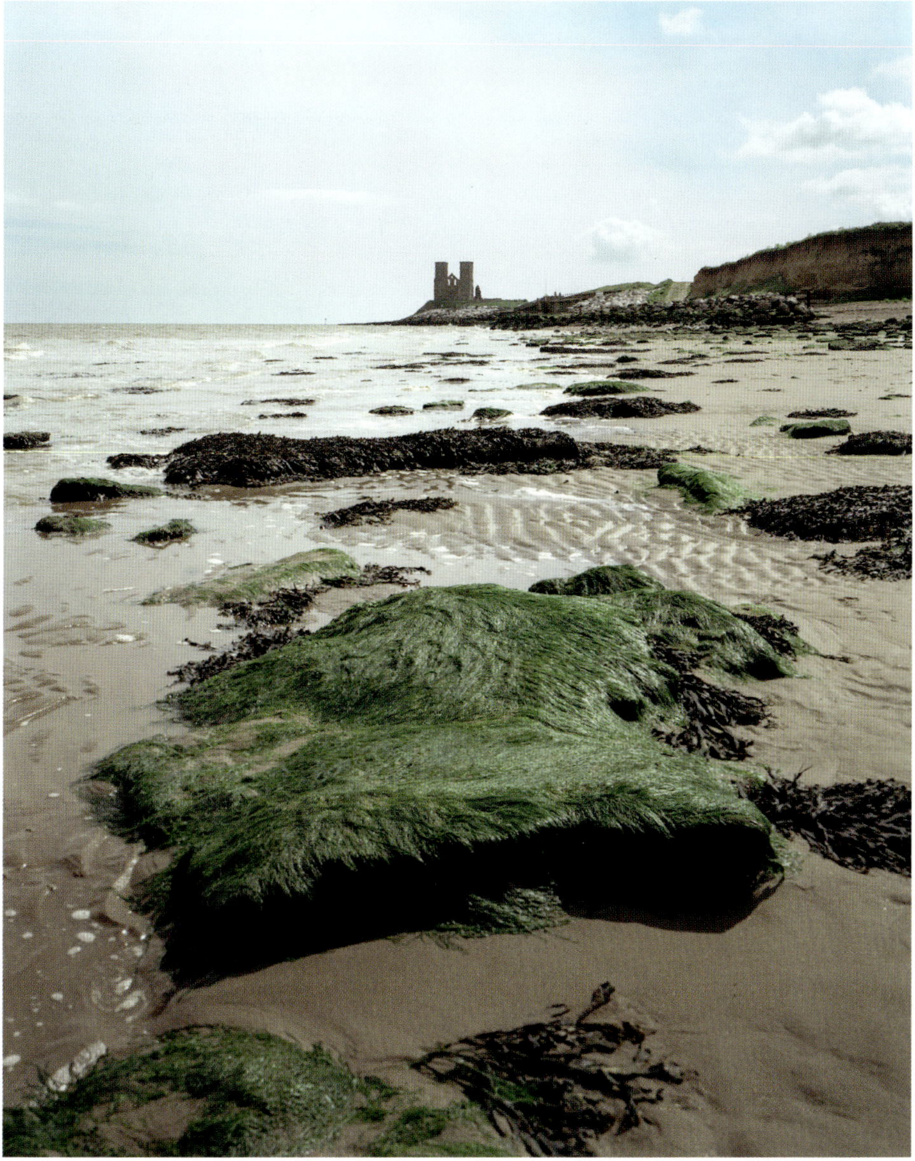

DEPTH OF FIELD

One of the aperture setting's most powerful roles in photography is controlling depth of field. This refers to how much (or how little) of a scene appears sharply focused. Here, a small aperture setting ensures that everything in the frame appears sharp, from the foreground rocks to the distant castle.

DEPTH OF FIELD

Unless you're completely new to photography, you'll be aware that when you cast your eye over a scene, everything in it seems more or less equally sharp, but in a photograph only part of the subject might appear to be acceptably sharp.

This zone of sharpness is called the 'depth of field', and it extends in front of and behind the point on which you actually focus. When most of the picture is sharp, it's described as having a large depth of field. When only part of the image is sharp, the depth of field is said to be limited.

The size of the zone is determined by three main factors: the size of the aperture, the focal length of the lens, and the camera-to-subject distance. Varying these three elements allows you almost complete control over the depth of field in a picture.

Aperture size

There's a simple relationship between the size of the aperture size and depth of field; the smaller the aperture, the more extensive (larger) the depth of field.

If you want to keep as much of a picture as possible sharp, you should set a small aperture, such as f/16 or f/22. Depending on the lighting conditions and your film speed, you may need to use a tripod or some other form of support at such small apertures, as the resulting long shutter speed will introduce the risk of camera shake.

If, however, you want to concentrate attention on just one part of the scene and throw the rest out of focus, you should select a large aperture. Exactly how large will depend on the maximum aperture of your lens: on a 50mm standard lens it may be f/1.4 or f/1.8, but on a zoom lens it might be f/3.5 or f/4.5.

For general picture-taking, when you want most of the picture to be in focus, you might want to set a middling aperture of around f/8 to f/11. This is what a programmed exposure mode would be likely to set when left to its own devices, but you can control the aperture yourself using aperture priority or manual mode.

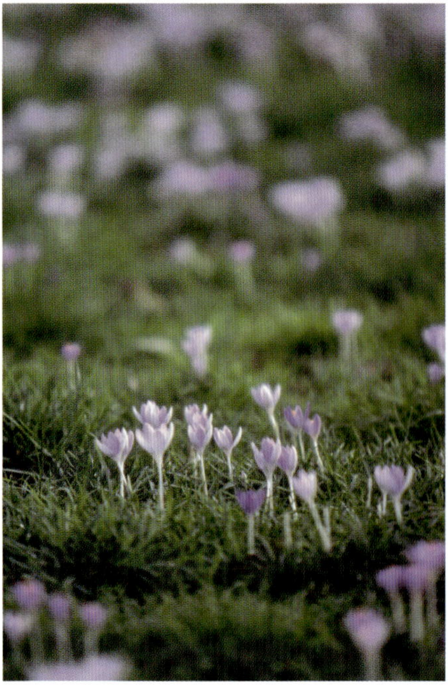

SHALLOW

A close subject combined with a wide aperture minimises depth of field, focusing attention on a single part of the frame.

Focal length of lens

In theory, depth of field does not change with focal length, but in practice it seems to. Slip on a wide-angle lens and you'll benefit from extensive depth of field, which will make it easy to keep everything in focus; the wider the angle of view, the greater the depth of field. If you choose a telephoto lens, the depth of field will immediately appear more limited. The longer the focal length, the more restricted the zone of sharpness will be.

Camera-to-subject distance

For various technical reasons, the closer you get to your subject the more limited the depth of field becomes. When shooting close-up subjects this can mean the depth of field extends to just a few millimetres in front of and behind the subject.

DEPTH OF FIELD ESSENTIALS

To maximise depth of field:

- Use a wide-angle lens.
- Set a small aperture (f/16 or f/22).
- Stand back from your subject.

To minimise depth of field:

- Use a telephoto lens.
- Set a large aperture (f/1.8 or f/2.8).
- Get closer to your subject.

EVERYTHING SHARP

Using a small aperture will maximise depth of field, but will also require a longer shutter speed, which can blur movement and cause camera shake if you don't use a tripod.

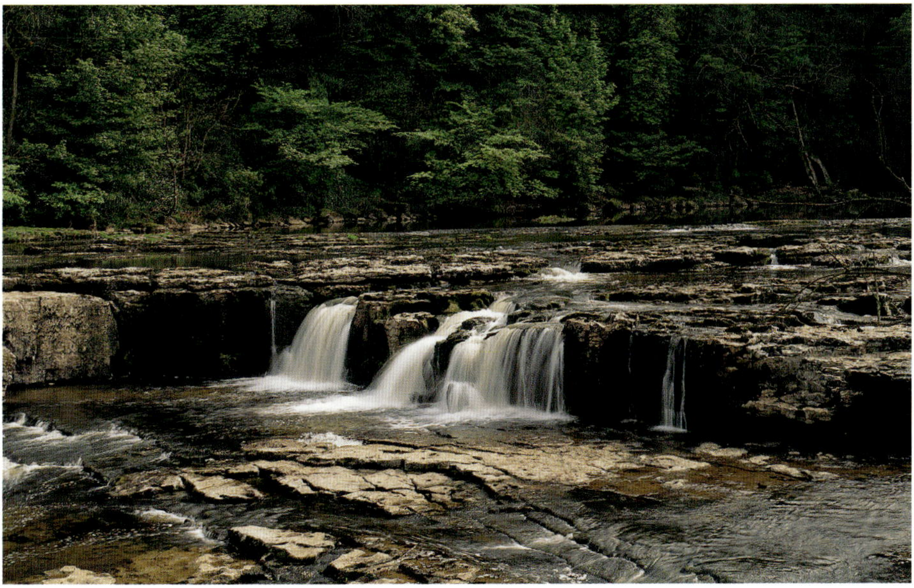

EXPOSURE MODES

Most 35mm SLRs and some compacts offer a selection of exposure modes that suit not only a variety of subjects and situations but also the photographer's preferred way of working. While some people like to leave the exposure decisions to the camera, others prefer to take control to gain creative flexibility.

Not all models offer all modes. The majority of electronic 35mm SLRs manufactured since the mid-1980s feature the four main modes – program, shutter priority, aperture priority, and manual – and some enthusiast models have additional subject-based modes. Earlier electronic cameras may not have program mode, while some mechanical cameras might not even have shutter and aperture priority, making them ideal for purists who want to work in a fully manual fashion.

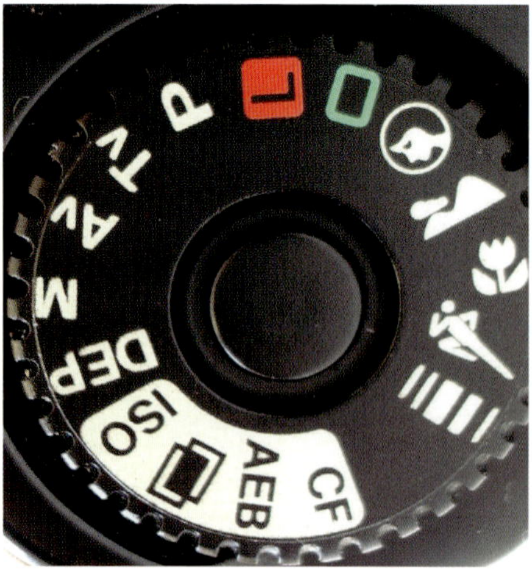

MODES

Exposure modes can typically be set using a dial on the top of the camera or selected electronically.

A wide range of exposure modes is less common on compact cameras. Inexpensive models often have systems that are fully automatic, offering no control at all, while some of the more sophisticated types may provide a modicum of manual control, even if it is subject-based modes.

In every case, the aim is the same: to allow the right amount of light to reach the film and make a good exposure. However, being able to take control of the aperture and shutter speed combination puts you in charge of how your photographs look, enabling you to produce images that are interesting and original.

PROGRAM

Program mode is indicated by the letter P on a camera's mode dial or electronic mode selector. In this mode, the camera chooses both the shutter speed and aperture automatically, so you don't have to worry about the exposure at all.

This is great when you're starting out in photography, because it guarantees good results while you're getting to grips with your camera, but the main drawback is that program mode doesn't know what it is you're trying to do creatively. It will typically set exactly the same shutter speed whether you're taking a portrait, landscape, or action shot. In practice, this means well-exposed but rather bland results.

This can be overcome to a certain extent if the camera has a program 'shift' option, which allows you to alter the emphasis – towards either the shutter speed or the aperture – but other modes are preferable if you want to take control.

APERTURE PRIORITY

As the name suggests, when you choose aperture priority mode (A or Av on the mode selector), you select the aperture and the camera provides the shutter speed that will give the correct exposure.

Aperture priority is a good mode to use when you want to control the depth of field to determine how much of the scene comes out sharp in the finished picture. Small apertures, such as f/11 and f/16, provide lots of depth of field, and keep most of the picture in focus, which is ideal for landscape photography and large groups of people. Large apertures, such as f/2.8 and f/4, restrict how much of the image appears sharp, and are great for concentrating attention on your subject when shooting subjects such as portraits.

In practice, many experienced photographers operate in aperture priority mode most of the time. This is because the aperture generally has more creative effect on the finished picture than the shutter speed. However, you still need to be aware of the effect the aperture you set is having on the shutter speed. If you choose an aperture that's very small, such as f/16 or f/22, this can extend the shutter speed to a level where there's a risk of camera shake.

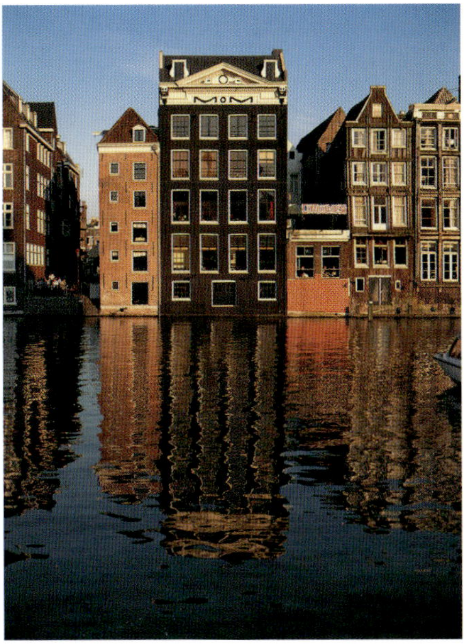

PROGRAM

The main concern with this photo was getting a good exposure. The exact shutter speed and aperture used were less important.

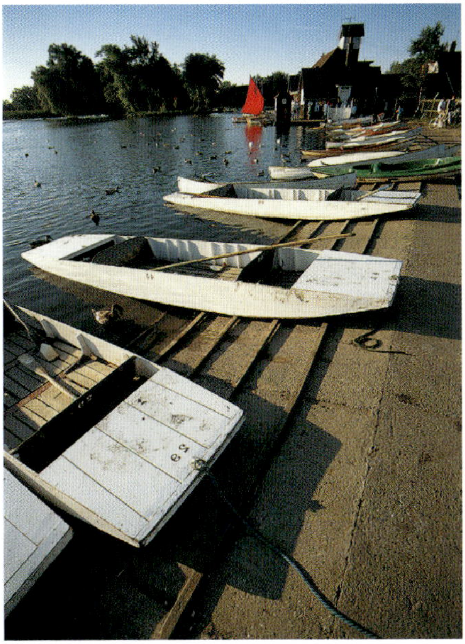

APERTURE PRIORITY

Aperture priority allowed a small aperture to be set, maximising depth of field and ensuring everything appeared sharp in the scene.

SHUTTER PRIORITY

When you use shutter priority mode (S or Tv on the mode selector), you select the shutter speed you want to use for your shot and the camera sets the aperture required for a correct exposure.

This makes it ideal for photographing action, as having direct control over the shutter speed allows you to match it to the movement of your subject, to ensure that it's perfectly frozen. For high-speed motor racing, for example, you'd need a speed in the region of 1/1000 sec. To capture someone running, a shutter speed of 1/250 sec would probably be sufficient.

You don't always have to freeze motion, though. Using shutter priority mode allows you to set a slow shutter speed that records movement as a blur; making fast-flowing water appear silky-smooth, for example.

Shutter priority can also be used to avoid camera shake, by setting a shutter speed that's faster than the reciprocal of the focal length of the lens in use. So, if you're using a 200mm lens you'd want to set a shutter speed of at least 1/250 sec; with a 50mm lens, 1/60 sec would normally be sufficient.

When setting a very fast shutter speed, you need to make sure there's enough light for the camera to be able to provide a matching aperture. There's usually a warning system if you go too far. You should also be aware that a fast shutter speed can require a large aperture, which limits depth of field. This means that focusing must be extremely accurate, especially when using a telephoto lens.

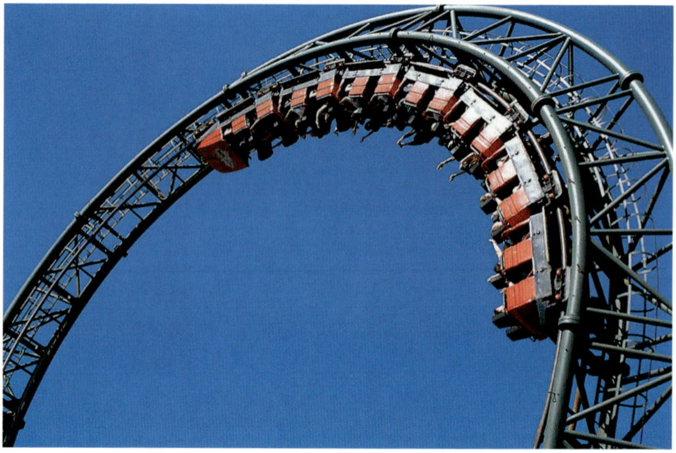

SHUTTER PRIORITY

When you want to freeze a fast-moving subject you need to have control of the shutter speed, making shutter priority your go-to mode.

MANUAL

When you want full control over the settings that provide the exposure, you should choose manual mode (M on the mode selector). This choice may be for a number of reasons. In some instances, you might be able to predict that the camera will give an incorrect exposure, so you want to override its suggestion, or you may prefer to take a reading with a separate hand-held meter. It could also be that your camera offers nothing in the way of automaton, as is the case with a lot of older cameras and most medium format cameras.

Although selecting both the shutter speed and the aperture independently gives you total control over your photographs, it is also more risky. Unless you're knowledgeable and experienced about exposure, it's much easier to make mistakes in manual mode.

The worst you can do in any of the automated modes is get the emphasis wrong – the overall exposure will still be correct (or close to correct), as the camera is at least partially involved in the process. However, if you make a mistake in manual mode, your pictures can be so over- or underexposed that they're unusable.

MANUAL
Backlit subjects can easily fool the camera into underexposing your shot, but you can avoid this by switching to manual mode.

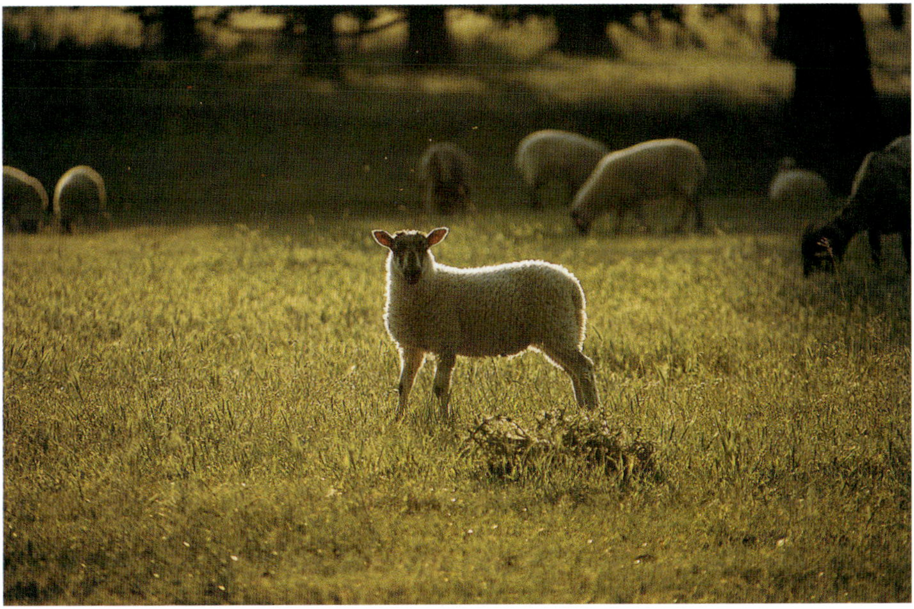

PICTURE PROGRAM MODES

Just like a lot of today's 'enthusiast' digital cameras, many electronic 35mm SLRs include modes designed to tackle a range of popular subjects, to help newcomers to photography get good results from the start. The four most common modes are portrait, landscape, action, and close-up, which are indicated by the following icons: a head, mountain, runner, and flower.

When you select one of these modes, the camera automatically sets what it considers to be the optimum shutter speed and aperture combination for the subject. Depending on the camera, it may also vary the metering pattern, choose single or continuous film advance, activate the camera's built-in flash, or select the most appropriate autofocus setting.

Although experienced photographers view these picture modes with disdain, they are capable of producing excellent results. However, to make the most of them you really do need to understand exactly what they're doing – or you might not get the results you expect.

PORTRAIT

Designed for taking pictures of people, portrait mode aims to concentrate attention on your subject by setting a large aperture to help throw the background out of focus. Typically, this will be in the region of f/6.7 to f/8, depending on the camera model and conditions.

Assuming you are using a lens with a focal length between 80mm and 120mm – which gives excellent perspective for portraits – and your subject is not too close to the background, this mode would produce an excellent 3D result. However, when you want to take 'environmental' portraits, showing your subjects in their surroundings, you should avoid portrait mode. Instead, switch to aperture priority and, if lighting levels allow, go for an aperture of f/11 or f/16 to keep everything sharp.

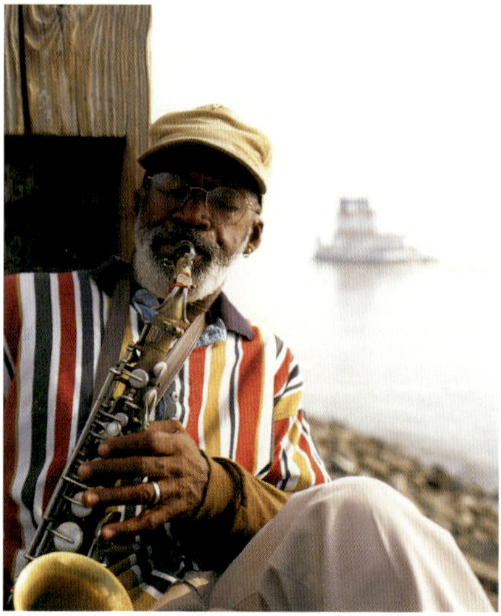

PORTRAIT

Portrait mode typically sets a wide aperture to limit depth of field.

LANDSCAPE

When you're shooting landscapes, you normally want as much depth of field as possible so that everything in the picture, from front to back, is in focus. Unsurprisingly, then, landscape mode aims to set as small an aperture as possible, to maximise depth of field.

Assuming you're using a wide-angle lens in good light, most landscape modes will provide you with an aperture of around f/16, which is more than sufficient to give the effect required, although Canon's EOS range is noticeably more cautious, and more commonly sets an aperture of f/8 or f/11. However, that should still be sufficient to hold everything in the picture in focus.

LANDSCAPE

In landscape mode, a small aperture is used to maximise depth of field.

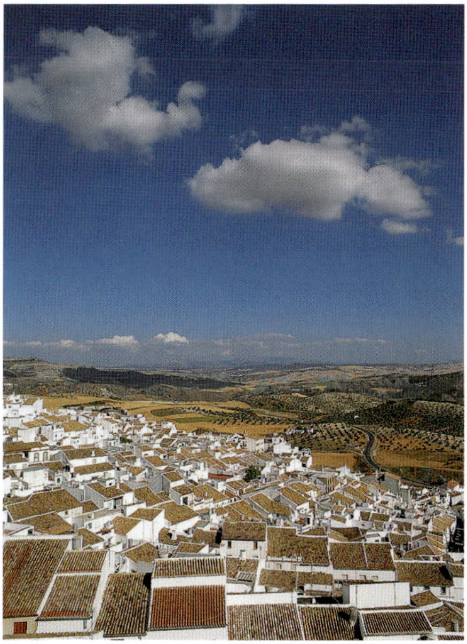

ACTION

As its name indicates, action mode is designed to tackle moving subjects and render them in sharp focus, whether it's racing cars hurtling round a track or skaters at a skate park. The first requirement when you need to freeze action is, of course, a fast shutter speed, and in bright conditions there's normally no problem achieving this. However, when light levels are lower or the maximum aperture of the lens is limited, things can be more problematic. In practice, if you load up with an ISO 400 film and shoot in sunlight, this mode will give you a shutter speed of around 1/500–1/1000 sec.

CLOSE-UP

Many photographers would like to tackle close-up photography, but are unsure exactly what settings are required. In fact it's a balancing act. The aperture needs to be small enough to provide an adequate depth of field, but a reasonably fast shutter speed is required to minimise the risk of camera shake and subject movement. The close-up mode on most cameras gets it about right, with the aperture typically set at around f/8, and the shutter speed chosen to match.

CLOSE-UP

Close-up mode uses a mid-range aperture to try and deliver a relatively fast shutter speed and reasonable depth of field.

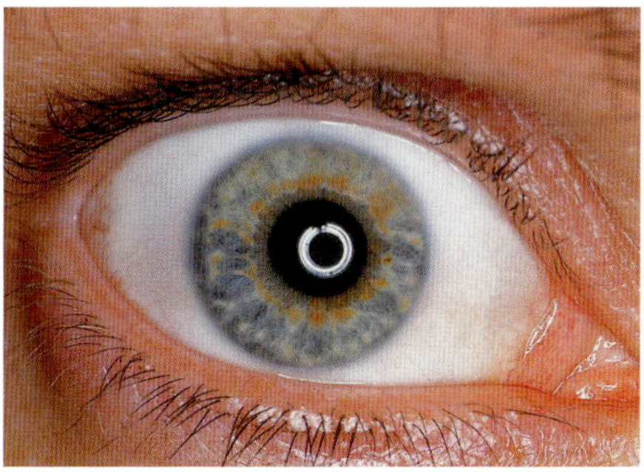

EXPOSURE METERING

Before a camera can start setting shutter speeds and apertures, it has to measure how much light is in the scene, and that's the job of the built-in meter. Most SLRs feature through-the-lens (TTL) metering, which measures the light passing through the lens using what is known as a 'metering pattern'. Some mechanical cameras have a single metering pattern, which would usually be centre-weighted, but top-end models often have two or more patterns to choose from.

Centre-weighted

This is a tried-and-tested pattern that most SLR cameras feature. The design is based on the assumption that the main subject will be in the centre of the picture, so most exposure emphasis is placed there. It's accurate in many situations, although more recent innovations now have the edge.

Multi-segment

This computer-based metering pattern has become increasingly sophisticated since it was first introduced in the mid-1980s, and continues to be used in the latest digital cameras. The metering sensor breaks the picture area down into segments, and compares the light level of each against information stored in its databank to give unparalleled exposure accuracy.

Partial

Less common than the other patterns described here, partial metering restricts the exposure measurement to a central portion of the viewfinder image – typically between 6 and 15 per cent depending on the camera model, and is often defined by the size of the focusing aid or autofocus envelope. Used with judgement, it can assist accurate exposure, particularly when used in conjunction with an AE-lock facility.

Spot

Spot metering limits the exposure reading to a very small area at the centre of the viewfinder image – usually no more than two per cent of the picture area. This makes it potentially a very accurate way of measuring exposure, but it will only give you good results if used correctly. The key point to understand is that exposure meters are calibrated to render whatever you read as a mid-tone. This is fine if the spot you choose is a mid-tone, but if it's significantly lighter or darker, you will get an incorrect exposure.

Multi-spot

This pattern takes spot metering a step further and allows you to take readings from a number of different points, averaging them out to give the exposure. On some models you can take a reading from the lightest or darkest points and press either a 'highlight' or 'shadow' button to make sure the exposure is biased towards them. It's a great system, but once again requires considerable understanding on the photographer's part to get good results.

WHY METERS FAIL

The important thing to understand about camera meters is that most of them are easily fooled. Why? Because they are calibrated on the basis that if you take all the tones in a subject – dark, middling, and light – and average them out, you'll get an 18 per cent mid-grey. While that's often true, or near enough not to matter, there are subjects and situations where an imbalance of light and dark tones will show how easy it is to trick your meter into giving the wrong exposure. But before you get alarmed and start losing confidence in your camera's meter, it's worth stressing that most of the time it will serve you very well indeed, delivering at least a 90 per cent success rate.

If you're serious about photography, though, that won't be good enough for you. You'll want to chase after the other 10 per cent of shots that get away. And you're right to – because it's in the tricky lighting situations (which fool meters) that the most successful pictures are taken – into-the-light shots and subjects projected strongly out of dark backgrounds, to name but two.

Getting the best from your meter is therefore about knowing when you're in a situation that is likely to fool the meter into giving the wrong exposure. The good news is there are only a handful of different situations, and once you learn to recognise them, you're in a position to take action to avoid exposure errors occurring.

HIGH CONTRAST

Getting the exposure right can be challenging in high-contrast conditions.

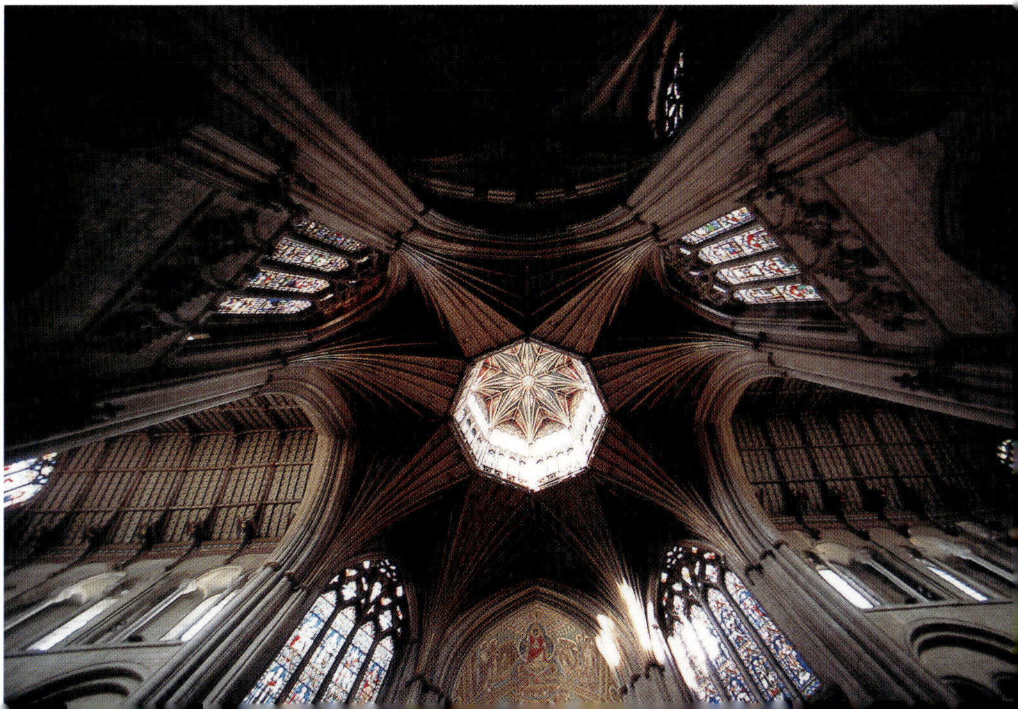

TRICKY SITUATIONS

Light subject

If the subject is unusually light, such as a bride in a white wedding dress or the wall of a Spanish villa, you'll get underexposure that will reproduce the white as grey.

» **To correct:** Increase the exposure by around 1–2 stops.

Dark subject

When your subject is unusually dark, such as a black cat or a school chalkboard, the meter will overexpose, making the black appear grey.

» **To correct:** Reduce exposure by around 1–2 stops.

Light background

If your main subject is in front of a light background, such as a person standing in front of a white wall or the sea, then the meter may be fooled by the background and the subject will be underexposed.

» **To correct:** Go in close and take a reading direct from the person.

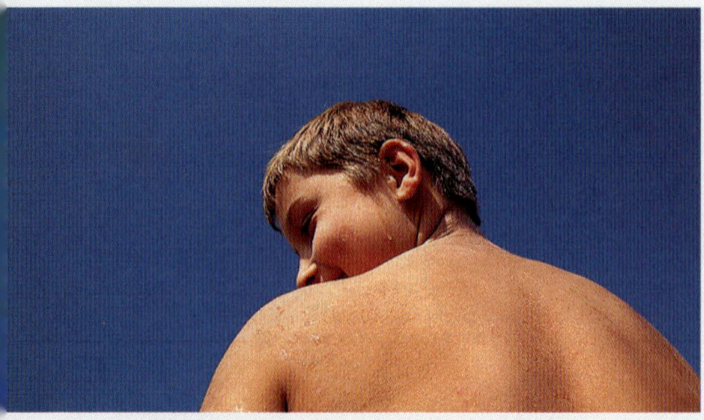

SHOOTING INTO THE SKY

Whenever there's a lot of sky in the picture, the camera's meter can easily be misled into underexposure, and adjustments may be needed.

Dark background

When the background is much darker than the subject, such as a spotlit performer, this can lead the meter into overexposing.

» **To correct:** Make sure you take a reading from the subject only, with the background excluded.

Into the light

In contre-jour, or into-the-light photography, the light streaming from behind the subject into the lens will cause underexposure.

» **To correct:** You should either take a reading from the subject only or increase exposure by around 2 stops.

Lots of sky in the picture

If you point your camera upwards to photograph a tall building, or shoot a landscape with a lot of sky, you may suffer underexposure as the meter is misled by all the light bouncing around.

» **To correct:** Take a reading that excludes the sky.

Light source in the picture

When the light source is actually in the picture, as with a setting sun or a lamp, there's likely to be underexposure. How much will depend upon the strength of the light source and where it is in the picture.

» **To correct:** Take a reading of the scene with the light source excluded.

COMPENSATION

Given that built-in meters are far from perfect, what can you do to ensure your picture is accurately exposed when faced with a tricky lighting situation? The answer is that you can compensate, increasing or decreasing exposure by the appropriate amount. Precisely how you do this depends upon your camera and its features. Here are the commonest ways of making adjustments.

Backlight button: A fairly unsophisticated way of compensating, and not as common as it was, the backlight button increases exposure, typically by 1½ stops. It's useful if you need to work quickly in into-the-light situations, but other options offer more accurate control.

AE-lock: This is a quick and effective way to improve your success rate. Simply go in close to your subject, or in the case of landscapes, tip the camera down to exclude the sky, and press and hold the AE-lock button. This will then store the correct exposure for the subject, allowing you to return to your original position and take the shot in the knowledge that the exposure won't be affected by other factors.

Exposure compensation facility: This is the most accurate way of compensating, provided you know how much you want to compensate by. On older cameras it usually takes the form of a dial; on more recent models it's often an electronic system accessed by buttons and input wheels.

Changing film speed: If your camera lacks any of the above, you can improvise exposure compensation by temporarily changing the film speed setting, with every doubling or halving giving a 1-stop compensation. If, for instance, you are using ISO 100 film and want to increase exposure by 1 stop, you need to alter the setting to ISO 50. To underexpose by 1 stop, switch to ISO 200. Remember to change the rating back afterwards.

Switching to manual: This is the most reliable way of controlling exposure, especially if taking a series of shots of the same subject. Take a reading directly from your subject, and enter the settings manually into the camera. You are almost guaranteed to achieve the correct exposure.

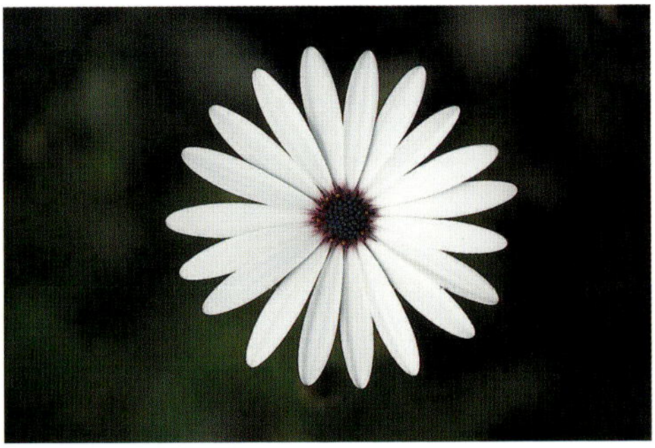

DARK BACKGROUND

Dark backgrounds can easily cause light subjects to overexpose, and care needs to be taken so that detail is retained.

LIGHT BACKGROUND

When the background is lighter than the subject, there's always a danger of underexposure.

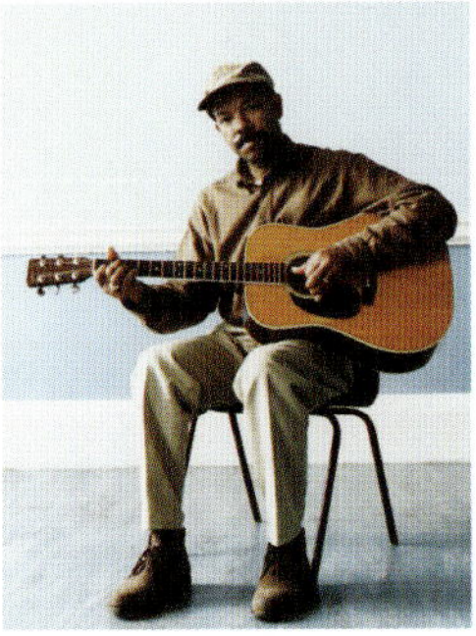

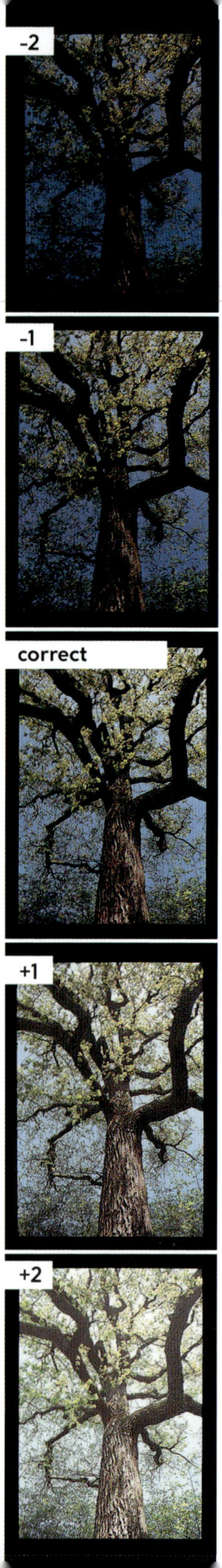

BRACKETING

Bracketing is a technique that should be part of the armoury of every photographer, and it's one that can be called upon whenever you are faced with taking an unrepeatable photograph in difficult lighting conditions.

This method involves taking a series of shots at exposures above and below what the camera believes to be correct. That way you know you're going to get at least one good shot. Unless your camera has an AEB (automatic exposure bracketing) control, which will do it for you, the easiest way to bracket is to use an exposure compensation facility. This allows you to increase and decrease the exposure quickly and accurately.

However, it's not a technique you should use every time. First, it's unnecessary – your camera will get the exposure right at least 90 per cent of the time – and second, it will cost you an arm and leg in terms of extra film and processing costs. How much should you bracket? It depends what kind of film you're using and what the situation is.

Colour print film is capable of giving acceptable results with exposure 3 stops above or below the correct level (black-and-white print film has an even wider range), so it's only worthwhile bracketing it in big chunks. In most situations, the best way to bracket when using colour negative film would be in three frames: correct exposure, 1½ stops above, and 1½ stops below.

Transparency film has much narrower latitude, and even ½ stop above or below the correct exposure can make a big difference. In this case, it is better to bracket in ½ stops, up to 1 stop above and below, as follows: correct, ½ stop above, 1 stop above, ½ stop below, and 1 stop below. In extreme situations it may be necessary to bracket even more widely than that.

Whatever method you choose, you need to take care – especially when increasing the exposure – that the shutter speed doesn't drop to a level that will potentially cause camera shake.

BRACKETING WITH SLIDE FILM

In tricky lighting conditions, such as when shooting into the sky, it may be worth bracketing exposures on slide film to ensure that at least one shot is correct. Here, the images have been bracketed in 1-stop increments, and the differences are clear: overexposure gives pale, washed-out images, underexposure gives dark, muddy results.

HAND-HELD METERS

The problem with all integral meters is that they measure the light reflected back from the subject, so there's always a danger, no matter how sophisticated they become, of uneven lighting misleading the meter and causing over- or underexposure. For that reason, it's still worth considering getting a hand-held meter that features an incident reading facility. This measures the light falling onto the subject, so it is not affected by unusually light or dark surroundings.

If you shoot colour negative film, this probably isn't necessary, because the film's enormous exposure latitude means that only very occasionally will you suffer any kind of failure – and that's more likely to be due to the printing than the exposure.

But if you're regularly shooting colour transparency film, which has less latitude and demands extremely accurate exposure, or tackling professional work where you need to achieve successful results every single time, then a separate meter is a worthwhile choice.

For most amateur photographers, though, the current in-camera meters are incredibly reliable, and more than sufficient.

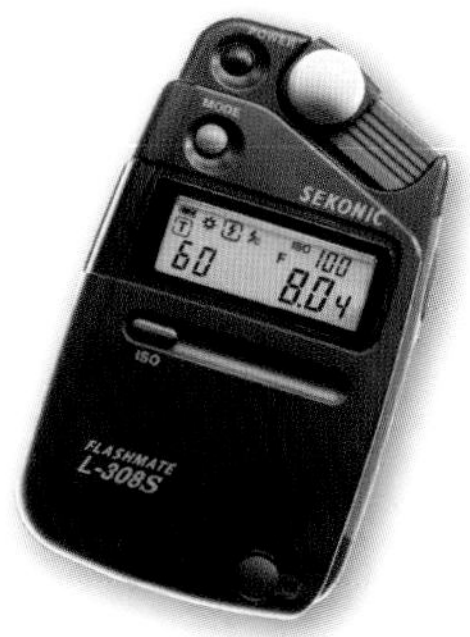

HAND-HELD METER

Using a separate light meter virtually guarantees correct exposures, whatever the circumstances.

ADVANCED ZONE EXPOSURE

The Zone System is an advanced and rigorous exposure system pioneered by the great American landscape photographer Ansel Adams (1902–1984). It breaks down the brightness range of a subject, from black to white, into ten zones – usually indicated by Roman numerals O–IX.

Each of the zones is 1 stop lighter or darker than its neighbour: Zone O is solid black, Zone IX (9) is pure white, and Zone V (5) is 18 per cent reflectance mid-grey, to which meters and grey cards are calibrated.

Through an exhaustive series of tests involving film speed (known as exposure index), developing times, and printing times, practitioners of the Zone System reach the stage where they are able to 'pre-visualise' exactly what the finished print will look like at the time of taking the picture.

It's worth saying that the Zone System was developed for black-and-white photography using large format cameras, although the principles can, to some degree, be adapted for colour and smaller formats. Find out more about the Zone System in two classic books by Ansel Adams: *The Negative* and *The Print*.

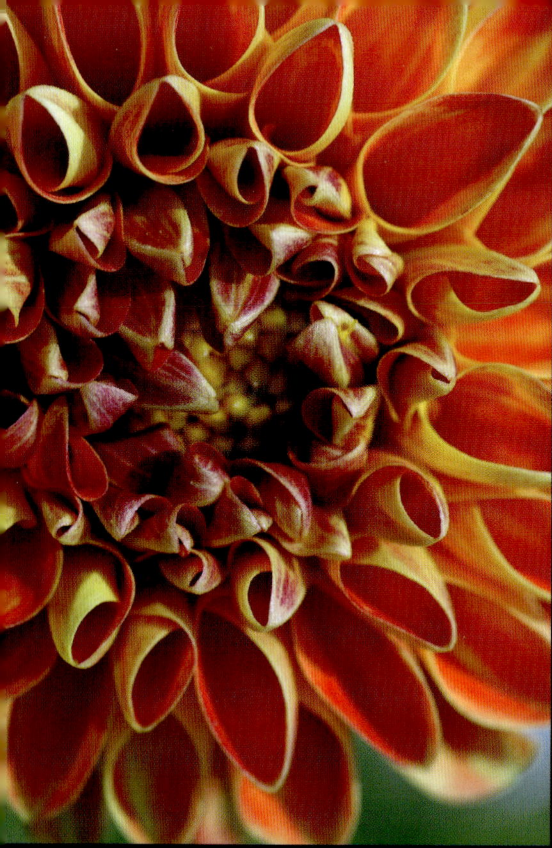
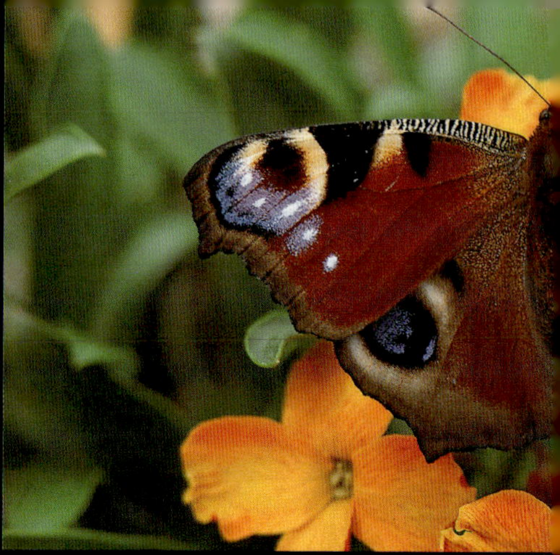
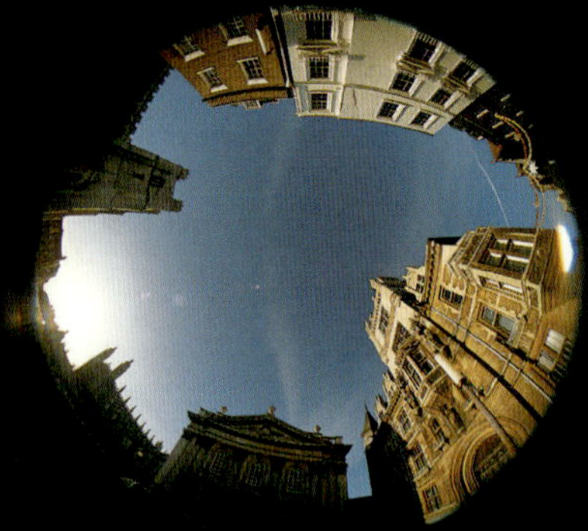
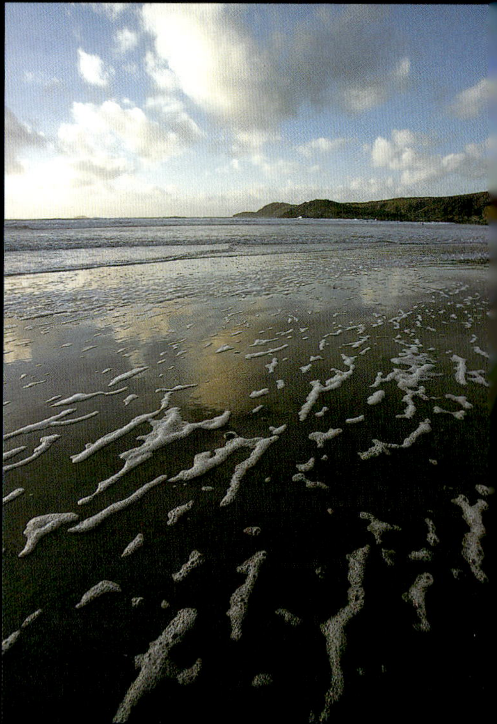

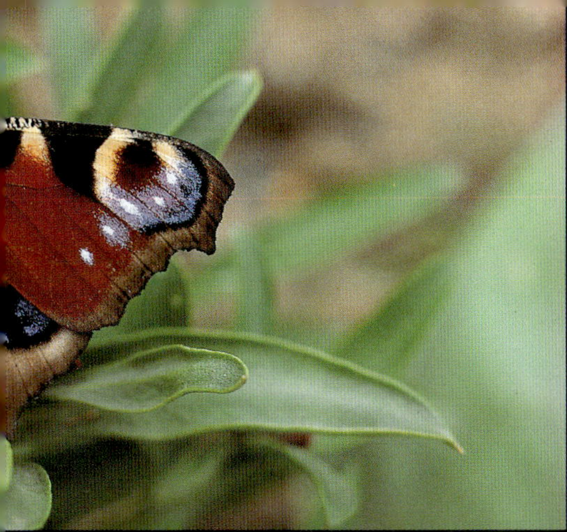

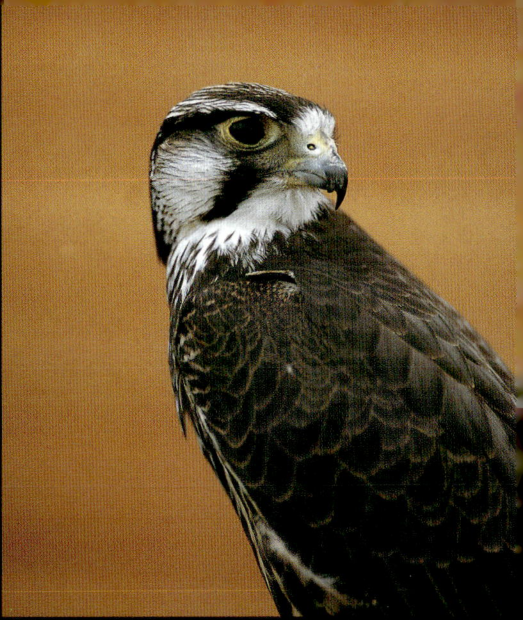

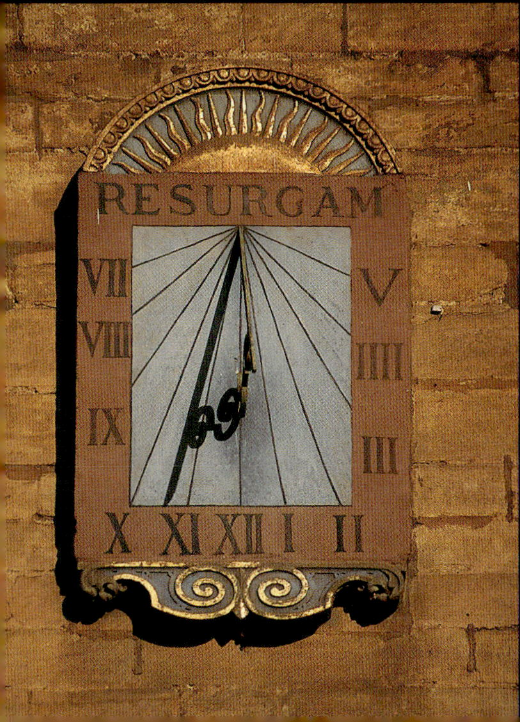
RESURGAM
VII
VIII
IX
X XI XII I II
III
IIII
V

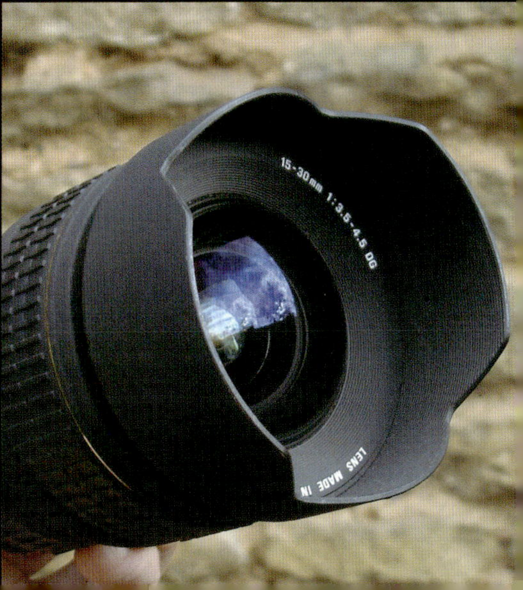
15-30mm 1:3.5-4.5 DG
LENS MADE IN

BUILDING A LENS SYSTEM

One of the biggest advantages of an SLR is its ability to take different lenses, which will allow you to tackle different subjects. But which lenses do you need? And which should you buy first? It all depends, of course, on what kind of pictures you like to take. In time you'll want to build up a comprehensive system that will let you handle just about any situation. But that takes time and money, and unless you have deep pockets, or an understanding bank manager, choices have to be made in the short term.

This section assumes that you either have an SLR (or rangefinder) with interchangeable lenses, or have an interest in learning about them. If you have a zoom compact, the information relating to various focal lengths and how to make the most of them will still be valuable, but you obviously won't have the option of changing from one lens to another.

The standard lens for most mechanical SLR bodies was a manual focus 50mm prime lens, while electronic cameras tended to be supplied with a standard zoom lens, covering focal lengths from around 28mm or 35mm, to 80mm or 105mm. Many second-hand cameras come with those lenses as standard, and they're a great way of getting started.

Over time, though, you'll probably want to add to your lens collection; perhaps you want a wide-angle lens for landscapes, a telephoto for portraits, or maybe just a faster lens to shoot in low-light. Whatever the reason, there are plenty of lenses available for most camera systems.

Unless you have a particular interest that demands a specialist lens, you'll find that 90 per cent of your picture-taking needs will be satisfied by just a couple of lenses covering the popular focal lengths, and they should be the first optics on your shopping list. It's important to choose them carefully, though, and try to think about your possible future needs, to avoid having to change lenses as your experience and interests develop.

LENS OPTIONS

Lenses come in many shapes and sizes. Most keen photographers build up a comprehensive system over time.

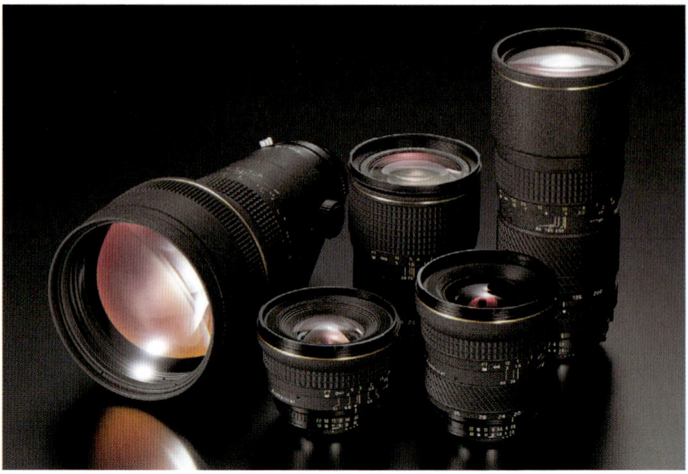

LENS TERMINOLOGY

- **Focal length:** This has both a technical and an everyday meaning. Technically, it's the distance between the principal point of a lens and the focal point, at which light rays from a distance are in focus. However, unless you know a bit about optics, that doesn't really tell you very much! At a more practical level, all you need to understand is that 50mm is a baseline reference point, considered the 'standard' or 'normal' focal length on a 35mm film camera. As you increase the focal length, the angle of view narrows and the magnification increases. The same object will, therefore, appear twice as large on film when photographed with a 100mm lens as it will with a 50mm lens. Conversely, as you reduce the focal length, the angle of view will increase and your subject will appear smaller in the frame. Any lens above 75mm is considered a 'telephoto' lens, and a lens with a focal length of 35mm or below is 'wide-angle'.
- **Angle of view:** The technical term used to describe how much of the scene a lens will take in is 'angle of view', which is always expressed in degrees. The larger the number, the greater the angle of view, or the 'wider' the lens. For example, a 50mm standard lens has an angle of view of 46°, while a 24mm lens has an angle of view of 84°, which allows you to include almost twice as much in the frame.
- **Maximum aperture:** This is the widest aperture setting on a lens. A 'fast' lens is one with a maximum aperture that is larger than normal for its focal length. For instance, a typical 300mm lens has a maximum aperture of f/4, but a fast 300mm has a maximum aperture of f/2.8. The extra light-gathering power allows you to set a faster shutter speed or achieve a shallower depth of field for creative effect, but you often have to pay a significant premium for this privilege.
- **Minimum aperture:** The minimum aperture of a lens is the smallest aperture available. This is often f/16 or f/22, although some lenses go to f/32. Having an extended minimum aperture offers no great advantage to most photographers.

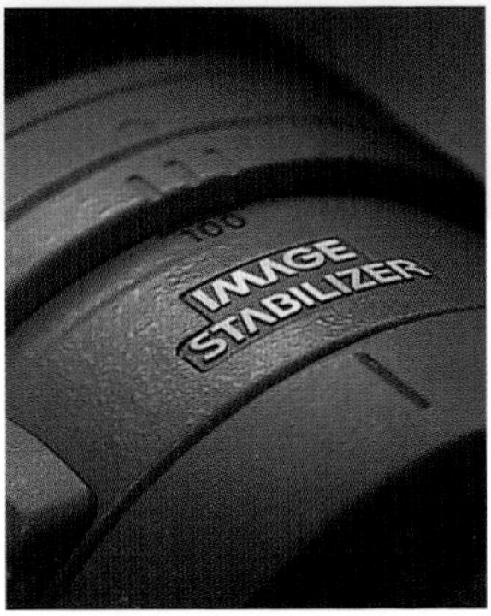

IMAGE STABILISER

Some modern lenses feature an image stabilisation system that compensates for photographer movement, allowing you to take pictures at slower shutter speeds without camera shake.

PRIME VS. ZOOM

One of the key factors to consider when building up a lens system is whether to buy zoom lenses or fixed focal length prime lenses – or a mixture of the two.

Zoom

Zoom lenses have a range of focal lengths in a single lens, which makes them incredibly convenient. If you want your subject to fill the frame a little more, you can zoom in, and if you want to record a wider scene, you can zoom out, without having to change your lens or camera position.

A single zoom lens can also be much cheaper than several prime lenses, which is why many photographers choose an outfit with two, sometimes three zoom lenses: a standard zoom with a focal length of 28mm or 35mm, to 80mm or 105mm; a telephoto zoom from 70mm or 80mm, up to 200mm or 300mm; and sometimes a wide-angle zoom. This is an excellent approach, and as you're not endlessly swapping from one lens to another you're always ready for the next shot. You'll use the standard zoom for everyday photography, the telezoom for details, portraits, and more distant subjects, and the wide-angle for group shots, buildings, and landscapes.

Some photographers opt for a superzoom, covering a 28–200mm or 28–300mm focal length range, which offers the ultimate in convenience.

However, designing complex zoom lenses is a matter of compromise, and generally these lenses aren't the optical equal of most primes, especially older zoom lenses from the 1970s and 80s. Aberrations are more often found on budget- to medium-priced zooms, with barrel distortion (where the image appears to bulge outwards) prevalent at wide-angle settings, and pincushion distortion (where the image is pinched in) common at the telephoto end.

The physical size of some zoom lenses when at full stretch can also make them difficult to hand-hold without causing camera shake at longer shutter speeds.

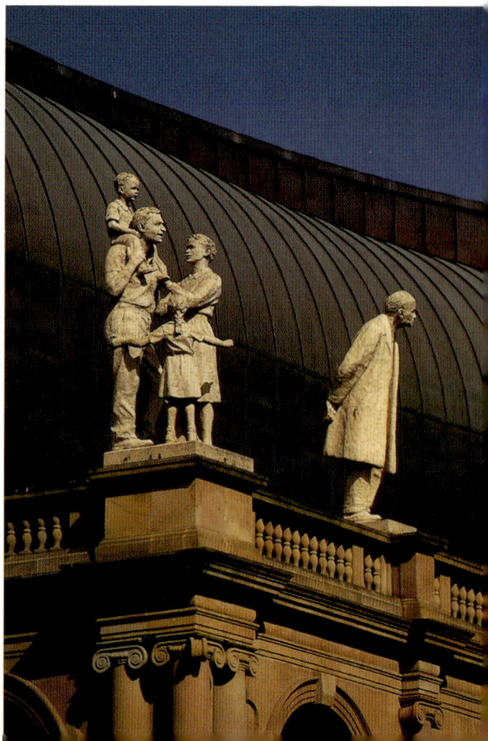

ZOOM

A zoom lens is ideal when you can't move physically closer to your subject, as you can zoom in to make your subject larger in the frame.

Prime

In comparison to zoom lenses, a prime lens is easier to optimise, as it has a single focal length. Consequently, both contrast and resolution tend to be superior in prime lenses. They're usually much smaller and lighter, making them easier to handle on the camera.

This is because a prime lens contains fewer lens elements and has a simpler configuration. A typical 28mm lens might have five elements in five groups, whereas a 28–80mm zoom might have 11 elements in nine groups, and a 28–200mm zoom may have 17 elements in 14 groups.

With less glass in them, prime lenses also tend to have larger maximum apertures. A 90mm or 135mm prime lens might offer a maximum aperture of f/2.8, while the maximum aperture on an average 70–300mm zoom lens may only be f/4 or f/5.6. Many fixed focal length lenses have a maximum aperture that's a full 2 stops larger than in the equivalent zoom lens. This not only gives you a brighter viewfinder image, but it also allows you to take pictures in lower light without the need for fast film or additional lighting.

Overall, you'll probably get sharper pictures if you shoot with prime lenses. If you can afford them, and don't mind carrying multiple lenses, this is arguably the best way to go if you are looking at older lenses.

However, modern zoom lenses are capable of high-quality images, which is why so many people use them on their digital cameras. You will need to check they are compatible with your film camera, but a modern zoom lens on a vintage camera body can strike a balance between convenience and quality.

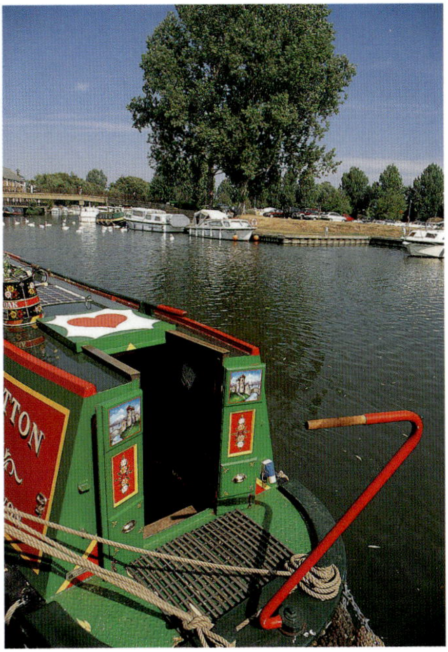

WIDE-ANGLE

For general wide-angle use, nothing beats a 24mm prime lens, especially if you go in close and fill the frame with a subject in the foreground and set a small aperture.

MARQUE VS. INDEPENDENTS

Today, the differences between marque lenses – those produced by the companies that make cameras – and most independently made lenses, tend to be slight. This was not always the case, and if you go back 50 years or so there was often a big performance difference between main camera manufacturers' lenses and those from an often bewildering range of third-party (indie) lens makers. Therefore, as a general rule, marque lenses are usually a better option when you're buying older film camera equipment.

At the same time, indie lenses can offer more choice, and because they were made in a range of fittings (gaining economies of scale), they are generally cheaper. If there is a particular 'exotic' focal length you want to experiment with – perhaps an ultra wide-angle, or a macro lens – an independent lens might let you test the waters without investing too heavily.

Generally, you get what you pay for with lenses, and since the optics are arguably the most important part of a camera system, it's always worth buying the best lenses you can afford.

HANDLING

Don't just buy a lens based on its specification. For example, the way a zoom lens handles in practice is also important. Is it comfortable and easy to use? Check the action of the zoom mechanism – is it just right, or too stiff, or too light? If it's an auto-focus lens, check the focusing ring in case you want to focus manually. Little niggles can grow into big ones when you use a lens on a regular basis.

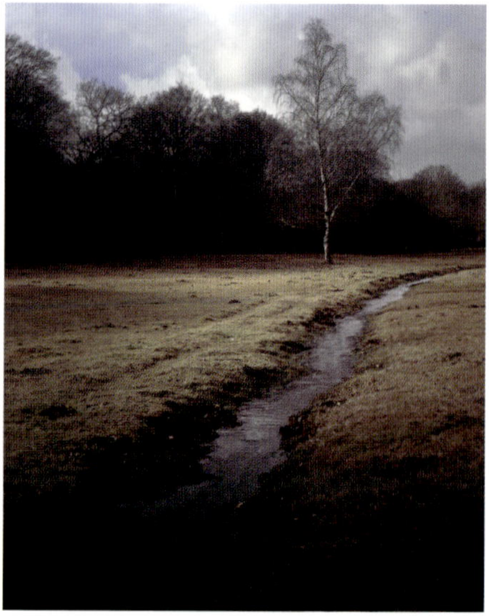

QUALITY

It doesn't matter how good your camera is, or who the manufacturer was, when it comes to image sharpness it is the lens that matters most. This image is packed with detail, thanks to the lens used.

LENS HOODS

Flare is caused when stray light enters the lens and scatters inside it, fogging all or part of the image, and resulting in a picture that lacks contrast and definition. Your pictures are most likely to suffer from flare when you're shooting directly into the sun on a bright day, and its strong light falls directly on the front element of the lens.

To prevent this, try to find a shooting position where the front element is shaded. Failing that, you can hold up one of your hands to block out the sun, although take care to ensure that it doesn't appear in the finished picture, or risk camera shake.

To minimise the risk of flare, you should also fit hoods to the fronts of all of your lenses. Whenever possible, buy a hood made for your specific lens, as it will be designed to offer the maximum protection. As a general rule, wide-angle lenses require extremely shallow hoods, telephotos benefit from far deeper types, and the lens hoods on zoom lenses tend to be a compromise as they have to cover multiple angles of view.

HOOD

A lens hood prevents stray light hitting the front element of your lens from the sides, which is a major cause of flare.

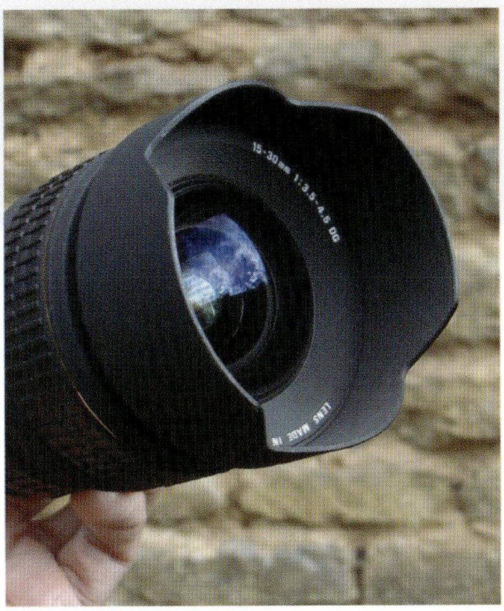

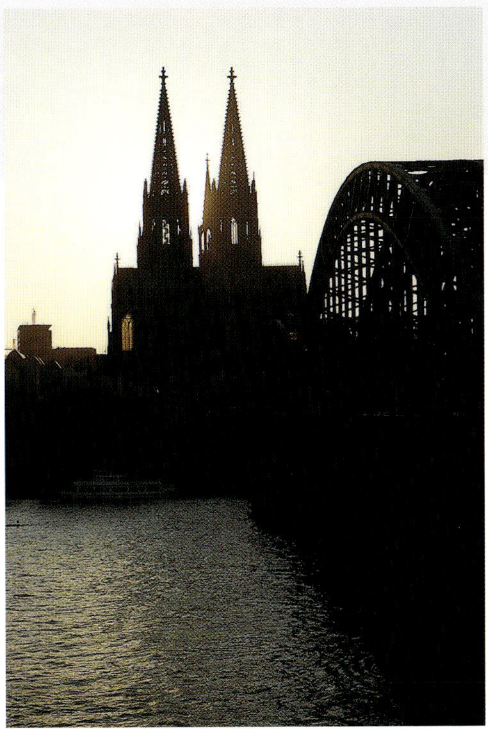

FLARE

When you're shooting towards a light source it can be impossible to avoid lens flare completely, but you can minimise it by positioning the light behind your subject.

APOCHROMATIC VS. NORMAL LENSES

Apochromatic lenses – more commonly known as 'apos' – have become popular in recent years, thanks largely to the pioneering efforts of Sigma, which was one of the first companies to offer a comprehensive range. But can you answer this question: what's the opposite of an apochromatic lens? Most photographers don't know the answer.

Normal – non-apo – lenses are technically called 'achromatic'. The key difference between the two is that achromats are corrected only in the blue-violet and yellow ranges of the spectrum, while apochromats are also corrected for the red wavelengths.

In practice, this means apochromatic lenses give sharper results. The improvement in optical quality is recognisable at all focal lengths, but is most significant with telephoto lenses. If you're shooting transparencies or having big enlargements made, an apo lens is a worthwhile investment if you have the choice.

LENS COATINGS

An important difference between older lenses and more modern ones is the coating that's now added to elements. When light hits an uncoated lens element, not all of it passes through; around 5–10 per cent is reflected back.

With a typical 70–210mm zoom lens containing 14 elements, that adds up to a lot of light sloshing around. The result is the loss of contrast and 'ghost' reflections that are referred to as flare.

To maximise light transmission, lenses are now given multiple coating layers, which can reduce reflection to as little as 0.2 per cent, minimising the danger of flare. The coatings used can also control the precise colour characteristics of the lens, and ensure that all the lenses in a particular range are optically matched for colour.

It's also worth noting that lens coatings contain a hardener that helps protect the front and rear elements from physical damage. For all these reasons, it's preferable to use a multi-coated lens if you are looking to get the highest quality images, although older, uncoated lenses can give your photographs a wonderfully vintage vibe.

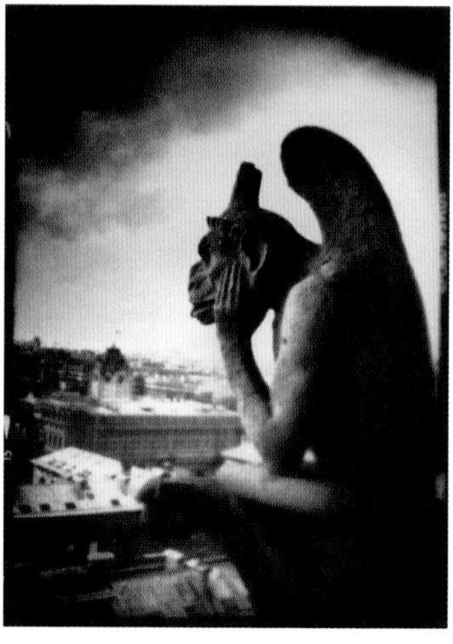

LO-FI

Vintage cameras and lenses can create distinctly 'lo-fi' photographs. This shot was taken using a folding camera from the 1930s, which has a lens that displays heavy blurring around the frame edges.

LENS DEFECTS

No lens is perfect, however well designed or made it is. Here are some of the most common optical aberrations and how to spot them.

- **Distortion:** The lens designer's aim is that the final picture represents the subject accurately. But the complexity of lens design, especially in wide-ranging zooms or fast-aperture lenses, means that this is not always possible. With subjects containing readily identifiable straight edges, such as buildings or artworks, distortion can become apparent when straight lines fall close to the edge of the picture. With barrel distortion, straight lines bend in at the corners of the frame; with pincushion distortion, the effect is reversed, with straight lines bending in at the centre. While some lens defects can be minimised or even eliminated by the chosen aperture setting, barrel and pincushion distortion remain the same no matter what the f-stop is.
- **Spherical aberration:** Light rays entering the edge of a lens element are bent more than those passing through the centre, and the spread of focus this produces results in a soft, low-contrast image. All lenses are subject to some spherical aberration, which is one reason why they tend to give sharper results as you close down the aperture – because less light from the edge is being used. Most lenses are at their optical best 2 stops down from maximum aperture. If the performance is significantly worse – with optimum quality 4 or 5 stops in – this is a sign of severe spherical aberration.
- **Coma (comatic aberration):** Compensating for spherical aberration is not difficult, but one of the effects of overcompensating is coma, which causes blurring near the edges of the image, with circles reproduced as 'pear' or 'comet' shapes. Once again, setting a smaller aperture will lead to a significant improvement in image quality.
- **Flare:** Flare is caused by non-image-forming light bouncing around inside the lens. Careful design, including multi-coated elements and anti-reflection measures inside the lens barrel can help, but it can never be eliminated entirely, especially when the sun or some other powerful light source is included in the picture. For that reason, it's always a good idea to use a lens hood.
- **Vignetting:** Less light finds its way into the corners of a picture, resulting in a darker 'frame' around the subject. This fall-off becomes greater as the angle of view increases, and is most often seen in lenses with a focal length of 24mm or less, although not all wide-angle lenses suffer from the problem. Setting a small aperture can help, as the smaller the aperture, the less the vignetting. With some lenses – especially wide-angles and those with large front elements – 'mechanical' vignetting may occur if you fit a filter or a lens hood that is too large. This is simply a result of the filter or hood encroaching into the frame.

FOCAL LENGTH

In the strictest sense, the focal length of a lens is the distance from its optical centre to the point at which the light rays passing through it converge and focus. Unless you're looking at a really old lens, this distance is typically given in mm, hence a 50mm prime lens, a 35–70mm zoom lens, and so on.

On a practical level, what the focal length tells us is whether a lens is a wide-angle lens, a standard lens, or a telephoto lens.

STANDARD LENSES

Until the 1980s, the majority of (primarily mechanical) SLRs were supplied with a 50mm prime lens, which was more commonly known as a standard lens. As electronic SLRs became more prevalent, standard zoom lenses appeared, offering focal lengths of around 28–70mm or 35–80mm.

In each case, they're called 'standard' because their 50mm focal length and 46° angle of view give a perspective that's very similar to the way we see the world with our eyes. This results in natural-looking pictures, making a 50mm lens the ideal choice when you want to record things faithfully, without distortion.

Most 50mm prime lenses are small, lightweight, and produce razor-sharp images. They also tend to have a maximum aperture of around f/1.8, which is ideal for taking photographs in low light without resorting to flash, as well as making it easy to throw backgrounds out of focus.

However, while a standard lens can be extremely useful, pictures can sometimes lack impact, simply because the perspective is so familiar.

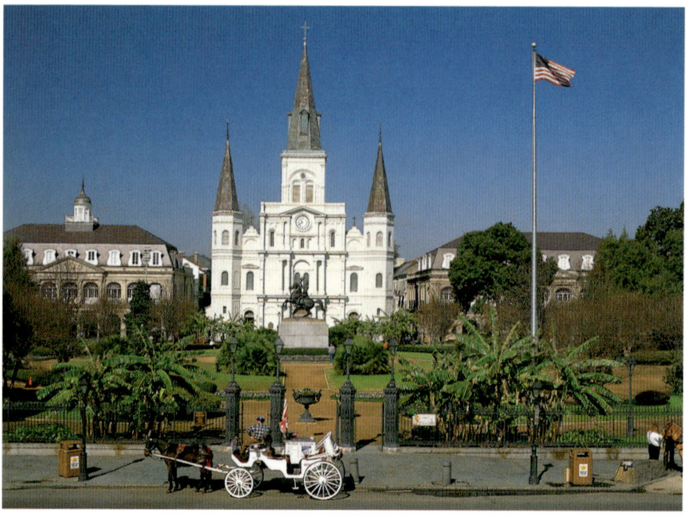

STANDARD LENS

A 50mm focal length is ideal when you want a natural perspective that concentrates attention on the subject rather than the photographic technique.

WIDE-ANGLE LENSES

Lenses that take in more of the scene than a 50mm lens are known as wide-angles. The most popular fixed focal length wide-angles are 28mm and 24mm, but the full range extends from specialised 8mm fisheye lenses up to 35mm.

The most obvious characteristic of a wide-angle lens is that it includes more of the subject in the frame. The wider the angle of view of the lens the more it will take in; a 21mm includes more than a 24mm, a 28mm more than a 35mm, and so on.

Wide-angle lenses also give a greater apparent depth of field, especially at small apertures such as f/11 and f/16. This ability of wide-angle lenses to keep everything sharp is legendary. If you set an aperture of f/22 and focus at 1m (39in), everything from 0.5m (20in) to infinity will be in focus. Even at more modest apertures, depth of field is extensive. In fact, when using a wide-angle lens, it can be difficult to throw the background out of focus when that is what you want to do.

Another useful aspect of a wide-angle lens is the dramatic perspective it can provide, with the parts of the scene that are closest to the camera looming large while elements further away seem to recede quickly into the distance. This effect is exaggerated if you tip the camera backwards or forwards. This creates what are called 'converging verticals', with the result that tall buildings appear to be falling over backwards.

There's always a danger when using a wide-angle lens that everything will end up looking a long way away, and the wider the lens, the greater the risk of this happening. However, by paying careful attention to your composition, and framing the subject so there is something of interest in the foreground, you can create a wonderful sense of depth and space in your pictures. With a landscape, for instance, you might find a vantage point with a rock or a boat close to the camera. With a building, the foreground might include some brightly coloured flowers or a statue. Or you could look for some kind of natural frame, such as an overhanging tree or a bridge, to place in the foreground.

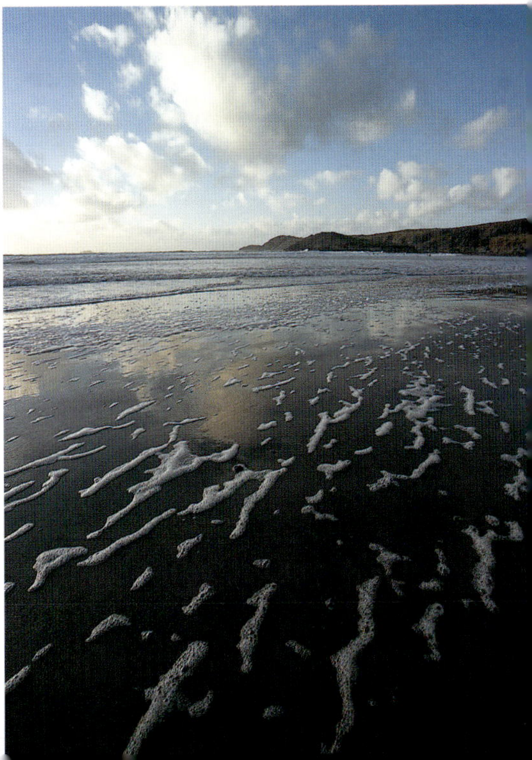

LANDSCAPE

To open up the perspective in this seascape, a 17mm lens was used from a low angle. The seafoam adds both a touch of foreground interest and draws the eye into the picture and up to the distant headland.

The two areas where wide-angle lenses are most commonly used are landscape and architecture photography. Both involve large subjects that cannot be photographed satisfactorily with a standard lens, and it's often not possible to step back to include more in the frame. When photographing the interior of a building, a wide-angle lens can make rooms look much more spacious than they really are.

Wide-angle lenses are also useful when you are photographing a large group of people and space is restricted. In this situation, care should be taken that you don't place those at the edges of the group too close to the edge of the frame, or they can end up looking distorted.

Wide-angle options

- **35mm:** The 35mm focal length used to be the most commonly used wide-angle, but hardly anybody buys it as a separate focal length now, apart from reportage photographers who work in close and want to include more than a 50mm lens will allow. If you want a fast, compact, moderate wide-angle lens, 28mm is arguably a better choice.
- **28mm:** With an angle of view of 75°, this is the first focal length at which wide-angle characteristics really become apparent. A 28mm focal length lends itself to pretty much any kind of photography, and is capable of taking in a broad sweep of landscape or the interior of a building with little in the way of distortion. At one time, 28mm prime lenses were phenomenally popular, but now they're more commonly the start of a zoom lens range.
- **24mm:** The 24mm lens marks the turning point between wide and ultra-wide. It's wide enough to give a distinctive and dramatic wide-angle sweep, but without significant distortion – and at a sensible price. Depth of field is extensive, even at wide apertures, and creates an exaggerated scale and perspective. If you ever find yourself wanting to photograph big buildings, vast landscapes, cramped interiors, or large groups of people, the 84° angle of view delivered by a 24mm focal length will let you cram a surprising amount more into your pictures.

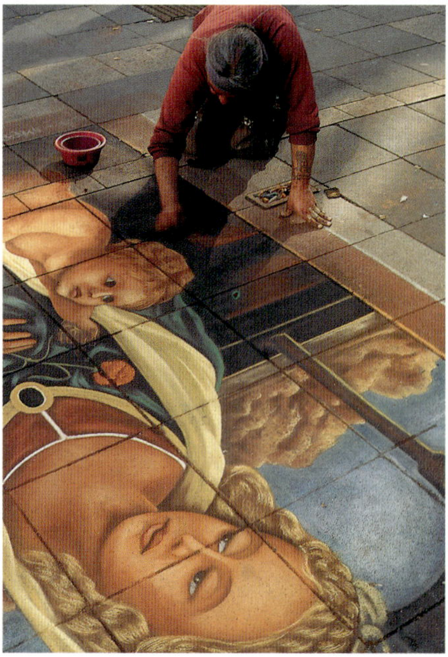

28MM

The look and feel you get from an image taken on a 28mm may not be as exciting as lenses with a wider angle of view, but they're great when you don't want to get too much into the frame.

- **20mm:** This focal length is loved by landscape photographers, due to its great covering power and sweeping perspective. Although it is never a cheap option, it's certainly worth considering, especially as most 20mm prime lenses have a maximum aperture of f/2.8, which makes it possible to shoot hand-held, even when the light levels start to drop.
- **17mm:** This classic ultra-wide-angle focal length swallows up an enormous amount of the world, and as soon as you tip it even a little, it will bend straight lines into curves. This is great when you really do want to cram everything in and produce dramatic results, but care is needed if you want to minimise the distortion. The amazing perspective offered by ultra-wide-angle lenses makes it possible to create striking images from virtually nothing, simply by going in close.

Wide-angle zooms

The advent of digital SLRs with small sensor sizes prompted manufacturers to produce high-quality, wide-angle zoom lenses at more affordable prices. As a result, you can buy zoom lenses that start from 15–20mm, and go up to somewhere between 30–40mm. As with other zoom lenses, image quality is not, in absolute terms, as good as prime lenses, but for most purposes it's more than sufficient. If you favour landscape, architectural, or group work, a wide-angle zoom lens is worth considering, assuming it is compatible with your film camera.

20MM

Lenses in the region of 20mm or 21mm give a distinctive, striking wide-angle look, but care is needed to prevent everything looking as if it's far off in the distance.

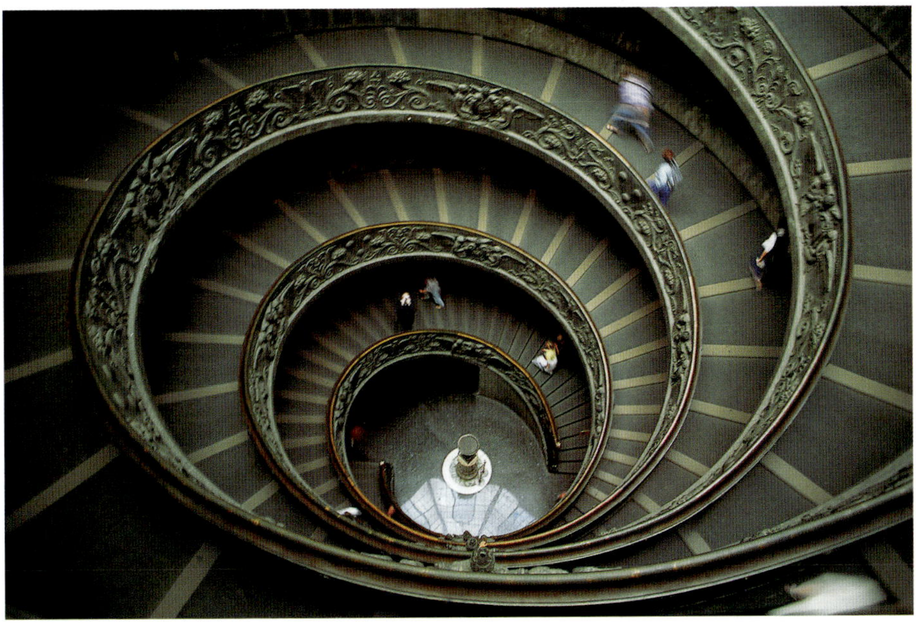

TELEPHOTO LENSES

A telephoto lens allows you to fill the frame with small and distant subjects, by narrowing the angle of view. Strictly speaking, any lens above about 70mm is a telephoto, but it's not really until you get to a 100mm focal length that you start to see an obvious telephoto effect, which gets stronger as the focal length increases.

The main reason most photographers want a long telephoto lens is to bring distant subjects closer. Certainly, if you want to photograph subjects such as wildlife and birds or sport and action, you won't make much impact without something reasonably powerful. But long telephoto lenses are also excellent for the subjects that most photographers tackle with a wide-angle – such as architecture and landscape.

With buildings, for instance, standing some way back and using a 200mm or 300mm lens enables you to take shots in which the verticals are perfectly upright. You avoid the convergence that happens when using a standard or wide-angle lens in close. Landscapes also take on a different dimension, allowing you to turn much-photographed scenes into interesting and unusual abstracts. Telephoto lenses enable you to crop in tightly on just a small part of the vast panorama in front of you – such as a lonely white house set in a vast valley. Zoom lenses up to 300mm are particularly versatile for this kind of work, allowing you a wide range of framing options.

CANDID SHOTS

Super-telephoto lenses are powerful enough to tackle most distant subjects – this candid portrait was taken from the opposite side of a road using a 600mm lens.

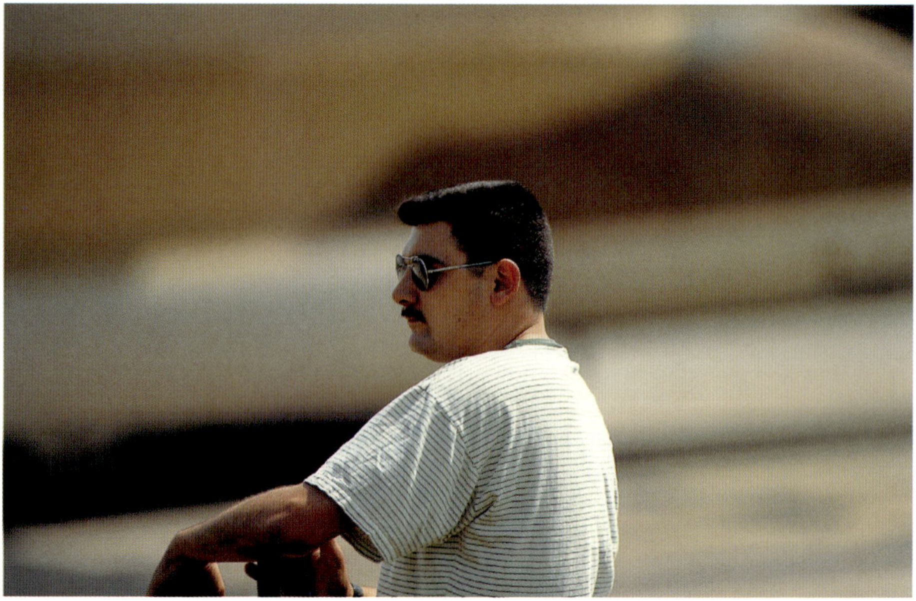

Even in portraiture, long telephoto lenses have a part to play. Most photographers recommend a lens with a focal length of around 100mm for flattering pictures of people, but try shooting with a 200mm or even 300mm, and you can make the person stand out extremely powerfully, thanks to the limited depth of field such lenses give, especially when used at maximum aperture.

Long telephoto lenses also have another characteristic that clever photographers can take advantage of – the way in which they appear to compress perspective. When you use a 300mm or 400mm lens, you'll find that subjects that are in reality a long way apart seem to 'stack up' so they look as if they're next to each other. This can be used to dramatic effect with a subject such as a row of trees or distant buildings.

You do need to be aware, however, that long telephoto lenses will show up any weaknesses in your technique. With the depth of field so limited, your focusing needs to be exact, because even the slightest error can lead to unsharp pictures. With an autofocus camera, this shouldn't be a problem, although camera shake might be. When hand-holding a long telephoto lens, remember to set a shutter speed that's at least the reciprocal of the focal length – 1/250 sec with a 200mm, 1/500 sec with a 400mm – and preferably faster still. Even that may not be enough. Whenever possible, you should use a tripod to stabilise it. Or when shooting sport and action, use a monopod, which combines stability with manoeuvrability.

ISOLATING DETAIL

Telephoto lenses are great for isolating details in the landscape; a 200mm lens was used to pick out this remote farmhouse.

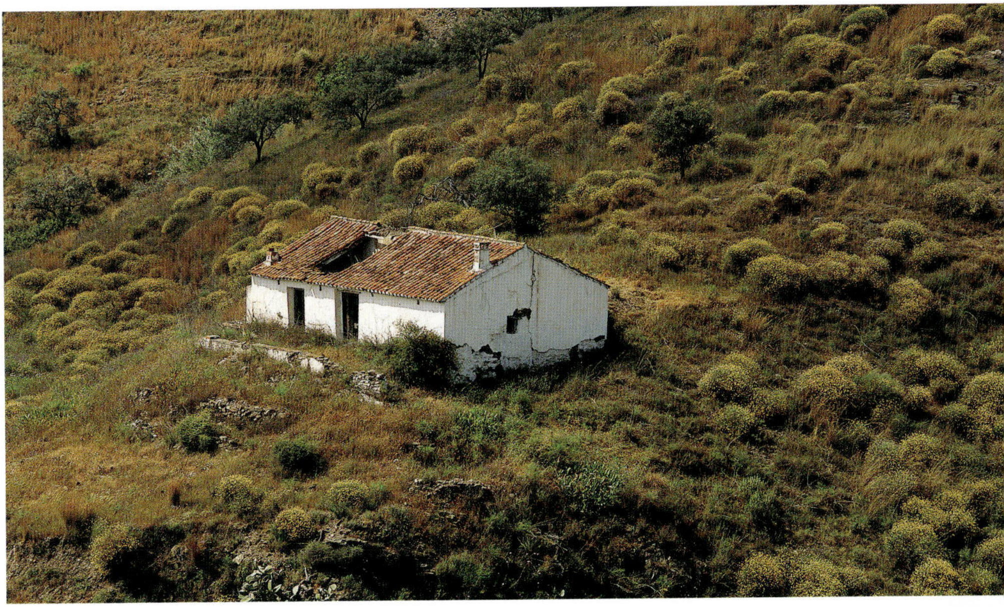

Telephoto options

In the days of mechanical 35mm SLRs, photographers would buy separate 90mm, 135mm, and 200mm lenses. It's now more common to take in these three focal lengths in a telephoto zoom lens, although as discussed previously there are still arguments for sticking with prime lenses.

- **Short telephoto:** Telephoto lenses with a focal length between 70mm and 105mm are more commonly known as portrait lenses. The perspective they give is perfect for creating flattering pictures of people. Short telephoto lenses are also excellent for a host of other subjects, from landscape to still life, where you want to crop in a little more tightly on a subject. The most common prime lenses in this sector have focal lengths of 85mm, 90mm, 100mm, or 105mm, and most camera makers offer one or two in their range, sometimes with options in respect of maximum aperture – 85mm f/1.8 lenses are particularly popular (and expensive).
- **Medium telephoto:** With a focal length of 135mm or 200mm, medium telephoto lenses are slightly more powerful, making them ideal for situations where you can't get quite so close to your subject, such as candid shots, accessible sports, pets, and architectural details. Prime 135mm and 200mm lenses are no longer as popular as they once were, as most people now prefer to buy a telephoto zoom lens, but this also means they no longer command high prices, making them a potential bargain for film photographers.
- **Long telephoto:** Longer telephoto lenses, from 300mm upwards, have extra pulling power that enables you to fill the frame with far-off subjects. This makes them the ideal choice for wildlife and sports photographers, and this is a sector that is particularly well served, both in terms of marque lenses and independents. For general long telephoto photography, a 400mm is probably the best choice, although there are also plenty of 300mm

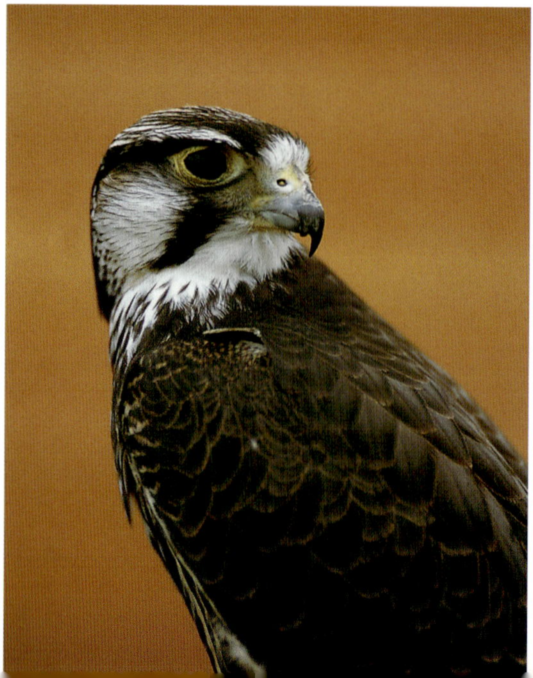

PHOTOGRAPHING BIRDS

At a falconry centre, it's possible to get sufficiently close to birds of prey to fill the frame using a telephoto lens.

lenses available. Longer telephoto lenses in the region of 500mm and 600mm are only worth considering if you want to shoot difficult subjects, such as wild birds and motorsport, while extreme focal lengths up to 1200mm are an extremely specialist option. Very long telephoto lenses are bulky, heavy, and expensive. Another option is a 1.4x or 2x converter when you need more pulling power.

Telephoto zooms

For many photographers – especially those using an electronic SLR – a telephoto zoom lens ranging from 70mm or 80mm to 200mm or 300mm, is the ideal second lens. A single, reasonably priced lens will give you access to a wide range of popular subjects out of the reach of a standard zoom. However, be aware that comparable lenses designed for mechanical SLRs are likely to be compromised in terms of image quality, making separate prime lenses a better option.

ARCHITECTURAL DETAIL

There are some things you can't get close to, such as this sundial on the side of a building. That's when you need a telephoto lens. Here, the top end of a 70–200mm zoom lens was used to focus attention on a small detail.

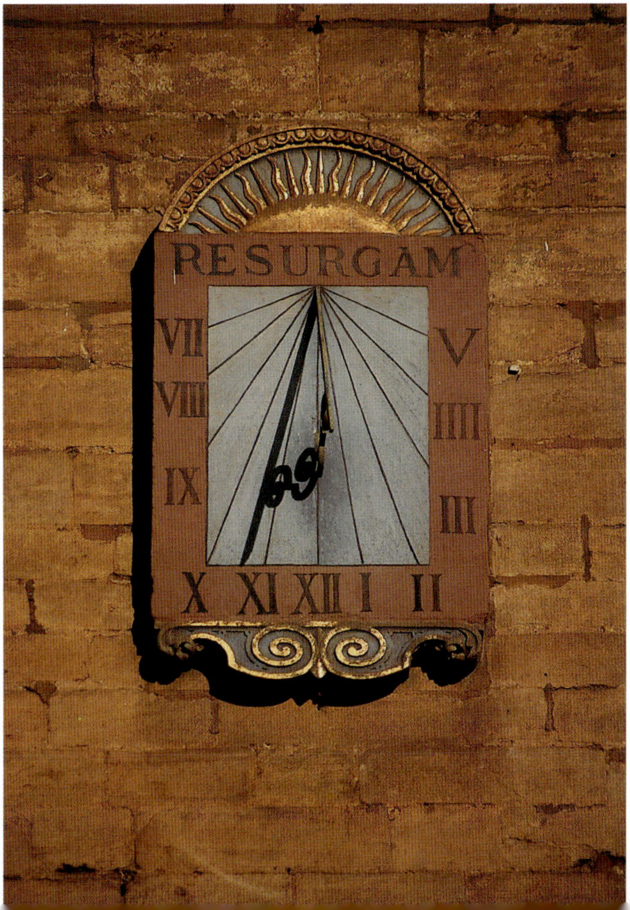

SPECIALIST LENSES AND ACCESSORIES

MACRO LENSES

Designed for close-up photography, macro lenses are available in two main focal length ranges: 50/60mm and 90/100/105mm. The former doubles as a standard lens, while the latter makes an excellent portrait optic. The short telephoto lens is also a better choice if you want to photograph insects, as you don't have to get as close to your subject.

While some macro lenses give half life-size reproduction, the true macro ratio is 1:1, which means your subject appears life-size on the film. When using a macro lens, accurate focusing is essential, as the closer you get to your subject, the more limited the depth of field becomes. At its closest focus setting, the lens may only offer few millimetres of depth of field, even at a small aperture, so it's best to focus manually, even if you have an autofocus camera.

SOFT-FOCUS LENSES

Most modern lenses, even budget-priced ones, are capable of taking high-quality pictures, with lots of detail and plenty of contrast. But for certain subjects they can sometimes be *too* sharp. While you could soften the image by fitting a soft-focus filter, you can also buy specialist soft-focus lenses. This type of lens has a ring that allows you to dial in soft focus when you want it, or use it as a normal lens when you don't. Soft-focus lenses aren't particularly common, but occasionally turn up on eBay or with second-hand camera dealers.

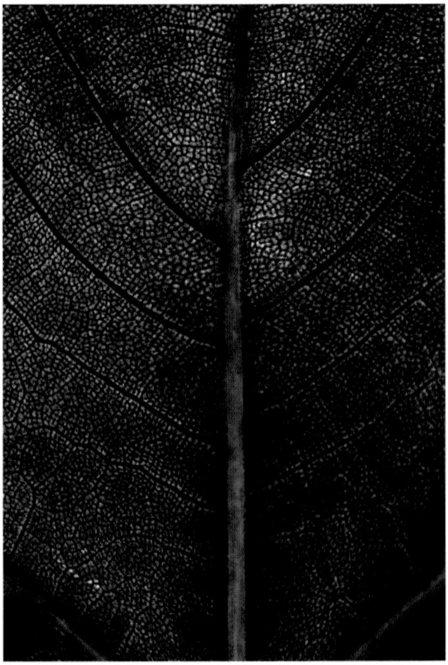

MACRO

A macro lens is the perfect choice for photographing small subjects or getting in close to tiny details, such as the veins in this leaf, which were given a 'sooty' black-and-white look.

PERSPECTIVE-CONTROL LENSES

Also known as tilt-shift lenses, perspective-control (PC) lenses make it possible to photograph tall buildings in confined circumstances without causing the converging verticals, which make buildings appear to be leaning backwards. This is achieved by means of a sliding control on the lens that allows the elements to be shifted up or down (hence the name) to control the perspective.

Shift lenses are easy to use because you can see the effect they're having in the viewfinder. Start by making sure the camera back is absolutely vertical – ideally using a hot-shoe spirit level – then simply adjust the degree of shift until a clear upright on the subject lines up with the edge of the viewfinder frame. Because of the fine control needed, this is a lot easier if you work on a tripod, which will have the added benefit of allowing you to set a small aperture, ensuring maximum depth of field.

A secondary control – 'tilt' – allows you to tilt the front of the lens forwards and back. This works in much the same way as the front standard on a large format camera and can be used to extend or reduce the depth of field at any given aperture. You can tilt the lens sideways to adjust the plane of focus and create a vertical 'slice' of sharpness in a photograph.

Whichever approach you choose, care should always be taken with exposure metering, as the process of shifting and tilting the lens can cause errors. The surest approach is to take your exposure reading *before* changing the perspective.

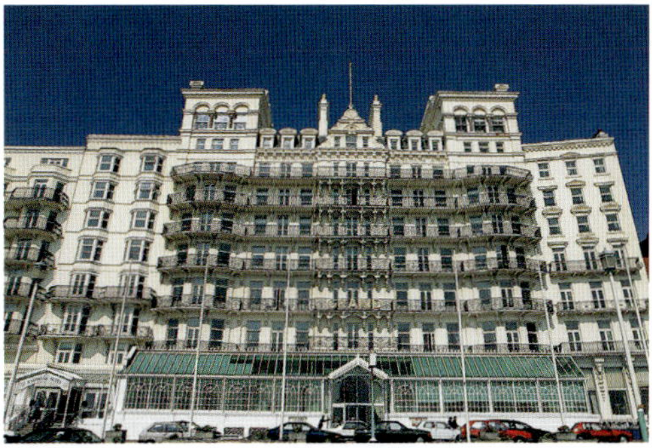

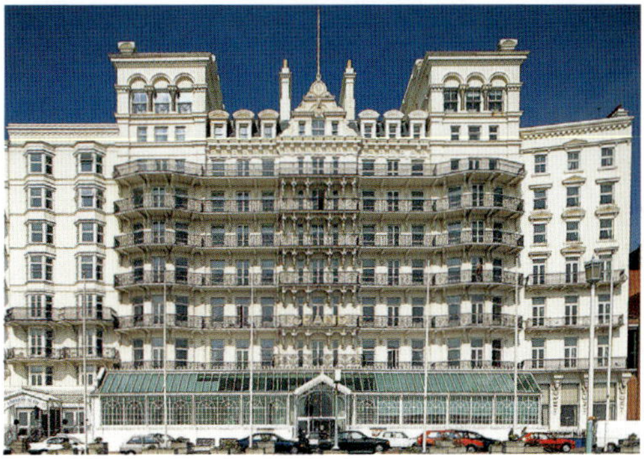

PERSPECTIVE CONTROL

Shot with a normal 24mm lens (top), this building appears to be leaning backwards. But when a 24mm PC lens is used (above), it's possible to correct the converging verticals.

FISHEYE LENSES

With an angle of view of 180°, fisheye lenses make all kinds of outlandish effects possible, although they can easily become overused, especially when you first get one.

There are two types of fisheye lens. The first is the circular fisheye, which typically has a focal length of 6mm or 8mm. As the name suggests, it produces a circular image on film, with a black border.

The second type of lens is the full-frame fisheye, with a focal length that's typically 15mm to 18mm. This type of fisheye lens produces an image over the entire frame.

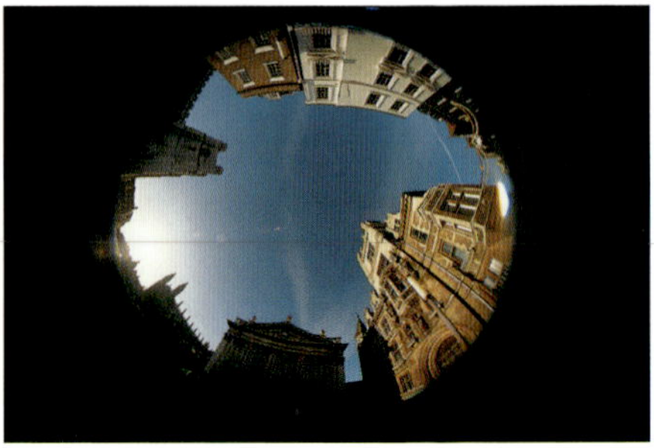

CIRCULAR FISHEYE

The characteristic circular image from a fisheye lens takes in a full 180°, so you need to be careful not to include your fingers or feet in the picture.

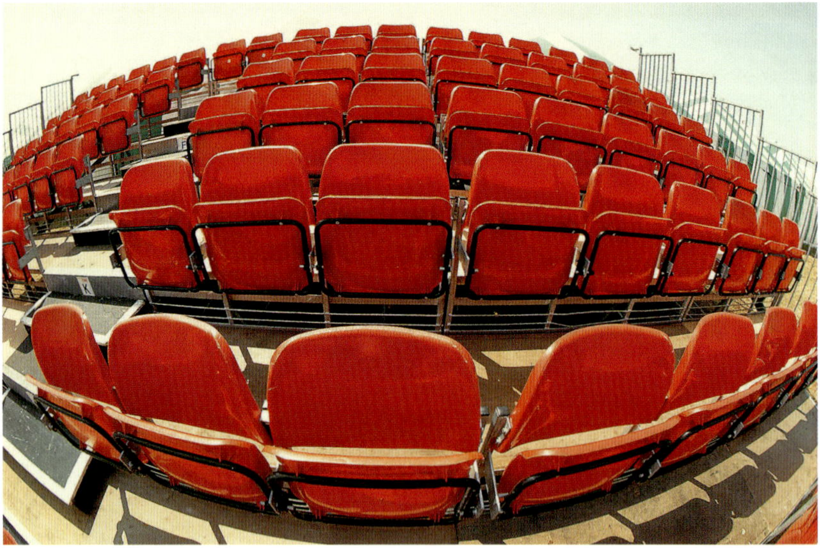

FULL-FRAME FISHEYE

Full-frame fisheye lenses, such as this 15mm lens, produce a standard 24 x 36mm image, but straight lines curve as soon as you tip the camera. Objects close to the camera look much larger than those further away.

TELECONVERTERS

Teleconverters are an inexpensive way of increasing your focal length. Fitting 2x and 3x converters to a 100mm lens (right) gives the equivalent of 200mm (centre right) and 300mm (far right) focal lengths.

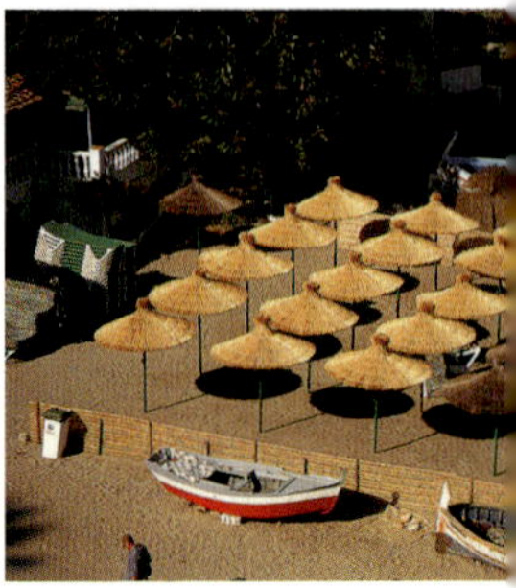

MIRROR LENSES

A mirror lens (or 'catadioptric' lens) is a kind of telephoto lens that uses mirrors rather than additional lens elements. This makes them far more compact and lightweight than traditional telephoto designs, so they are considerably easier to carry around and use.

However, the nature of the design also means that a mirror lens has a fixed aperture – typically f/8 on a 500mm lens – so you have no real control over the shutter speed. If you're hand-holding the camera you'll want to set a shutter speed that's at least equivalent to the focal length of the lens in use. With a 500mm mirror lens, the minimum shutter speed to be safe is 1/500 sec. On a sunny day, you *might* be able to shoot at 1/500 sec using ISO 100 film, but it makes more sense to load up with a faster film, or use a tripod. Because of the fixed aperture, you will need to work in aperture priority or manual exposure modes.

The design of a mirror lens also produces a distinctive 'doughnut-like' effect on out-of-focus highlights (which you'll soon tire of) and the large front element and mirror design makes these lenses prone to flare and low-contrast images. If you want a cheap long telephoto lens then a mirror lens is an option, but you may quickly find it too restrictive.

TELECONVERTERS

A teleconverter is an optical device that fits between the lens and the camera body. It increases the focal length of the lens by a factor of 1.4, 2, or 3 times, depending on the converter. It is a simple and inexpensive alternative to buying another lens of a longer focal length, with a 2x converter effectively turning a 50mm lens into 100mm, a 300mm into 600mm, and so on. This also applies to zoom lenses. If you use a 2x converter with a 28–105mm lens, it would effectively become a 56–210mm zoom lens.

However, there are two problems. First, a teleconverter degrades the image quality, resulting in a picture with reduced sharpness and lower contrast. The amount it's degraded by depends primarily on the quality of the lens. Prime lenses tend to give good results when used with a converter, but results from a zoom lens combined with a converter can be disappointing.

A second drawback is that converters absorb light. A 1.4x converter absorbs one stop, a 2x converter two stops, and a 3x converter loses three stops. This reduces the maximum aperture of the lens, so an f/2.8 lens with a 2x teleconverter attached would behave as if it had a maximum aperture of f/5.6. To compensate, you may need to use faster film, which further compromises image quality.

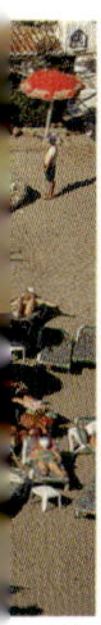

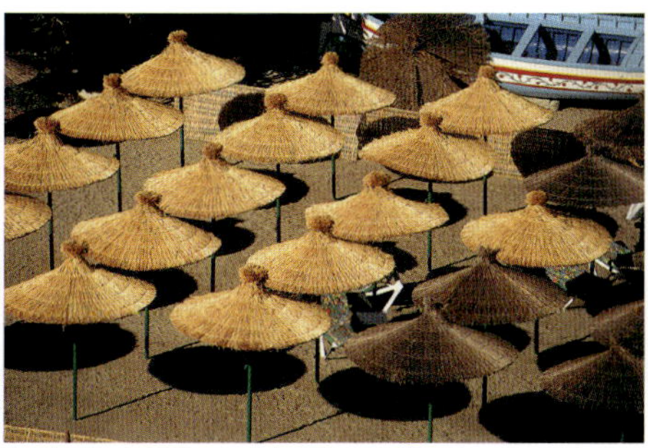

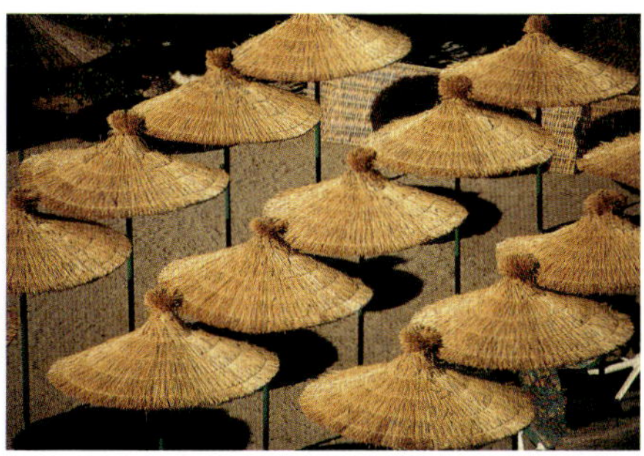

CLOSE-UP ACCESSORIES

Looking for a new challenge? Then why not have a go at shooting some close-ups? Start thinking small and you'll soon find yourself immersed in a fascinating world. Many of the most beautiful things are tiny – think of the wings of a dragonfly or the petals of a flower – and for just a small investment you could start capturing their beauty on film.

To start with, it's important to be clear about the terminology, because the terms 'close-up' and 'macro' are often treated as interchangeable, when in fact they have very specific meanings. The key lies in understanding what 'life-size' means.

A life-size photograph is one in which a subject is reproduced on film exactly the same size as it is in real life. If you were to take a life-size photograph of an object measuring 24 x 36 mm, it would completely fill the picture area. This is said to be a reproduction ratio of 1:1. If the same subject filled half of the picture area it would be half life-size, or 1:2. And if only half of it could be fitted in, that would be twice life-size, or 2:1.

Technically, close-up photography is concerned with pictures in the range 1:10 to 1:1. That is, from one tenth life-size to actual life-size. So suitable subjects include insects, coins, small flower heads, stamps, and so on. Macro photography covers life-size to ten times life-size, from 1:1 to 10:1. Magnifications greater than 10:1 fall into the area known as micro photography.

To be able to shoot close-ups successfully you really do need an SLR, with its reflex viewing system that allows you to look through the taking lens. Compact cameras are wonderful for a great many subjects, but close-up photography is not one of them. The parallax errors caused by the separate viewing and lens systems mean it's impossible to frame the shot accurately. Nor can you see precisely the effect of any close-up accessory you may have added.

Many people think expensive specialist equipment is required to shoot close-ups, but nothing could be further from the truth.

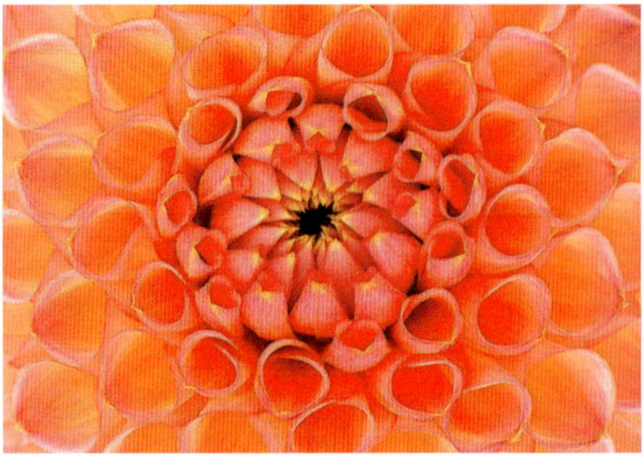

MACRO LENS

When it comes to close-up photography, nothing beats a good quality macro lens for clarity, detail, and sharpness.

In fact you may already have all that you need to get started. The standard 50mm lens will focus down to around 0.5m (20in) and fill the frame with something the size of an A4 page. This makes it suitable for closing in on larger subjects such as flower heads. A telezoom lens will take you even closer. Specifications vary, but many telezoom lenses allow you to produce quarter life-size images. However, if you want to magnify things more than this, you'll need to invest in some accessories.

The great thing about close-up photography is that there's such a wide range of accessories available. You can dip your toe in the water by buying a simple screw-in filter and then, if you find you like shooting close-ups, dive into the deep end and invest in a macro lens.

CLOSE-UP LENS

Supplementary close-up lenses fit over the front of your lens like a filter and are typically available as screw-in types.

Close-up filters increase the magnification achieved by reducing the focusing distance. They come in a range of different strengths, measured in dioptres. The weakest is +1 dioptre and the strongest +10 dioptres. For general close-up work, a +4 dioptre lens is the best choice, and will allow you to fill the frame with something the size of a butterfly.

The advantage of using close-up lenses is that there are no problems with exposure. You can rely on your camera's meter for accurate results. There is some slight loss of quality when working with these lenses, but this can be minimised by shooting at a small aperture of f/11–f/22. This also has the advantage of giving you plenty of depth of field to keep everything sharp. You can also combine multiple close-up lenses for even greater magnification, although the loss of image quality will be compounded.

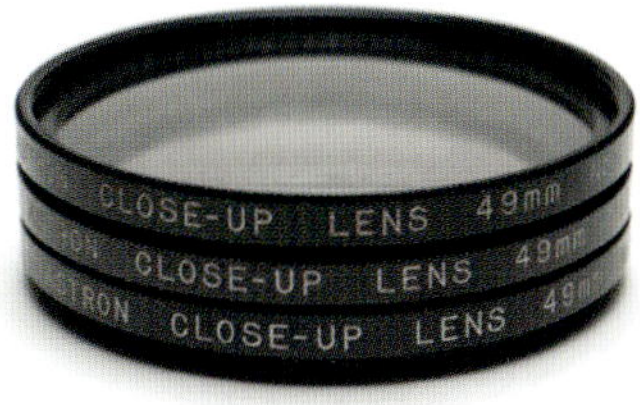

CLOSE-UP LENSES
Close-up lenses come in a range of strengths, measured in dioptres – the higher the number the closer you can focus.

GETTING CLOSER
Although inexpensive, supplementary close-up lenses produce high-quality images quickly and easily. To capture this butterfly, a +4 dioptre lens was used on a 50mm standard lens.

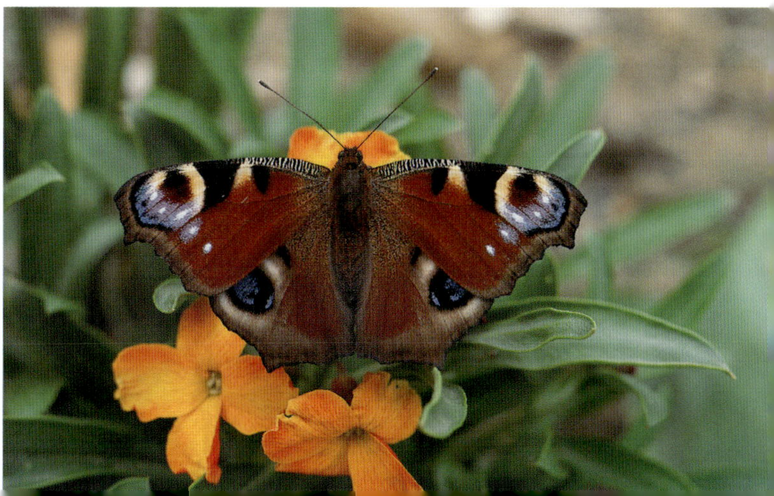

REVERSING RING

A lens reversing ring is a simple adapter that allows you to reverse the lens so that the front element faces the camera body, producing an extremely powerful and high-quality close-up accessory. The degree of magnification depends upon the lens in use: a 50mm lens will give 1:1 (life-size), a 28mm delivers 2:1 (twice life-size), while a 100mm produces 1:2 (half life-size).

The versatility of this set-up improves if you use a reversing ring with a zoom lens. A 28–105mm zoom would enable you to vary the reproduction ratio from half life-size to twice life-size, albeit with a slight loss of image quality.

EXTENSION TUBES

Extension tubes are simply hollow tubes that increase magnification by extending the distance between the camera body and the lens. Independent manufacturers generally sell tubes in sets of three different sizes that can be combined to give a wide range of extensions. The degree of enlargement can be determined by dividing the amount of extension by the focal length of the lens in use. For example, a 50mm lens with 52mm of extension (21mm plus 31mm) will give you 1:1 (life-size) reproduction. Extension tubes also work well with telephoto lenses, giving smaller magnifications but greater camera-to-subject distances. The quality is top-notch, because no additional glass is introduced. Extension tubes are the best general accessory for close-up and macro work, but make sure you buy a set that maintains automatic linkages.

REVERSING RING

A 50mm prime lens is ideal for use with a reversing ring. The brand of lens you use isn't important; the main thing is that you can set the aperture manually.

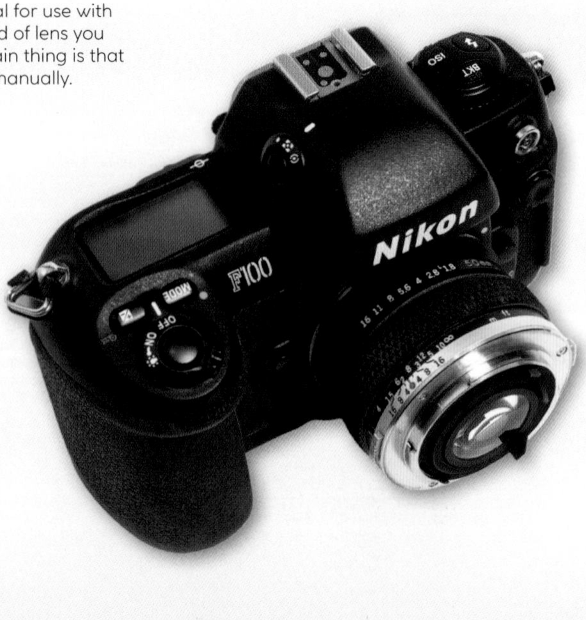

BELLOWS

The ultimate tool for macro enthusiasts is a set of bellows, which can be infinitely adjusted to produce the required magnification. Typically they can be extended up to 130mm, giving magnifications of up to 2.6:1 (2.6 x life-size) with a 50mm lens. Such extension increases exposure considerably, though, and a tripod or flash is recommended if sharp results are to be obtained. Unless you're willing to get involved in a lot of complex calculation, auto bellows – which maintain metering connections – are essential, and it's useful to retain autofocus as well.

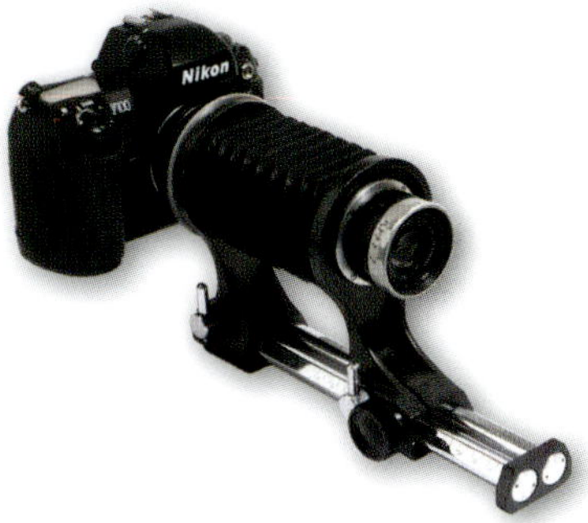

MANUAL BELLOWS

A set of manual bellows is all you need for extreme close-up photography, although a set of auto bellows will make exposure metering easier.

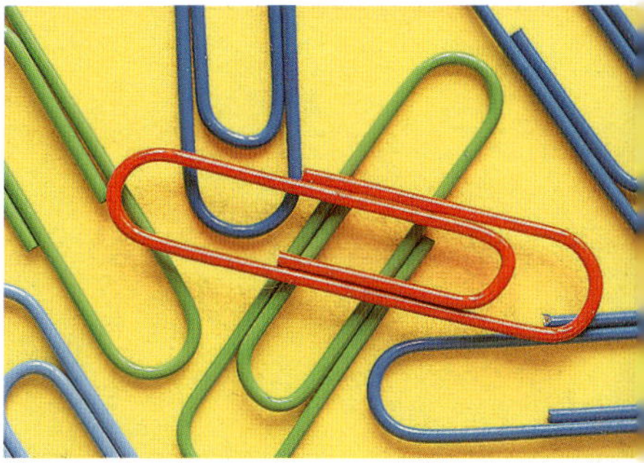

EXTREME CLOSE-UPS

A set of bellows enables you to magnify tiny objects beyond life-size for a dramatic new perspective on everyday items.

DEPTH OF FIELD

No matter what close-up accessories you use, focusing is critical in macro photography, as the depth of field is reduced significantly.

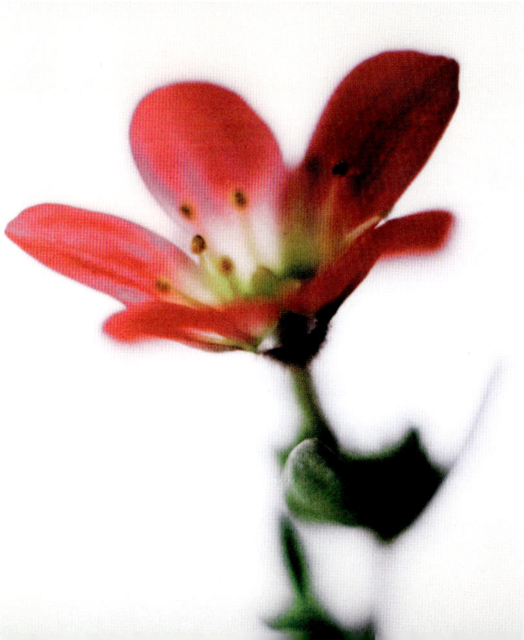

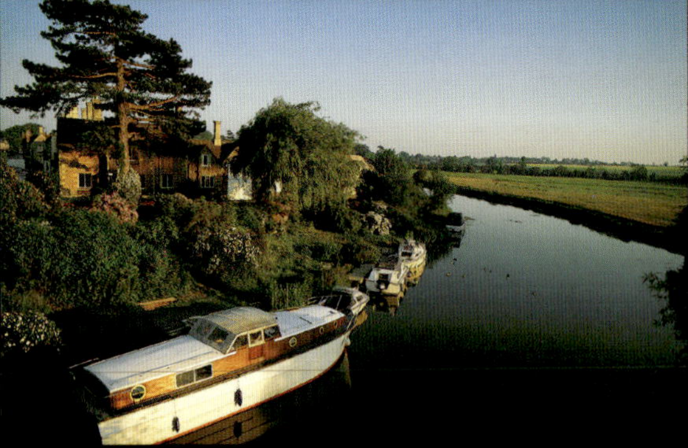
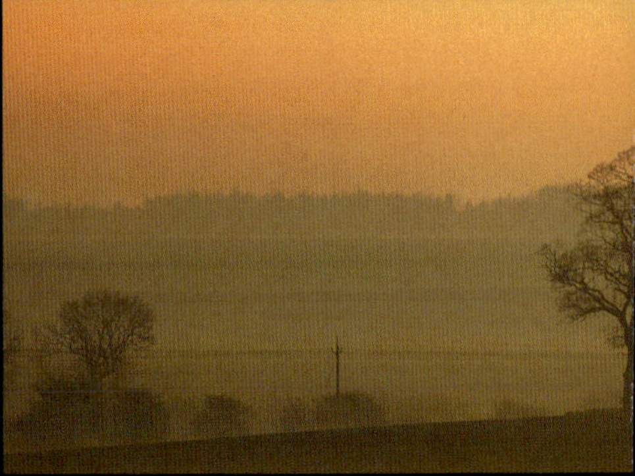
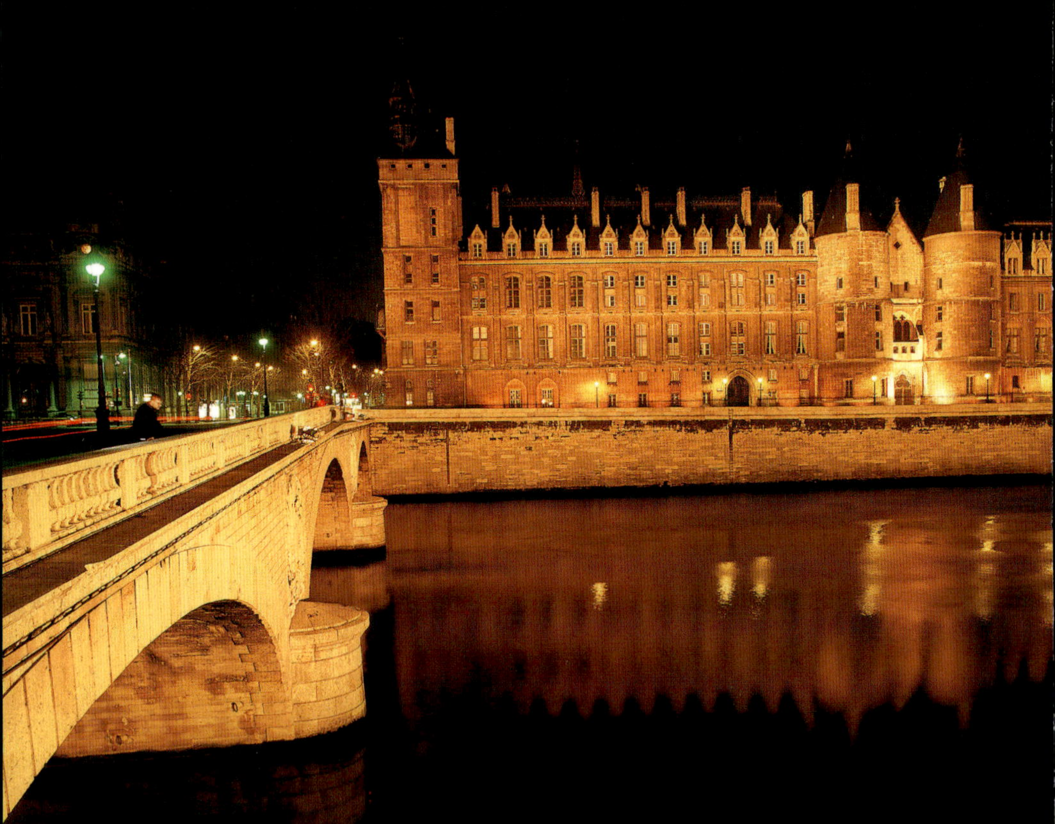

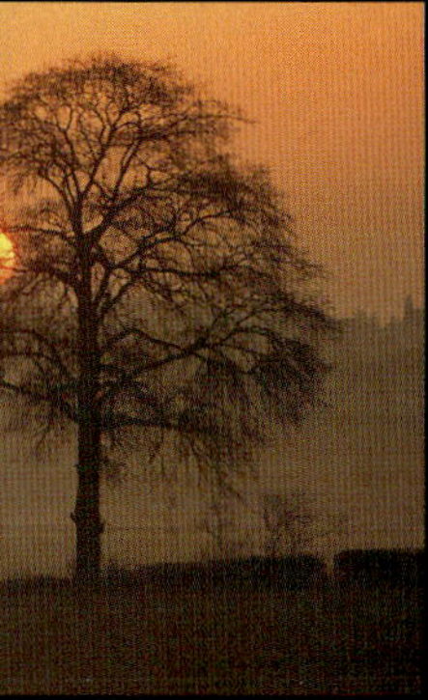

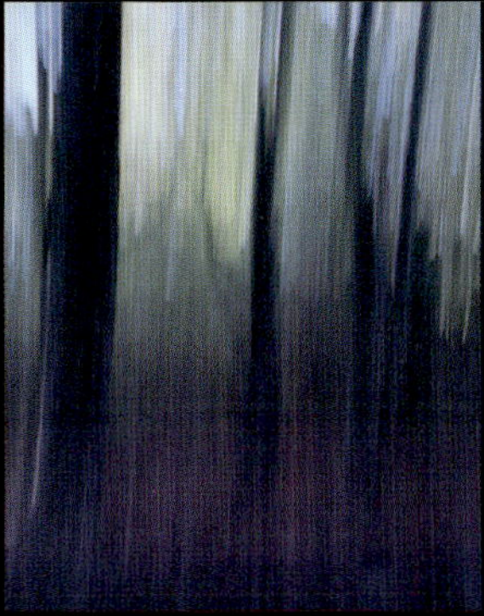

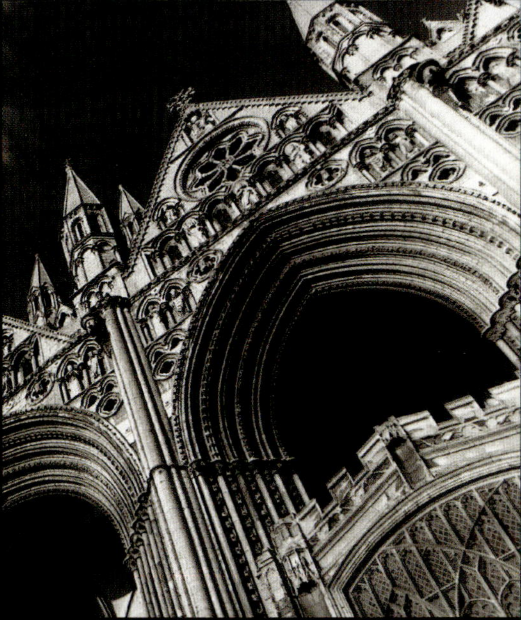

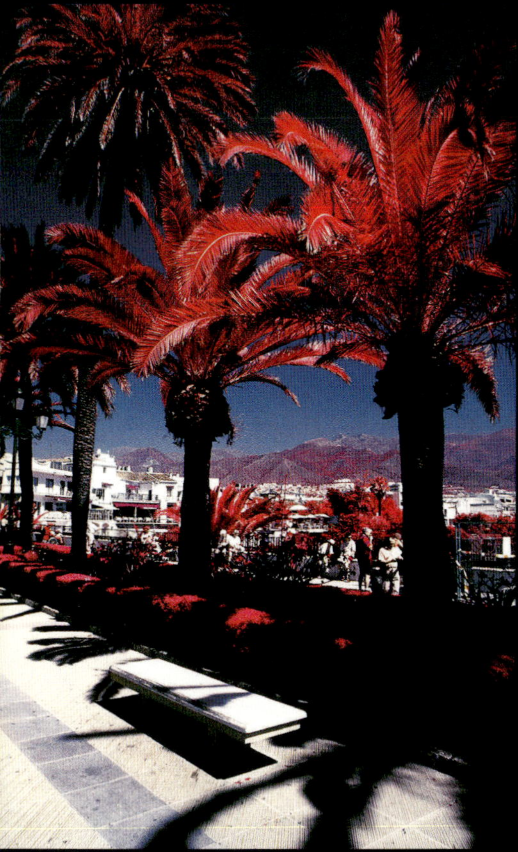

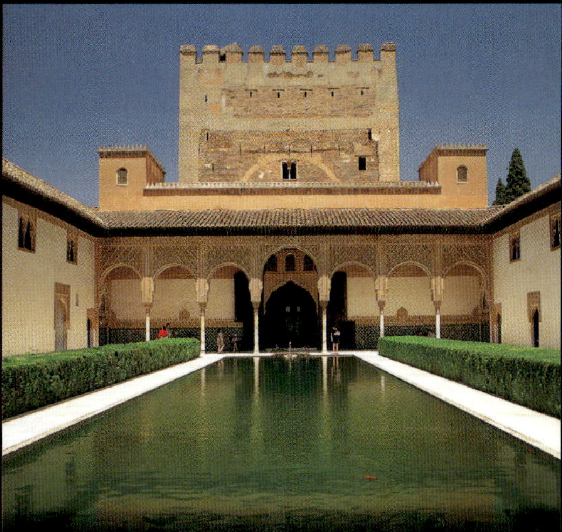

FILM AND ACCESSORIES

WHAT FILM?

Film plays an extremely important role in the life of an analogue photographer. The type you choose and how you use it can make an extraordinary difference to how your pictures come out. In fact, it's no exaggeration to say that the whole look and feel of an image is determined by film choice. Consequently, this choice demands careful consideration based on the subject, the situation, what you want to do with the pictures, and most importantly, your personal approach to photography.

SLIDE OR PRINT?

The first decision you need to make is whether you want to make conventional photographic prints direct from film. If you do, negative film is the preferred choice, and with high-quality modern emulsions it's hard to get bad results. For a reasonable price you get your film processed and a set of prints made, and if you take an outstanding shot and want a big blow-up, you can get that done as well.

However, if you're looking to scan your film photographs (and let's face it, most of us will digitise our film at some point), then slide film is an option. Although very few people can be bothered to set up slide projectors and screens anymore, there's no denying the power of a pin-sharp and well-exposed transparency, and it can be far easier to scan slides than negatives.

Slide film is much more demanding, though. It is far less tolerant to exposure errors than negative film, so your technique needs to be up to the mark, and your camera metering has to be accurate.

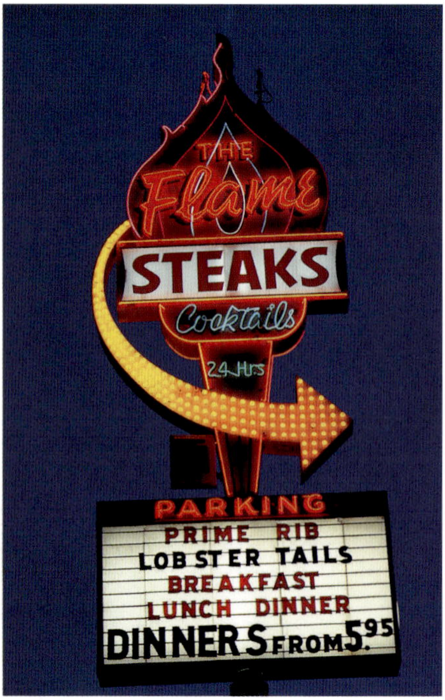

TRANSPARENCY
Slide film can deliver richly saturated positive images, which are ideal for scanning.

COLOUR OR BLACK AND WHITE?

The next decision is whether to go for colour or black and white. Once again, for many photographers this is an easy choice to make – they prefer the natural, realistic look of colour, and wouldn't consider anything else. The rich, saturated colours of modern emulsions make it easy to get wonderfully true-to-life images.

Black-and-white photography has a lot going for it, however. If you want to go beyond merely capturing a memory, and you are setting out to produce creative or artistic images, then monochrome emulsions – because of the way they reduce everything to a series of tones – can be a great medium to work with.

Although there are a couple of black-and-white slide films available, the vast majority of photographers working in monochrome shoot negative film, as it is far easier to work with and there is much greater choice.

Black-and-white negative film falls into two categories: traditional emulsions that use silver halide crystals to form an image, and chromogenic films that use dye clouds. The advantage of the latter is that it can be processed using standard C41 colour chemistry, with prints made on colour paper. Ilford's XP2 Super is currently the only available example of this type of film.

However, when it comes to the alternative – traditional silver halide emulsions – you are spoilt for choice, with a wide range of films available, from ultra-slow low grain ISO 50 films, up to fast, gritty ISO 3200 films. If you fancy processing film yourself, this is the ideal starting point, as it's an incredibly forgiving medium.

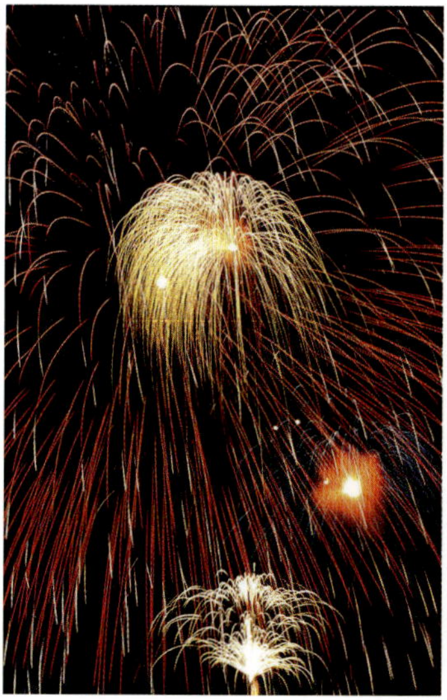

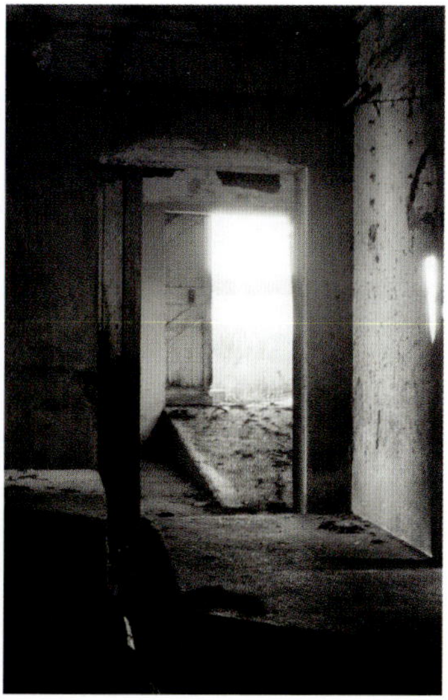

CHOICE

Sometimes your film choice will be driven by your subject. Fireworks are naturally suited to colour, for example, but black and white was a better match for this atmospheric interior.

PROFESSIONAL FILMS

It's worth saying a word or two about films designated 'professional'. The obvious connotation is that these films will give better results than 'non-professional' films, but in fact the opposite can be true.

This is because professional films are designed to be shot and processed immediately to ensure the greatest consistency between rolls in terms of colour and contrast. If you leave a roll of professional film in your camera for a couple of months before processing, the results will probably be inferior to those from an off-the-shelf amateur brand.

You also need to be aware that there may be tonal differences in professional films that may not suit your photography. Professional colour films made for wedding and portrait photography, for instance, have muted colours and a soft tonality that don't bring out the best from many everyday subjects.

TUNGSTEN VS. DAYLIGHT

Most colour films are intended for use in daylight or with electronic flash, so they give neutral-coloured results. However, if you use them under a tungsten light, such as a warm household lamp, you'll get a strong orange cast. This can be corrected by using a blue correction filter, or you can use a tungsten-balanced film (of which a few options are available). Tungsten film can also be used in daylight to give a cool look to your images.

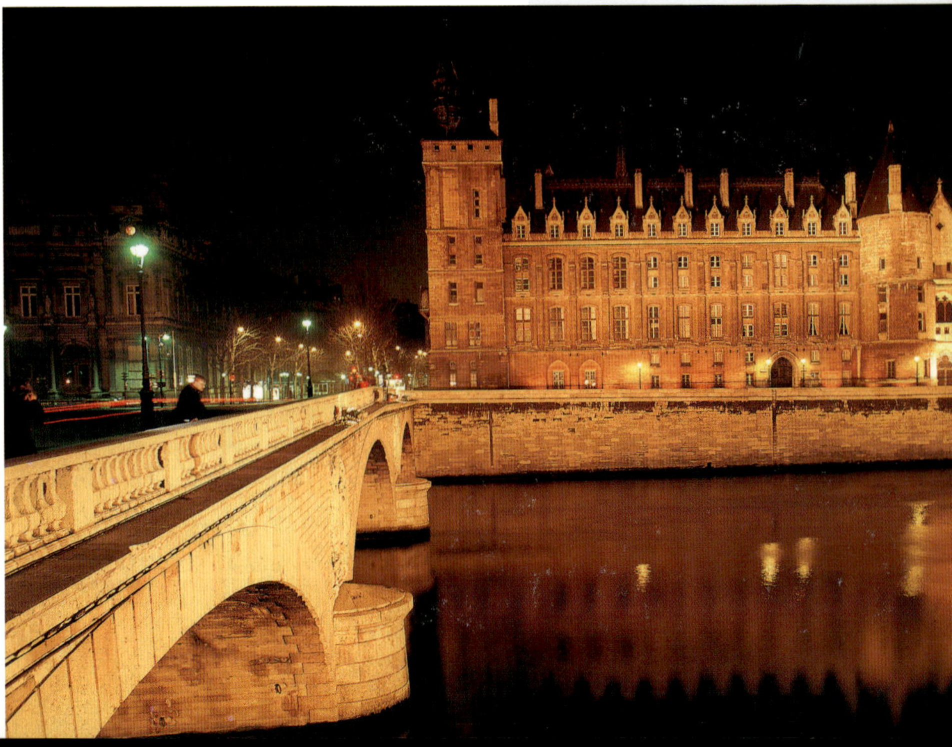

INFRARED FILM

Beyond the mainstream films are a host of other specialist emulsions that are well worth investigating. One of the most interesting is infrared (IR), which is currently only available in black and white. As well as recording visible light, IR film also captures invisible infrared wavelengths, which can give your images an otherworldly look.

Colour infrared film could create some truly 'alien' images, as shown below – but it was discontinued a long time ago. Although rolls sometimes appear for sale on eBay, they tend to be at unrealistically inflated prices given there is no guarantee the film will still produce an image.

At the time of writing, LomoChrome Purple film is about the closest there is to a colour IR film, although it simply delivers false colours rather than true infrared capture.

TUNGSTEN FLOODLIGHTING

Unless you use blue filters or a tungsten-balanced film, floodlit buildings tend to come out orange. This can work well, though; removing the warm colour would take away the mood of this picture.

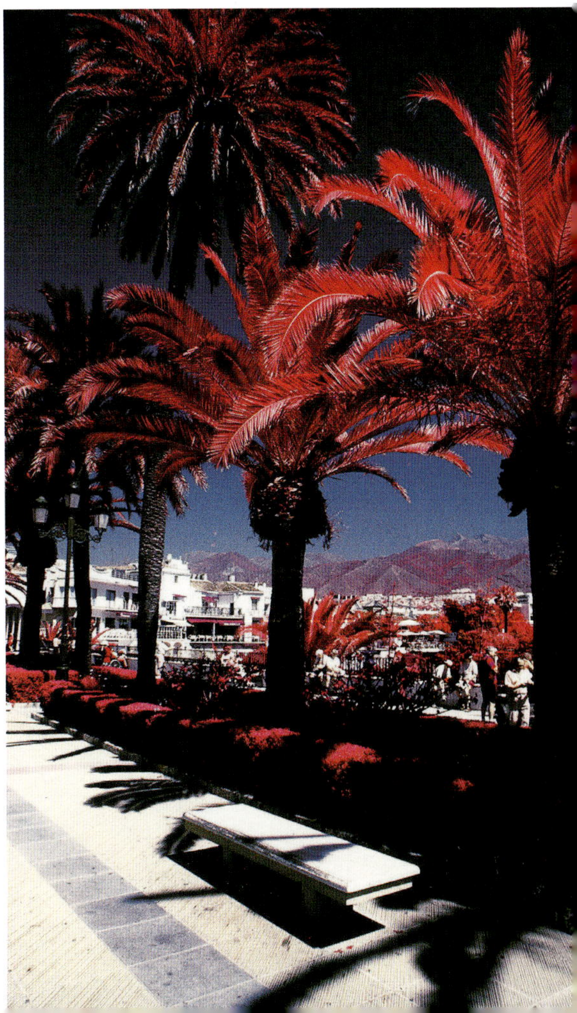

INFRARED FILM

The rich colours of this Mediterranean scene have been transformed through the use of infrared film and a yellow filter over the lens.

FILM SPEED

Whether you shoot slide film or negatives, colour or black and white, the one thing they all have in common is a nominal speed or ISO rating. This indicates how sensitive the film is to light, from 'slow' films, which require a lot of light to make an exposure, to 'fast' films that require less light. Which one you choose depends on your chosen subject(s) and the look you are after.

Slow

Slow films are those with an ISO of up to 100. When only the highest possible quality will do – for a big enlargement or publication – slow films are the first choice, because grain is virtually non-existent and colours are rich. The only problem is that the relative insensitivity of the film means you need good light or to use a tripod – possibly both.

Medium

For general purpose picture-taking, a medium-speed film (ISO 200) is the one to go for. It gives excellent quality, and will enlarge well beyond 8 x 10in, while still being very usable. At smaller print sizes, it's almost impossible to detect any difference between ISO 100 and 200 films, but the extra stop of speed offered by ISO 200 gives more options with exposure settings.

Fast

A fast film (ISO 400–800) will start to reveal grain in enlarged images, which for some photographers is no bad thing (it is, after all, one of the key differences between analogue and digital images). With colour film, the colours will also be softer and the pictures not as punchy, but again, some photographers welcome this.

SLOW FILM

Although you may need to use a tripod when light levels fall, slow film, such as the ISO 50 emulsion used here, offers superfine grain, excellent sharpness, and rich, vivid colours.

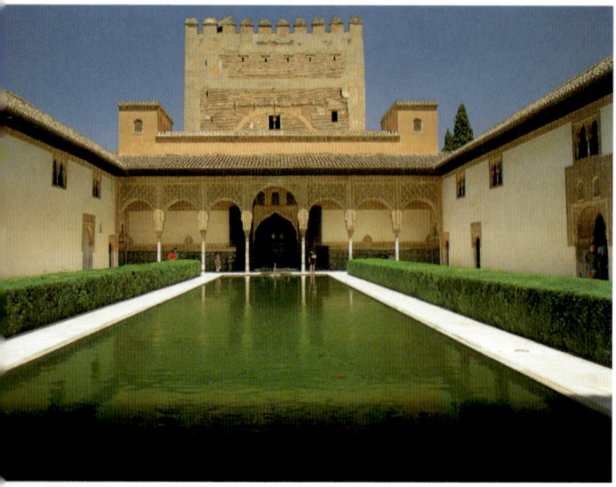

Ultra-fast

Once you exceed ISO 800, you will start to see grain at even normal levels of enlargement. But these films can be useful tools in the right circumstances – such as taking pictures hand-held in really low light, or if you need fast shutter speeds. You can either regard them as 'get-you-out-of-trouble' films or use their pastel graininess to deliberate creative effect.

UPRATING AND DOWNRATING

In the past, when few films were faster than ISO 400, a technique called 'uprating' was very popular. This involves deliberately treating the film as if it has a higher ISO setting, so you might load ISO 400 film, but tell your camera it is ISO 1600. This will effectively underexpose the film, but the development would be increased to compensate (you would need to let the processing lab know so they process your film accordingly).

For technical reasons, this is only possible with slide film and black and white, and it tends to be used for creative effect, as it increases grain and contrast significantly.

The opposite technique – downrating – can be an effective way of reducing contrast when faced with a harshly lit subject, although it is rarely used.

FAST FILM

When the light levels start to fall, you'll need a slightly faster film. ISO 400 is a good choice – you'll get strong colour and good sharpness without excessive grain.

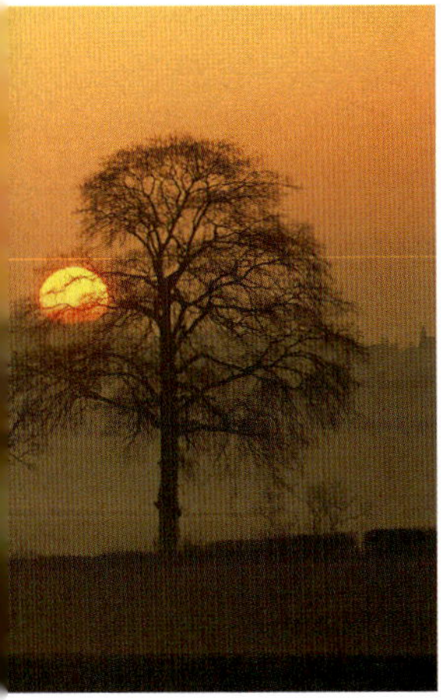

UPRATING

Uprating is an excellent way to squeeze more sensitivity out of a film. Here, an ISO 400 film was rated at ISO 1600 and push-processed to compensate.

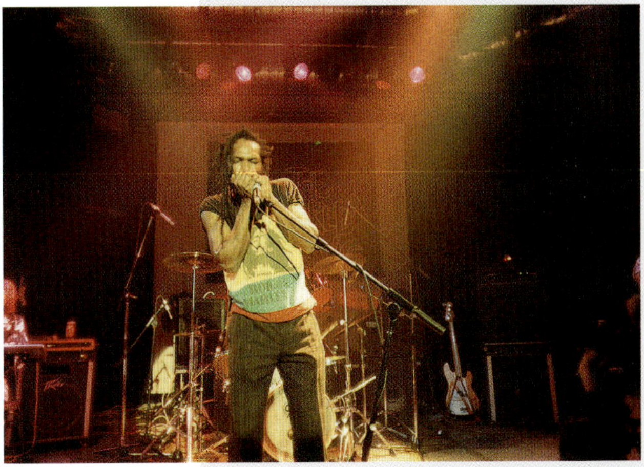

FLASH

Most electronic SLRs and compact cameras have a built-in flash. Most are of low power, but as a rule of thumb, an integral flash will give you a working distance of up to 3–4m (10–13ft), making it good for pictures of people, domestic interiors, and other relatively close subjects.

However, because the flash is fixed in place close to the lens, there's little you can do to improve the quality of light it gives out, which is both hard and direct. If you're serious about using flash, this means a built-in unit is quickly going to limit your creativity, and you'll need to think about investing in a more versatile and powerful flash. For most photographers this means a hotshoe flash, which can either sit on top of the camera or – with the appropriate cable – be used off-camera.

Power

For built-in and hotshoe flashes, flash power is given as a guide number (GN), with an associated distance and ISO. Built-in flashes typically have a GN in the region of 12 (or, more specifically, 12m (40ft) at ISO 100), which isn't particularly powerful. For a hotshoe flash, you want something with a GN in the region of 30–50m (100–164ft) at ISO 100, which lets you work with smaller apertures and/or at greater distances.

Control

Many SLRs – both mechanical and electronic – have a dedicated flash facility, meaning there's some interchange of information between the flash and the camera. Exactly what you get depends to a large degree on the system you're using, but almost all set the flash sync speed automatically. Beyond that, external flashes can offer a variety of working modes, from TTL (Through-The-Lens) flash to fully manual control, perhaps with a few automatic options in between.

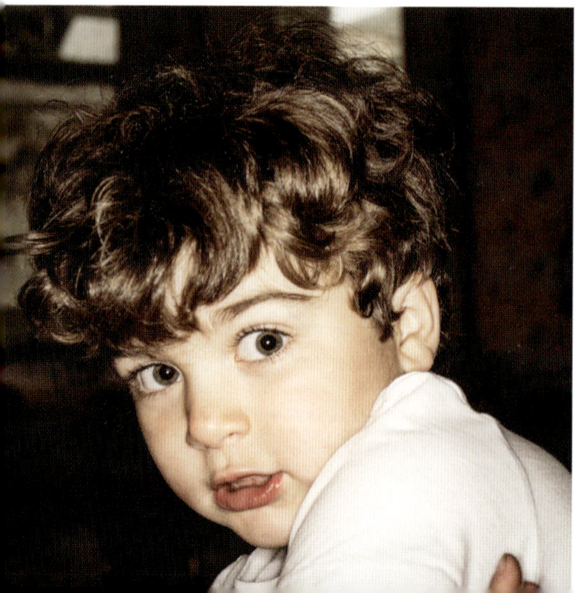

BUILT-IN FLASH

A built-in flash is fine for subjects relatively close to the camera. While the quality of the light is not perfect they produce crisp, sharp images.

Bounce and tilt

Although it's not essential, a flash with a bounce-and-tilt head is definitely recommended. It enables you to turn the flash in the hotshoe and bounce the light off a ceiling or wall, which is a sure-fire way of improving your flash photography by softening the light and making it less direct.

Coverage

If you're a fan of wide-angle photography, check the angle of coverage of the flash. This is often the same as a 28mm lens, which is fine for general photography, but if you use a wider lens the edges of your pictures will come out dark. Some hotshoe flashes have a flip-out diffuser that widens the spread.

Other features

Advanced features, such as second-curtain sync, multi-flash, and slave flash facilities can open up further possibilities and fire your creativity, but whether you use them or not largely comes down to the type of photography you do. A lot also depends on the camera and flash you use.

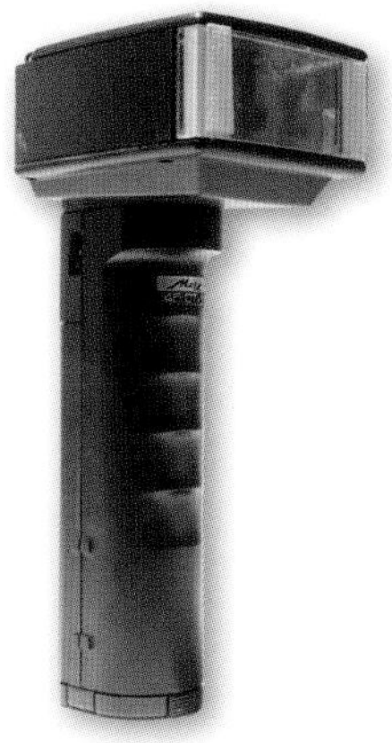

HAMMERHEAD FLASH

This type of flash unit is designed to fit alongside the camera on a bracket. It is typically more powerful than a hotshoe flash.

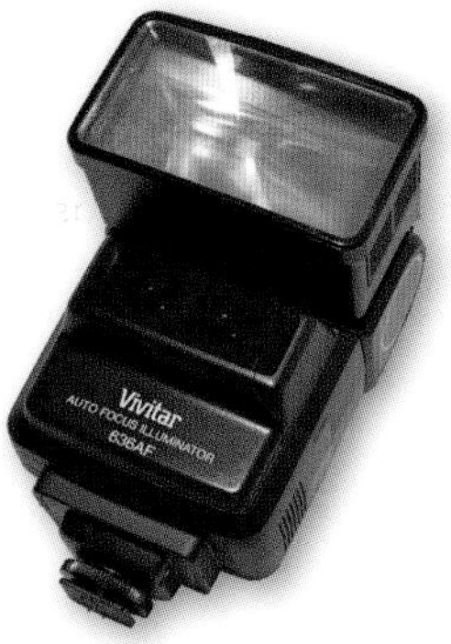

HOTSHOE FLASH

A good hotshoe-mounted flash will have a bounce-and-tilt head.

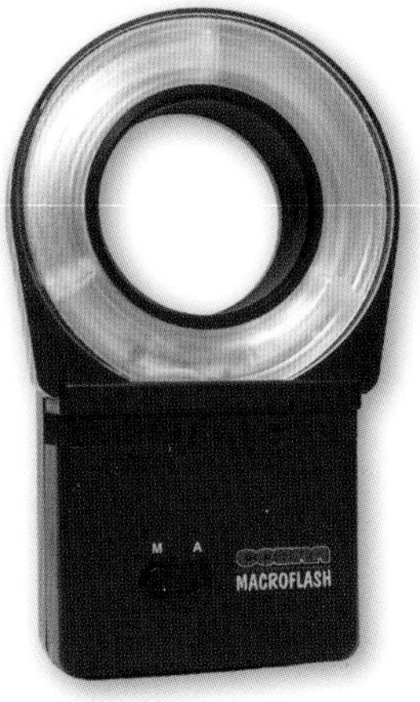

RING FLASH

A ring flash delivers a shadowless light that is ideal for macro photography, although it is also widely used in portrait and fashion shoots.

FILTERS

Filters that physically sit in front of the lens are far more important in film photography than they are in digital photography, simply because it's more important to get things right when you make your exposure. The filters mentioned here are arguably the most useful, and should be in every film photographer's bag. But beyond them there are dozens of different types – from the wacky to the downright weird.

The first filters that most photographers acquire are skylight or UV filters, which are left in place more or less permanently to protect the fronts of lenses from dust and damage. The only time you might want to take them off is when you need to clean them, or when you're using other filters that serve the same purpose.

In general, it's a good idea to fit as few filters as possible at any one time, because every piece of glass or plastic you place in front of the lens risks degrading the quality of your final image. In practice, adding one filter will normally make no difference, and you may not be able to spot any difference using two, but adding three or more filters is definitely something to be avoided. You should also take great care when handling filters, as any finger marks or scratches can cause further loss of quality.

SQUARE OR THREADED FILTERS?

The decision to invest in one filter system over another should really come down to how versatile it is. If you work exclusively with a single camera and lens, life can be pretty straightforward, but ideally you need a filter system that can grow with you and adapt as you add to your camera kit.

Slot-in filter systems score highly over traditional screw-in brands in this respect, because you can fit the square filters to different lenses simply by investing in another adapter ring. However, if you go for a slot-in system, make sure it's big enough to cope with all your lenses. The 84mm Cokin P size is about the smallest you should consider, but 100mm systems are far more versatile, especially with wide-angle lenses.

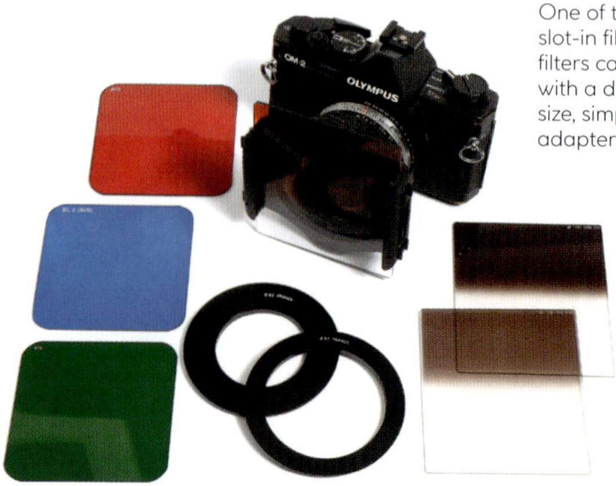

FILTER CHOICE

One of the main benefits of slot-in filters is that the same filters can be used on lenses with a different filter thread size, simply by changing the adapter ring.

By comparison, round, screw-fit filters are designed to fit a specific thread size. This is fine if all your lenses share that same thread, but not so good if they don't, as you will need to buy stepping rings to increase or reduce the size. There's also a significant risk of vignetting if you use two or more screw-in filters together on wide-angle lenses, due to the combined depth of the filter mounts. Flare and reflections can be caused by the parallel glass surfaces being close together, and screw-in graduated filters offer no control over alignment.

That's not to say you should rule out round filters altogether. If you use only one filter at a time, or need a particular filter for a specific application, they're ideal. A larger number of glass filters are made with the round screw-in design, so optical quality and durability can be higher.

WARM-UP FILTERS

A useful range of filters for film photography is the 81 series of warm-up filters. These come in a range of strengths from 81A (pale straw) to 81EF (rich orange) and – as their name suggests – these filters give a picture an attractive, warm glow. In portraiture they can create a sunkissed look, while for landscape and travel photographs they give a glorious sense of warmth. To enhance the effect, use two filters together.

Another orange filter, 85A, is required for colour correction when tungsten-balanced film is used in daylight.

COOL-DOWN FILTERS

Sometimes, the warmth of the natural light can be too great, or you may want to produce a cool, melancholic feel in your picture. For these situations you can turn to the blue 82 series of filters.

When taking pictures under tungsten lighting using normal daylight-balanced film, the much stronger 80A blue filter helps you avoid a strong orange cast. Like most filters, this reduces the amount of light reaching the film, but TTL (Through-The-Lens) metering systems automatically compensate for the loss.

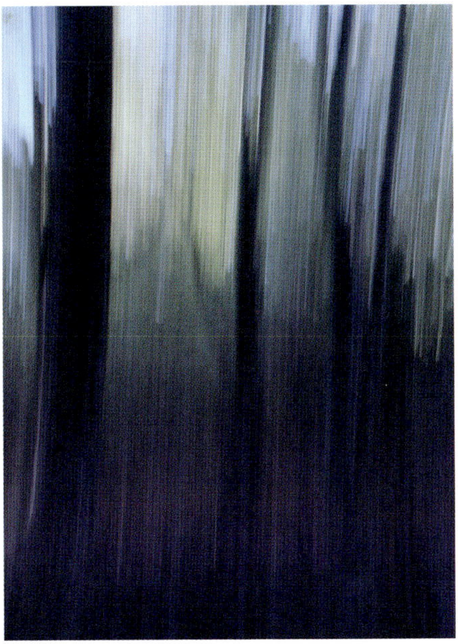

COOL

A cooling (blue) filter was used on this motion-blurred photograph of trees to enhance its abstract nature.

GRADUATED FILTERS

With some filters, you need to be more careful with metering, and this is true of graduated filters. These are half-coloured (or half-tinted) filters that are typically used to add density or colour to bland skies in landscape, travel, and architectural shots. The best way to get accurately exposed results when using graduated filters is to tip the camera downwards and take a meter reading from the foreground with the sky excluded – before fitting the filter.

To produce a natural-looking effect you need to line the filter up so that the point at which it changes from clear to coloured lines up with the horizon. This is where square, slot-in filter systems come into their own, allowing you to slide the filter up and down in the mount until it's exactly where you want it. You can't do that with a round filter. Setting a large aperture, such as f/4 or f/5.6, will also help to make the line less obvious. This is especially important when you're using a wide-angle lens.

Which graduated filter you choose is largely a matter of personal choice. Some photographers favour the natural effect created by grey or neutral density graduated filters, while others prefer to add drama with a tobacco or blue gradient. It's also possible to use graduated filters together – with one upside down to colour the foreground, for example.

SUNSET FILTER

Sunset filters are effectively graduated warm-up filters that can add an overall warmth to an image (bottom) and density to the sky area.

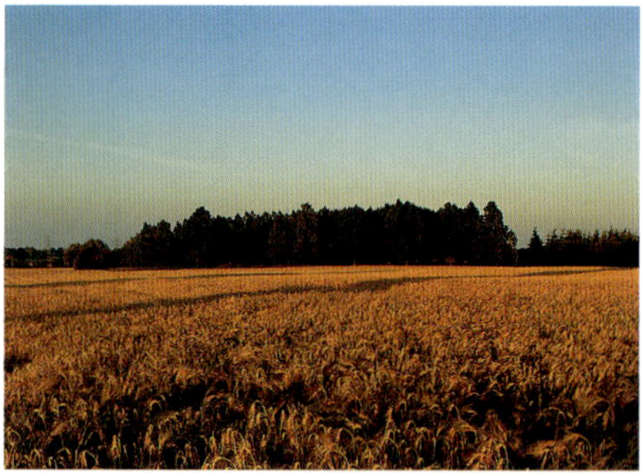

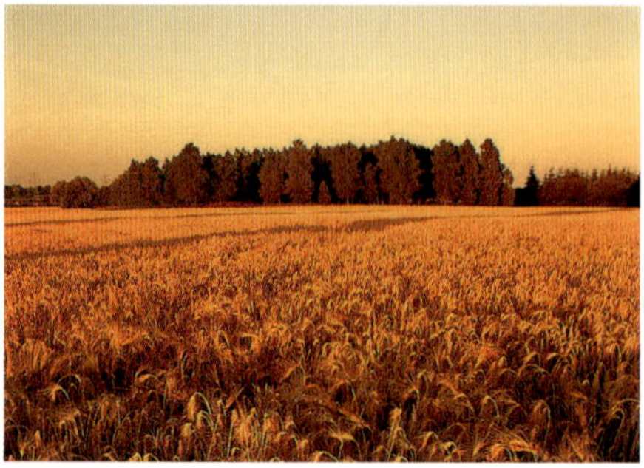

GRADUATED FILTER

The sky in this evening scene was grey and lifeless, but using a blue graduated filter balanced the exposure and added richness to the shot.

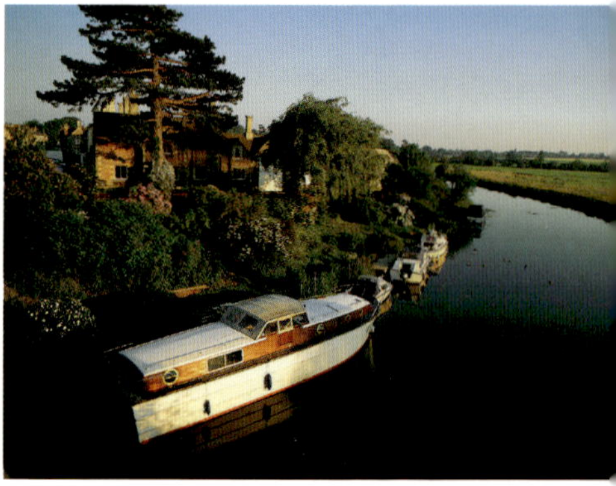

POLARISING FILTERS

Overall, one of the most useful filters you can buy is the polariser for film photography – in fact it's pretty near indispensable in sunny weather. As well as deepening the blue of the sky, it also increases the overall saturation of an image. Add to that its ability to take away surface reflections from glass and water, and you have a filter that's worth its weight in gold.

The degree of polarisation that is produced depends on the position of the filter, and as you rotate it you will see through the viewfinder the effect it's having. You'll get maximum polarisation when you have the sun to the side of you, but you'll need to take care if you're using a wide-angle lens that one part of the sky doesn't end up darker than the other.

There are two types of polarising filter: circular and linear. This has nothing to do with the shape of the filter, but refers to the alignment of the polarising material. If you have an autofocus camera, or one with spot metering, you will almost certainly need the more expensive circular type to prevent the filter affecting focus or exposure.

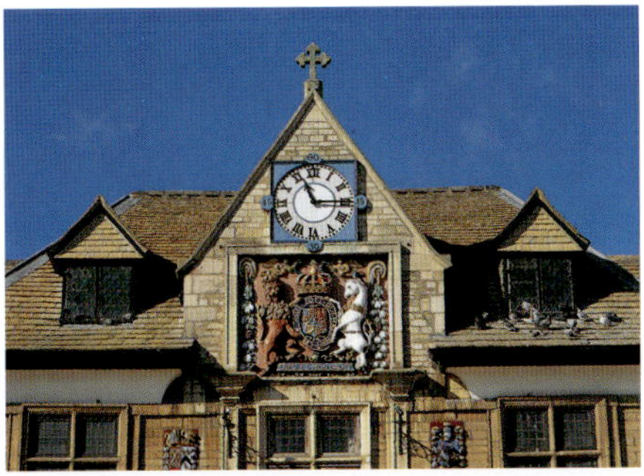

POLARISING FILTER

By deepening the blue of the sky and enhancing contrast (below), polarising filters can produce images with much more punch.

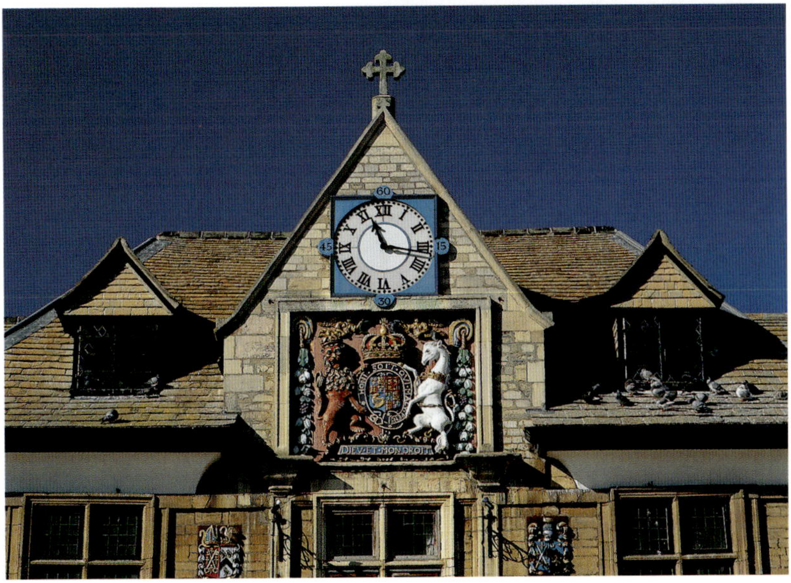

FILTERS FOR BLACK AND WHITE

When you take a black-and-white photograph, the various colours in the subject are all recorded as shades of grey. But it is possible to manipulate the tonality and contrast of a scene – to a surprisingly large degree – with the use of plain coloured filters. These filters lighten their own and associated colours, and darken complementary colours.

The most widely used filters in black-and-white photography are yellow, orange, and red filters, which lighten yellow, orange, and red tones, while darkening blues and violets. They are a great way to progressively increase contrast and deepen skies in landscape, architecture, and travel photographs.

Yellow improves things a little, but the best result is usually achieved using orange, producing white clouds against a dark sky and strong contrast. Red gives results that are very dramatic, although it can sometimes be a bit 'soot and whitewash', with black skies and bleached-out foliage. Red filters are also used in black-and-white infrared photography.

Yellow and orange filters are also excellent for portraits, lightening Caucasian skin tones and blonde hair and helping to hide skin blemishes. A pale to medium yellow filter gives the most natural-looking effect; an orange filter lightens skin further but may also lighten lip colour and darken eye colour too much. Red won't give you flattering portraits, but it is good for creative, experimental work.

Although few photographers use a green filter, it can help to differentiate foliage tones in landscapes, allowing you to produce prints with fine nuances. Green can also be good for portraits where you want to darken skin and lip tone, such as in character studies of older people.

Blue is a useful filter when photographing under artificial light, which can muddy the tonality of the shot, but it is another monochrome filter that is not often used.

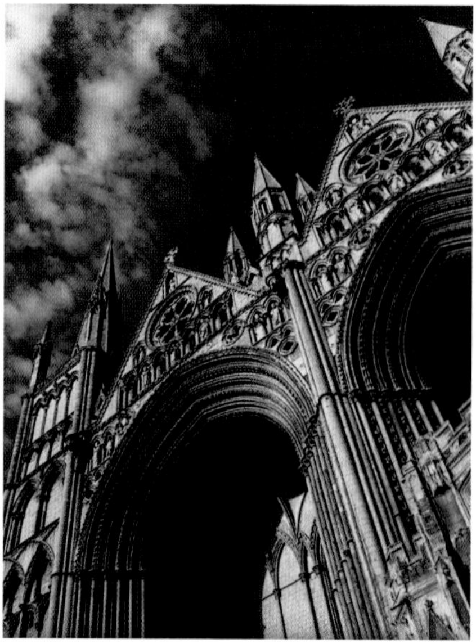

RED FILTER

Red is the most dramatic monochrome filter, creating deep, near-black skies with stark white clouds in outdoor images.

DIFFUSER

One filter that can be used equally well with colour and black-and-white film is the diffuser or soft-focus filter. It comes in various strengths to give an atmospheric mood to many subjects.

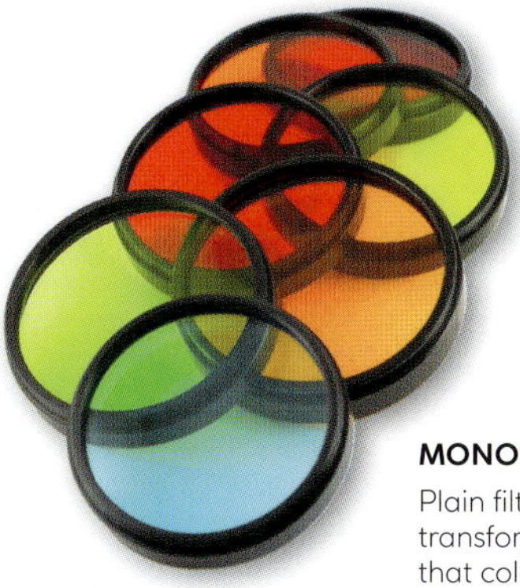

MONO FILTERS

Plain filters can transform the way that colours appear in black-and-white photographs.

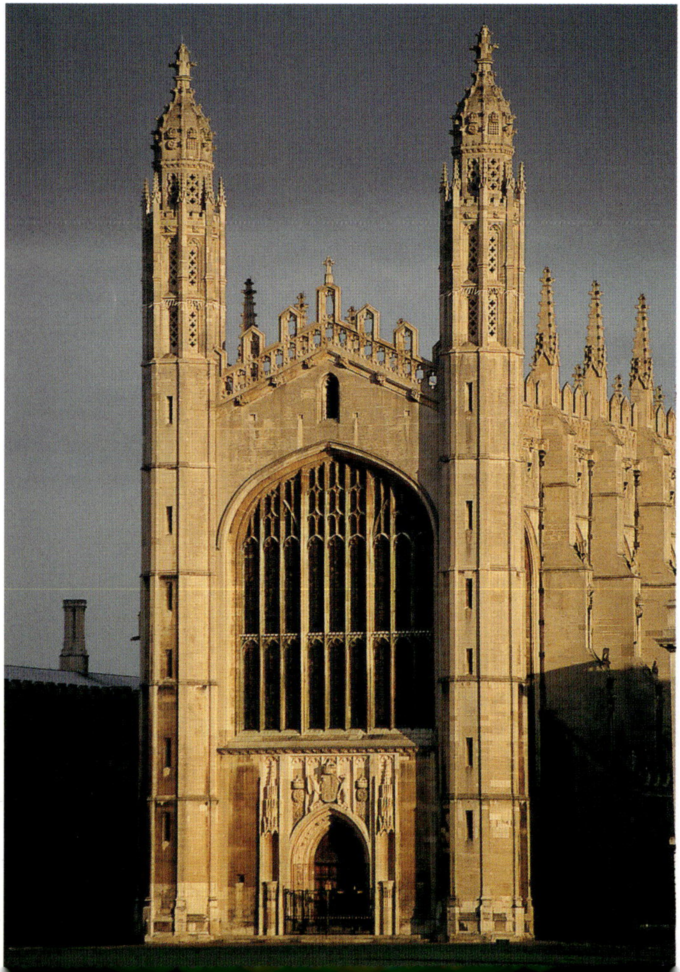

SOFT-FOCUS FILTERS

Soft-focus filters offer a quick and easy way to give an attractive, atmospheric feeling to images of all kinds.

CAMERA SUPPORTS

Of all the accessories you can spend your hard-earned cash on, none can so dramatically improve the quality and range of your picture-taking as a tripod. Why? Many photographers overestimate their ability to hand-hold a camera without shake – especially when they're using a zoom or telephoto lens.

The well-known rule of thumb, which says it's safe to hand-hold your camera as long as the shutter speed matches the focal length of the lens you're using, sounds highly scientific and plausible. But photographers vary enormously in their ability to hold a camera steady. Some are as steady as a rock and capable of shake-free results using a 300mm lens at 1/8 sec in a force nine gale, while others are so wobbly that they need 1/500 sec to get sharp shots from a 28mm wide-angle.

Mounting your camera on a tripod does away with any concerns regarding shake, because once it's firmly anchored you can safely use whatever shutter speed you want. Using a tripod also makes it possible to take more creative and interesting pictures.

For instance, at the moment when it starts to get dark you may pack your camera away, load up with a faster film or reach for the flash. But if you fix your camera to a tripod you can take advantage of the often atmospheric and moody illumination you get when the daylight level drops – such as the gorgeous colours of the early morning or fascinating night scenes – without compromising on image quality.

You can also use a tripod to explore longer shutter speeds – perhaps by photographing a waterfall or a fairground ride. Other creative options include being able to pan the camera during the exposure for a dramatic 'motion blur' effect, or trying your hand at advanced techniques such as 'painting with light' using a torch or flash with a long exposure.

Of course, one of the most obvious advantages of working with a tripod is that it gives you greater control over depth of field. You're free to choose the aperture you want for the effect you have in mind, not the one that is forced upon you by circumstances.

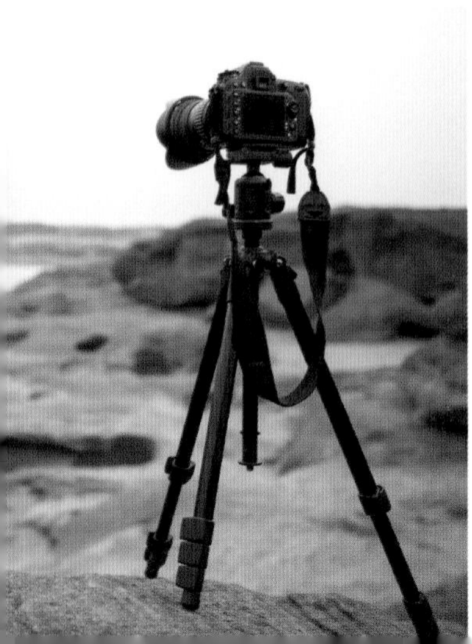

TRIPOD

A full-size tripod not only helps alleviate camera shake, but also opens up more creative options.

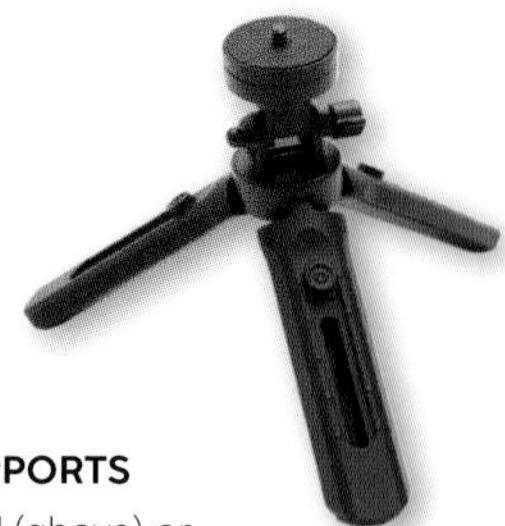

OTHER SUPPORTS

A mini-tripod (above) or monopod (below) is more portable than a full-size tripod.

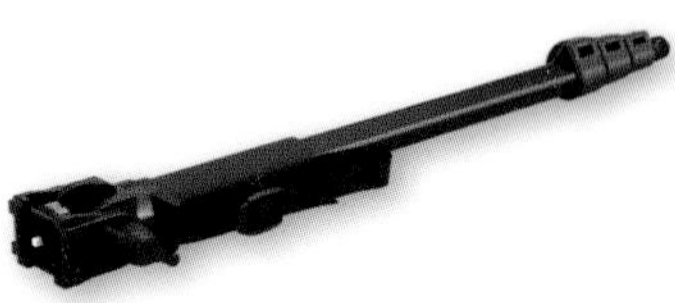

CHOOSING A TRIPOD

When buying a tripod you should go for a model that's stable but not too heavy, otherwise you'll be tempted to leave it at home. It should ideally extend to at least 1.5m (5ft) – higher if possible. An adjustable head is essential, and it is also useful to have legs that can be splayed out for work close to the ground and/or a reversible centre column.

OTHER SUPPORTS

A mini-tripod that's small enough to slip into your gadget bag and light enough to carry around all day is also useful to have. The most stable models tend to extend to a height of 60cm (2ft) and have three- or four-section legs.

Monopods – which are essentially one leg of a tripod with an adjustable head on top – don't offer the stability of a tripod, but they're ideally suited to sports and wildlife photography, where you need more mobility.

Another versatile support is a bean bag filled with expanded polystyrene, which acts as a stable cushion for the camera and lens. You can rest it on a fence or a half-opened car window.

SHUTTER RELEASE

When using a tripod, you'll need some way of operating the shutter without putting your finger directly on the release, as this can introduce camera shake. A simple option when photographing static subjects is to use the camera's self-timer, but if the timing of your shot is more critical you will need a remote release instead.

Older cameras have a simple screw thread, allowing you to buy an inexpensive cable release, while electronic SLRs and some compacts use an electronic release. Also available are infrared remote control systems, which enable you to fire the camera from a distance.

GETTING THE BEST FROM YOUR TRIPOD

DO

- Spread the legs wide to give a low centre of gravity.
- Make sure the locks on the legs are fully tightened, so there's no risk of slippage.
- Secure the camera tightly to the tripod platform.
- Use the rubberised feet on slippery surfaces and the spiked feet on rough terrain.
- Use a remote cable release to fire the shutter.
- Hang your gadget bag at the point where the legs join if you need extra stability.
- Invest in a proper carrying bag – you're more likely to take the tripod out with you if it's easy to carry.

DON'T

- Hold on to the tripod, as you're more likely to cause vibration rather than stop it.
- Extend the central column any more than you have to – it's certain to create unwanted wobble.
- Put cameras with long or heavy lenses on flimsy tripods meant for lightweight systems.
- Fire the shutter release by hand.

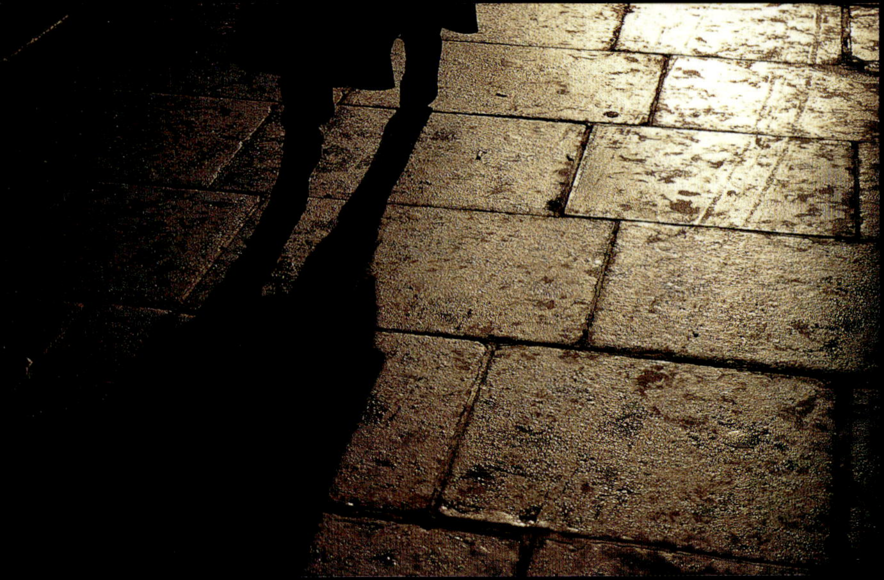
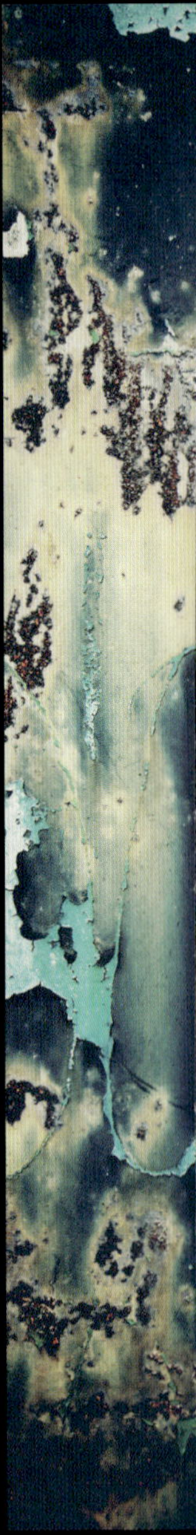
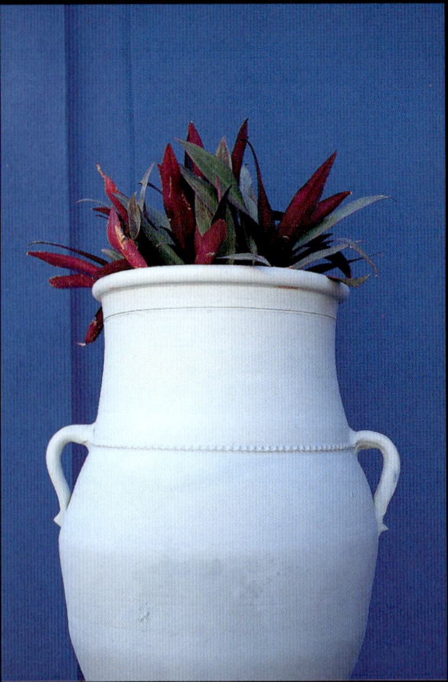
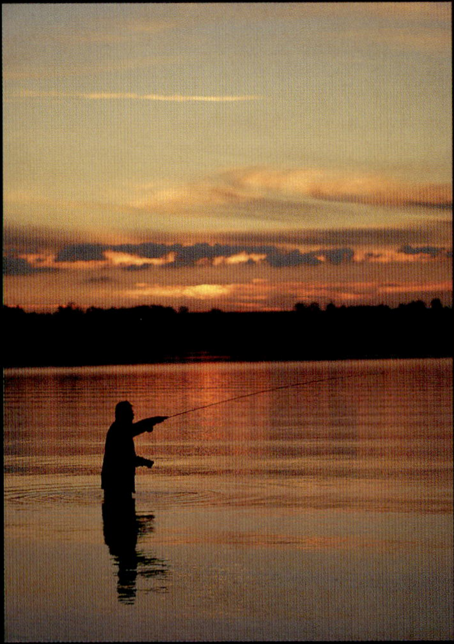

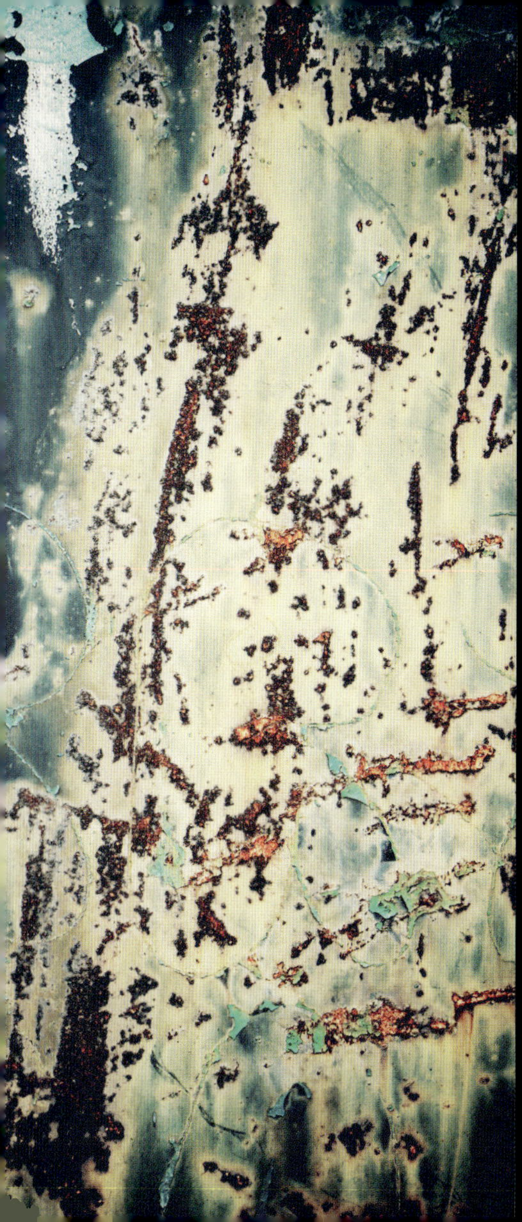

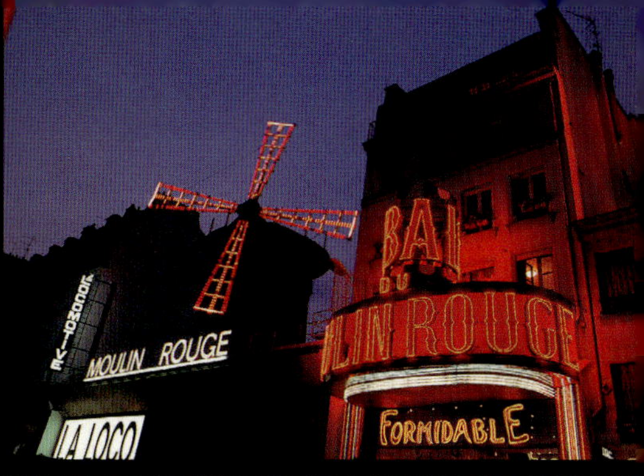
LOCOMOTIVE
MOULIN ROUGE
LA LOCO
BAL
FORMIDABLE

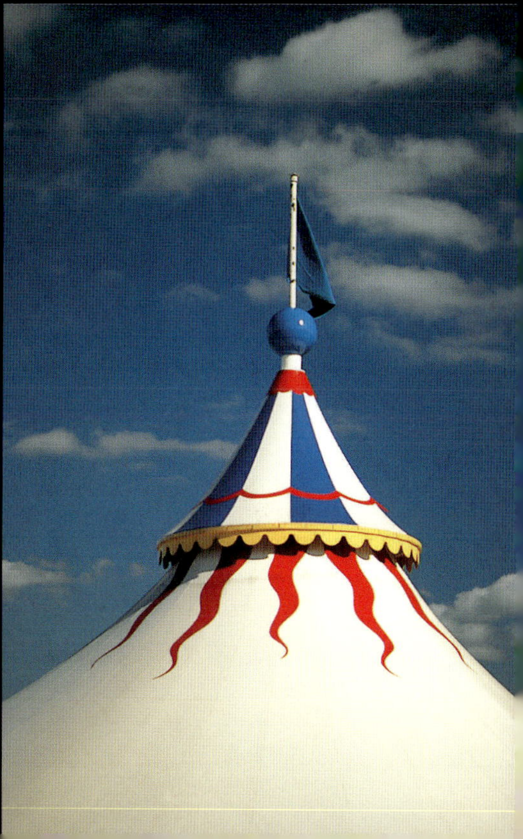

UNDERSTANDING LIGHT

It's a common misconception among photographers that certain kinds of light are 'good' while others are 'bad'. They'll often glance out of the window, decide the weather isn't suitable, and pack their equipment away for another day.

But all light is useful in certain situations, and the secret of success in photography is simply a matter of matching the right subject to the right light. Even the flat, grey light of a rainy, overcast day has its uses, while the intense, contrasty light of a summer's day has as many disadvantages as it has advantages.

It's not an exaggeration to say that light is the single most important element in any picture. In many ways it's the photographer's raw material. You can have all the cameras, lenses, and accessories in the world, but without light you won't get very far. But it's the way you use light that makes all the difference. It doesn't matter how attractive or interesting your subject is, if the lighting's not appropriate, your picture won't work. Yet it's astonishing how few people pay any real attention to light; so eager are they to press the shutter release and get the picture in the bag they don't really think about how to make the light work for them.

The most fascinating thing about light is its sheer diversity. Contrast, intensity, colour, and angle are the four attributes of most interest to photographers, and it's the many ways in which they combine through the day and in different weather conditions that gives so much choice and control.

CONTRE-JOUR

Shooting into the light on a city street late in the day creates an enigmatic image.

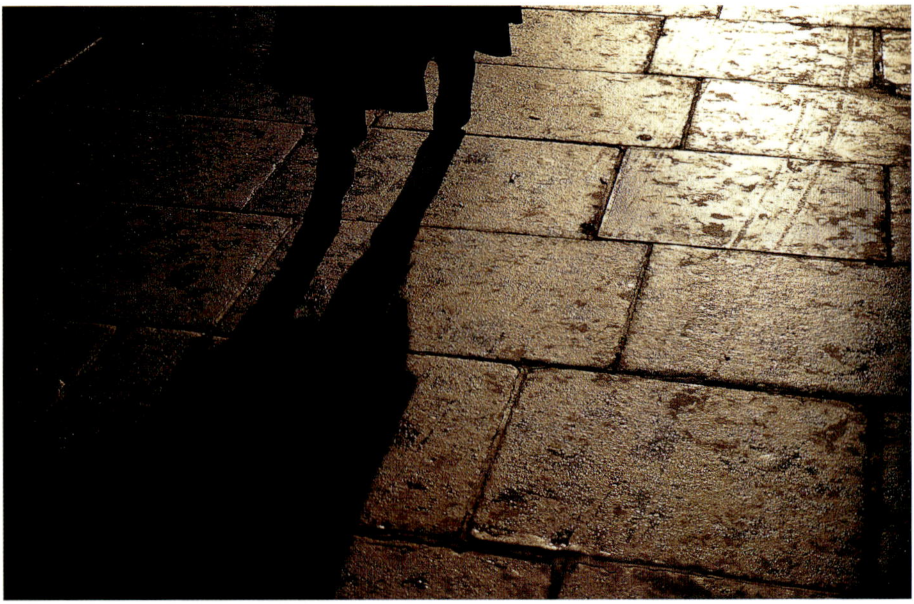

QUALITY OF LIGHT

One of the principal things to understand about light is that quality is far more important than quantity – more doesn't mean better. In fact, the opposite is often true and the most evocative results are achieved when the light is subtle and directional, rather than intense and overwhelming.

Bright sunny days certainly have a lot going for them, with the high levels of light giving the option of fast shutter speeds and small apertures. However, this light can be exceptionally 'hard'. This is particularly true around noon, when the light is direct and shadows are not only short, but also heavy.

This hard light can work well with black-and-white photography, but if you're shooting in colour, the high contrast can be too much. Instead, try shooting early in the morning and late in the afternoon, when the lower angle of the sun produces longer, more photogenic shadows.

In winter, the sun sits low in the sky throughout the day, producing a characteristic 'raking' light that's ideal for bringing textures and patterns to life in black and white or colour. This is particularly true of buildings and architectural details, which are great subjects for winter photography, along with the barren landscapes you find at this time of year when there's little foliage around. The way in which the light strikes the subject is important; the narrower the angle the more detail is revealed.

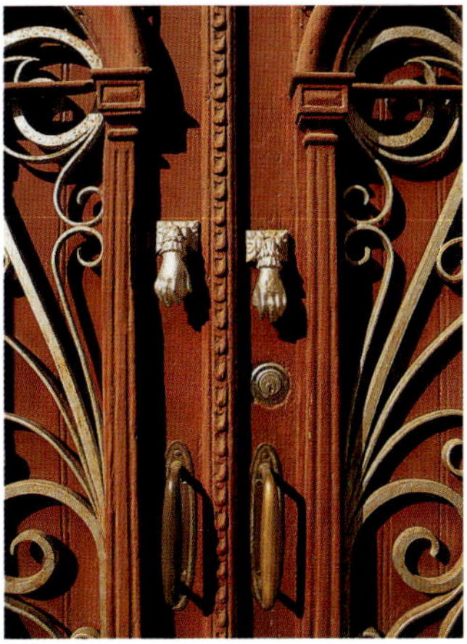

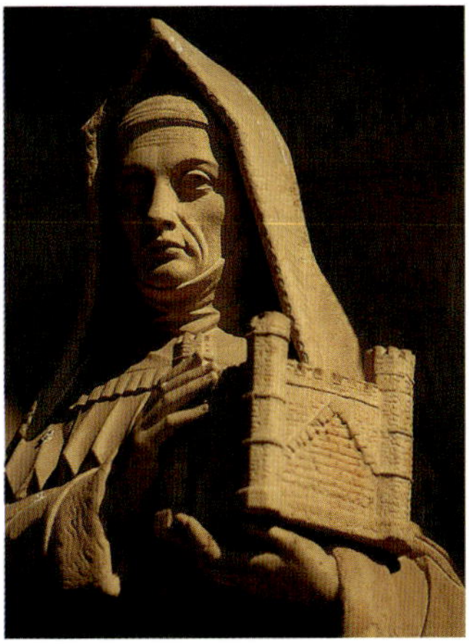

SIDE LIGHTING

Some architectural details are more absorbing than the buildings they're on, such as the pair of hands spotted on a door (far left) and this statue (left). The relief of such details is best brought to life under hard side lighting.

DIFFUSED LIGHT

For close-ups, where you want to preserve the maximum amount of detail, soft, diffused lighting is ideal. Most garden photographers avoid sunny days in favour of more overcast conditions; some even like to shoot when it's raining.

This is also a great time to improvise still-life images by gathering together a number of related or contrasting items. Items of food – such as bread, fruit, or vegetables – can make up an appealing theme, or you could have a go with anything from tools to crockery to jewellery. Simply find a suitable shaded spot outdoors, spread out a piece of fabric or a sheet of card, and arrange your subjects on it in an interesting way.

When it rains or the weather's colder, there are fewer outdoor subjects that work well, but you can move indoors and create your still-life images there instead. Position your subject(s) close to a window and use the soft light to illuminate them. If you want to reduce shadows, try using a reflector on the opposite side of your subject to bounce some light back. Your reflector doesn't have to be anything too complicated – a sheet of white card will often suffice.

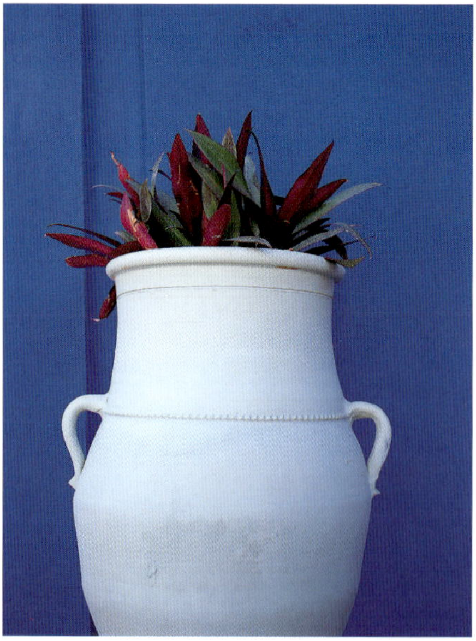

DIFFUSED LIGHT

The extremely soft light found on the shaded side of a building doesn't suit every subject, but works well for the pastel shades of this large pot.

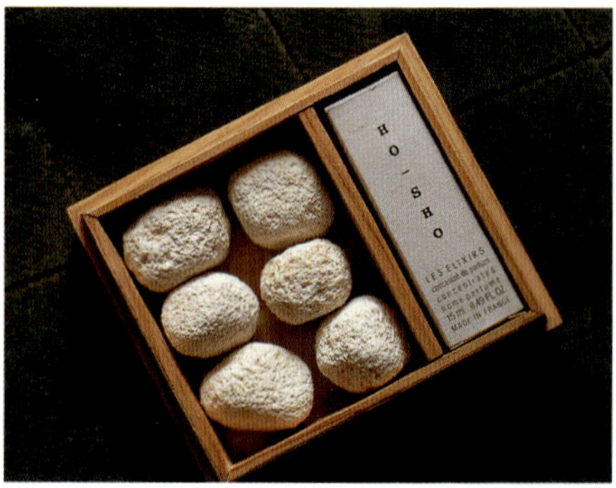

USING NATURAL LIGHT

You don't need fancy lighting for a lot of still-life work, just window light – as here – and a tripod to ensure sharp results if the light levels are low.

LIGHT FOR LANDSCAPES

Light is particularly important in landscape photography. In fact, it is arguably the most important element in emphasising shape and form, and this is affected by the time of year, time of day, and the weather.

If you want to reveal all the curves and contours of a scene, shadows are essential, and this means that the sun has to be shining for landscape photography to be worthwhile. The flat, shadowless light you get on an overcast day is generally the kiss of death to scenic work – although in stormy weather the dramatic skies can sometimes compensate for lack of excitement on the ground.

The position of the sun in relation to the camera is also crucial. You don't want it behind you, as the shadows will fall away and be hidden, producing bland, uninspiring pictures. The best place for the sun is 90° to the left or right, so that it casts shadows that fall right across the picture, giving a strong sense of shape and depth.

In the right circumstances, shooting into the sun can be effective, with shadows falling towards the camera, but care must be taken to expose correctly and to avoid flare.

The longer the shadows, the more dramatic the effect, which is why the best summer landscapes are often those that are taken early in the morning or late in the evening, when the sun is low in the sky. There are numerous apps you can use to help plan a shoot, and perhaps the most popular of these is The Photographer's Ephemeris. This handy app allows you to determine the position of the sun at any given location and at any given time, so you can catch it in the best light. If you want to shoot at night it also tells you where the moon will be (and when) and its phase, as well as the best time to photograph the Milky Way.

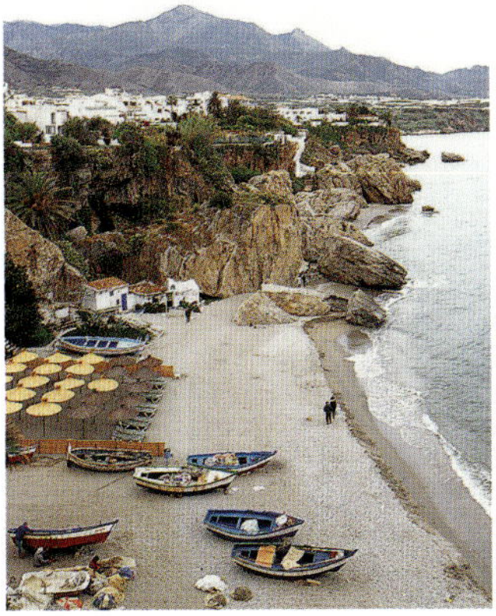

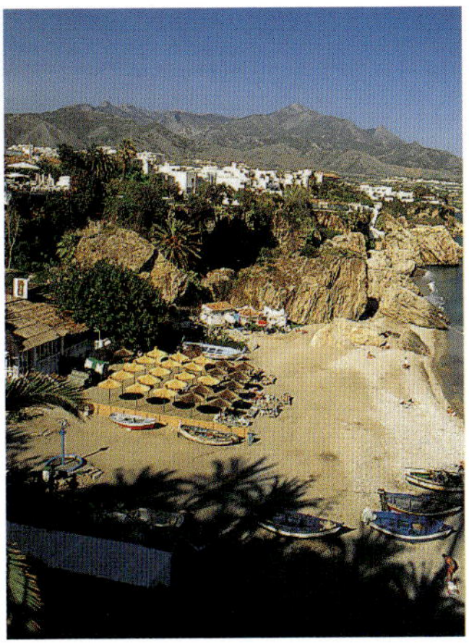

THE RIGHT CONDITIONS

Light makes all the difference to landscape photographs. Seen on a grey day with a washed out sky, this coastal town looks pretty unappealing, but under a blue sky in the early morning sun it is completely transformed.

THE COLOUR OF LIGHT

We've probably all seen the warm glow of a sunset, which looks completely different to the colour of light around lunchtime. The fact is, all light has a colour temperature, which indicates how warm (orange) or cool (blue) it is. At noon, daylight appears neutral in tone, or may even have a slight blue tint, especially in the shade, but the closer you are to sunrise and sunset, the warmer (more orange) the light will be. Artificial lighting can look different still – head out into a town or city at night and you are likely to see a range of colours in lit buildings, from the green glow of fluorescent lighting in office buildings to the deep oranges of tungsten bulbs.

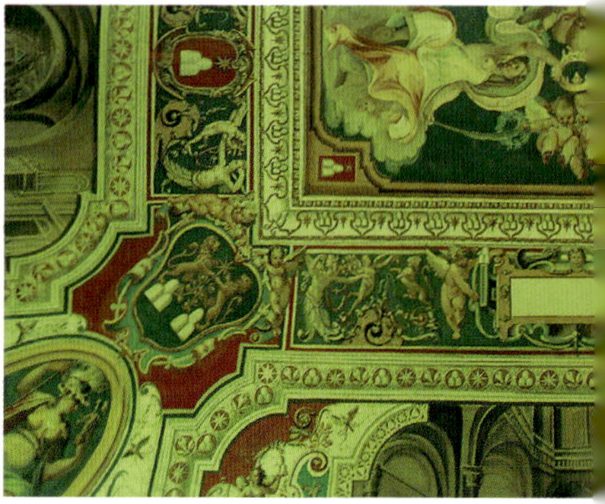

FLUORESCENT LIGHTING

A colour-correction filter is highly recommended if you're shooting under fluorescent lighting on colour film; there are very few situations where the distinct green colour cast is desirable.

EVENING LIGHT

Warm, dappled evening light can often be relied on to bring a subject to life. Without it, this church doorway would probably not have been worth photographing.

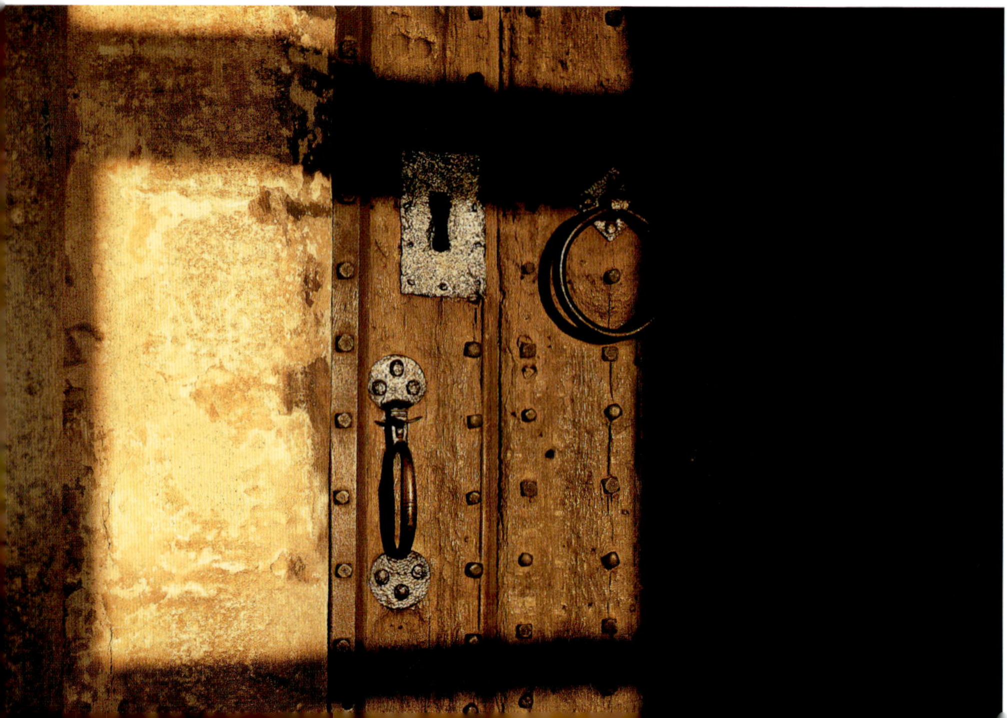

The Kelvin scale

Saying that light is a 'bit blue' or 'slightly orange' is a vague way of describing it, which is why a more scientific method is used – the Kelvin scale.

In photography, think of colour temperature as being based around noon daylight, which has a colour temperature of approximately 5500K (Kelvin). Daylight film is designed to produce natural colours under this light, and flash also has a colour temperature of 5500K.

As the blue content of the light increases, so the temperature rises. On a bright summer's day with a vivid blue sky, or at high altitudes in mountainous regions, the colour temperature may be as high as 10,000K. Photographs taken in such conditions can exhibit a blue colour cast, that requires an orange filter to correct the balance.

At sunset the colour temperature falls to around 3000–3500K, which is a much warmer, more orange colour. Theoretically, you should use a blue filter to get a neutral result on daylight-balanced film, although most photographers prefer to keep the warmth of a sunset in their photographs, so they shoot without a filter.

The colour temperature of tungsten lighting is similar to that at sunset, but in this case it is a good idea to use a correction filter (or tungsten-balanced film), as the strong orange cast usually looks wrong. Filters are also desirable when you're shooting under fluorescent lighting, which has an unappealing green colour.

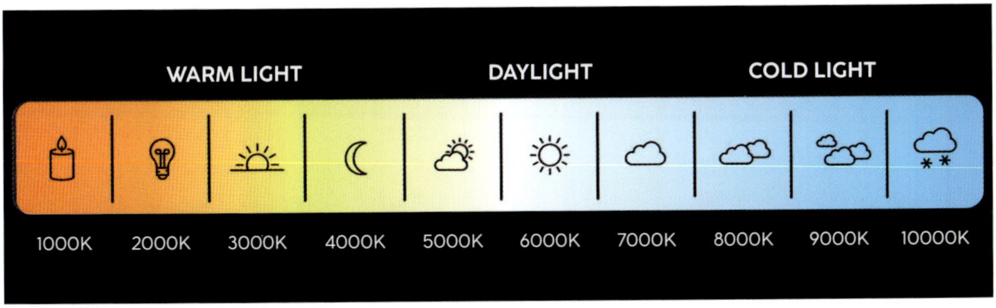

KELVIN SCALE

Most colour film is balanced for daylight (5500K). When the light has a higher temperature, images will appear cooler (more blue), while a lower colour temperature will lead to a warmer (more orange) colour cast unless you use a colour-correction filter.

COMPOSITION

Composition is all about arranging the elements in a scene so they hold the attention of the viewer by soothing, captivating, surprising, or even disturbing them. It is, therefore, vitally important.

Of course, whenever you take a picture it has to be composed, but unless you pay conscious attention to what you're doing, you can end up with an image that's bland and boring. When you start actively thinking about how best to frame the picture and trying different things, your photographs will quickly improve. Over time, these thought processes will become natural, and you'll instinctively know what works and what doesn't. In other words, you'll develop visual awareness – an eye for a picture.

THE 2:3 FORMAT

One of the great things about 35mm film is its 2:3 ratio format, which is not only pleasing to the eye, but also allows you to compose pictures both horizontally and vertically. It's perhaps not that surprising that the majority of pictures are taken in the horizontal format, because that's the way in which it's most comfortable and convenient to hold the camera and, frankly, because a lot of photographers never think of turning their camera on its side.

However, many subjects will benefit from being photographed in the upright format, so make it a habit to consider which orientation would work best every time you're sizing up a scene.

FOREGROUND INTEREST

Wherever you go, you'll find ways to add interest to an image. Here, walking some way down the road from this building (below left) produced a more interesting composition with the traffic light gantry in the foreground (below right).

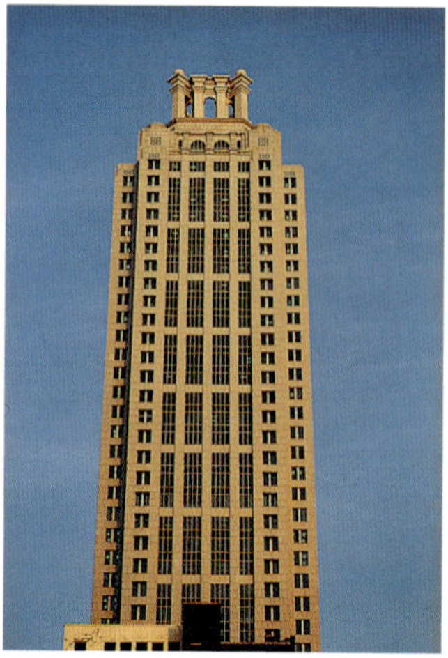

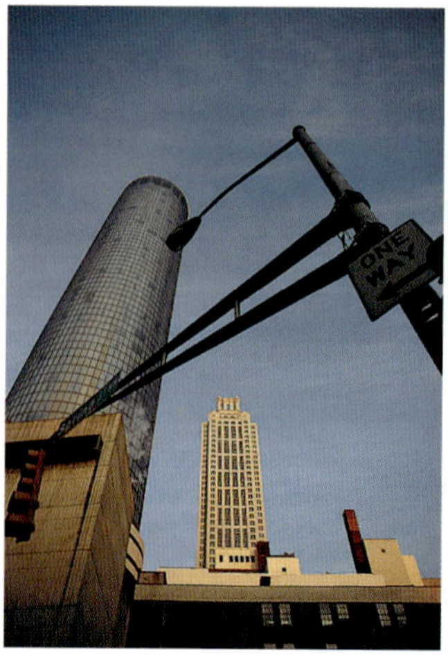

If you use the horizontal format for pictures of people, for example, you'll include quite a lot of their surroundings. This can be a good thing if you want to show someone in their environment, but if you want to concentrate attention on your subject it will almost certainly be better to turn the camera on its side and frame tightly, ideally by using a telephoto lens. On the other hand, when you photograph two people together, or a group, it's more satisfactory to keep the camera horizontal.

When it comes to landscapes, many photographers automatically use the horizontal format in order to get the broad scene in front of them into the frame. This approach can work extremely well, but can also sometimes result in a weak picture in which everything seems to be far away – especially if a wide-angle lens is used. Turning the camera on its side, and including something of interest in the foreground, can often create a greater sense of depth.

In architectural photography, the format you choose will depend to a large degree on the nature of the building itself and on how much of the surroundings you want to include. Ordinary buildings, such as houses, which are long and low, generally benefit from a horizontal treatment, while skyscrapers and other high-rise structures often require an upright treatment.

If in the end you can't decide which format is best, the answer is simple: shoot both so you've got the options covered.

RULE OF THIRDS

The rule of thirds is a classic concept of composition. Essentially, it suggests placing your subject at the intersection of an imaginary grid that divides the frame into thirds vertically and horizontally. In doing so, your picture will look perfectly balanced.

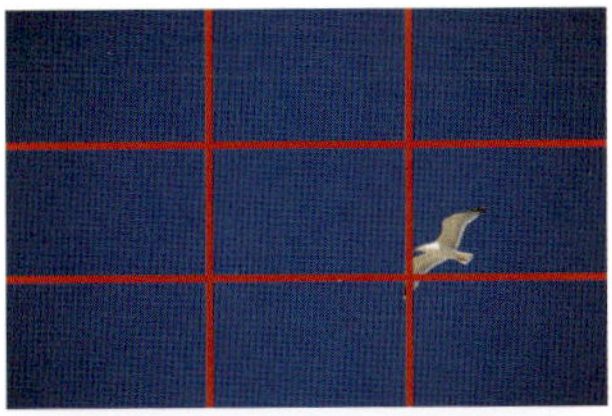

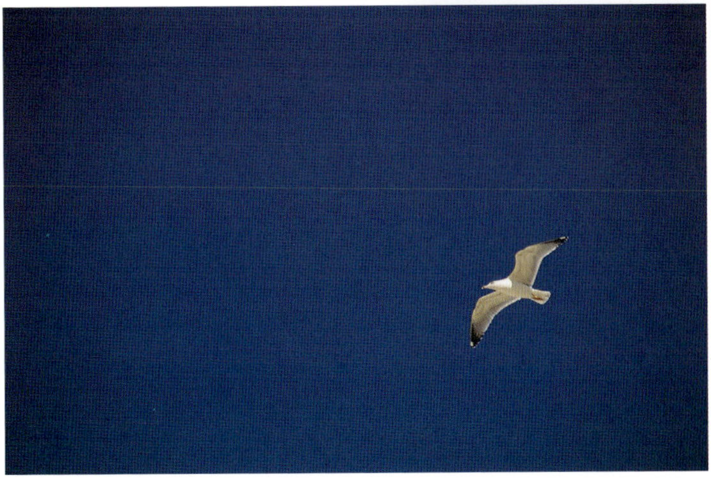

FOCAL POINT

If a picture is to hold the attention of the viewer, it must have a focal point – a centre of attraction on which the eye can settle. That point can be any size, from a barely discernible dot on a landscape to a person filling most of the frame.

Many photographers simply place the most important part of the scene at the centre of the frame. Although this often works very well, it can get rather boring. If you want to add variety to your picture-taking, try putting the subject somewhere else.

One of the classic compositional techniques to follow is the rule of thirds. All you need to do is mentally visualise a grid that divides the picture into thirds vertically and horizontally, and place your subject at one of the four intersection points. This gives a strong sense of balance and harmony.

The rule of thirds can also prove useful in landscape work when it comes to positioning the horizon. Placing it in the centre of the picture produces a balanced composition, which can be static and lacking in interest; try placing it on the upper or lower horizontal thirds line instead.

Of course, it's not always harmony you want, so don't be afraid to break the rules and create a little discord by placing your focal point elsewhere. With the subject at the top of the frame, for example, you get an unsettling and top-heavy image. The point of interest seems to hover in the air and the eye struggles to balance it against the space around it.

The left-hand side of the frame is an excellent place for your subject. Because we read from left to right, the eye naturally starts with the main point of interest and uses it as a springboard to explore the rest of the picture.

Images with the main point of interest at the bottom centre tend to feel grounded and stable, making for good, solid compositions.

Including more than one focal point is an effective way to create tension. The eye can't decide where to settle so it wanders from point to point, taking in the whole picture as it goes.

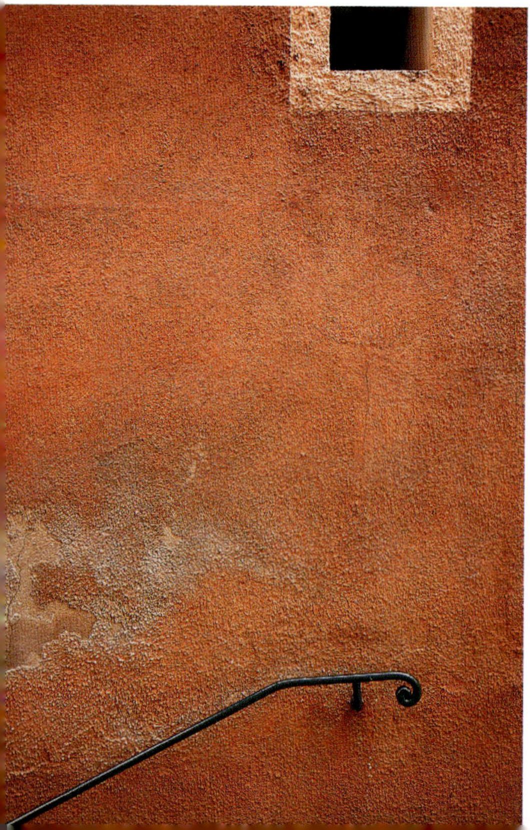

DUAL FOCAL POINTS

Having two points of interest at opposite ends of the frame creates a feeling of tension, making it difficult for the eye to settle on any one place in the photograph.

FRAMES AND LINES

To add an extra dimension to your photographs you can exploit the many natural and man-made frames you'll find around you, such as overhanging branches, arches, and window frames. They focus attention on your subject and may also help to fill out large areas of sky or obscure distracting details.

Frames are a great way of giving your pictures a strong sense of depth. If there's nothing suitable around, placing an object in the foreground can achieve the same effect. The foreground interest establishes a relationship between the front, middle, and back of the scene, and is particularly valuable in landscape work.

You can do similar things with lines. Diagonal lines provide the most dynamic compositions, whether some element of the picture cuts it in half or several elements are arranged along a diagonal line. Some diagonal lines are straight, and the most dynamic, while others are meandering, such as a road or a river in a landscape.

Horizontal lines give a strong sense of stability, while vertical lines are vigorous and active. In circular compositions, a line can sometimes seem to spiral down to the centre of the picture, taking the viewer's eye with it on a journey of discovery.

Converging lines draw the eyes very quickly from the foreground of the picture to something in the distance. The effect is easily achieved if you find a subject with strong parallel lines and tilt a wide-angle lens backwards.

DIAGONALS

A tight crop was chosen for this shot of a colourful boat, and the camera was deliberately angled to give the composition more impact and dynamism from the strong diagonal lines.

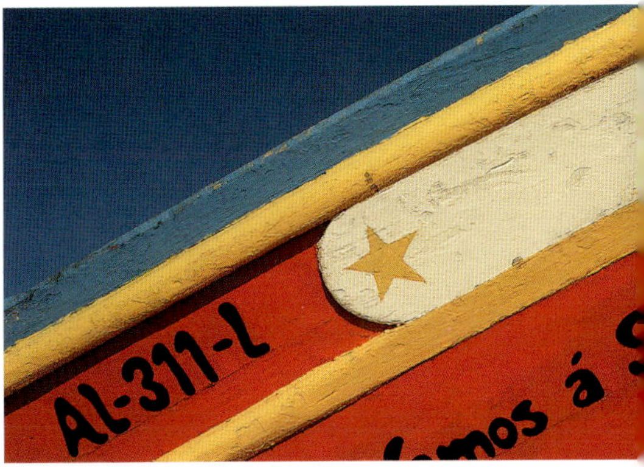

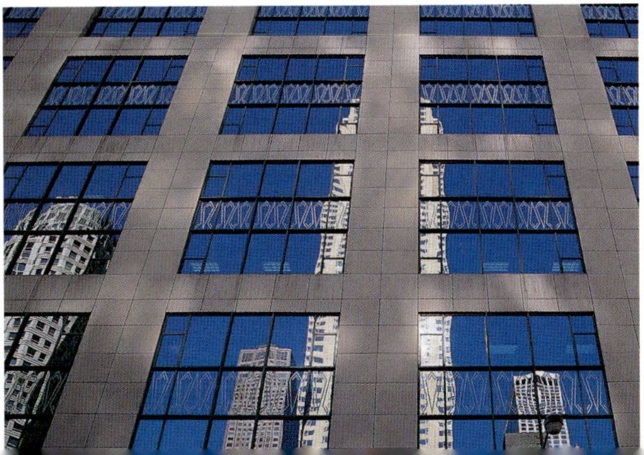

REFLECTIONS

Sometimes, the most intriguing architectural images are the least obvious, as this reflection in the windows of a building in the shade demonstrates.

SHAPES

It can be useful to see compositions in terms of shapes that give structure to a picture and help lead the viewer's eye through it.

Triangles create dynamic compositions, with the eye flitting between three different points along diagonal lines.

Squares are solid and stable shapes that are common in the human-made world, and you'll be able to make good use of them if you regularly photograph subjects such as buildings. Positioning squares full in the frame can produce strong, but occasionally rather dull compositions.

Rectangles offer more interest than squares, because the sides are of irregular lengths. The effect is enhanced by choosing a subject that is long and thin, and matching it to the upright format.

Semi-circles are more active than full circles, but both can be strong elements.

Crosses create pictures in which a lot seems to be going on, with the crossing lines intersecting the picture. Though not as prevalent as other shapes, they're worth looking out for because of the interest they bring to even the simplest of photographs.

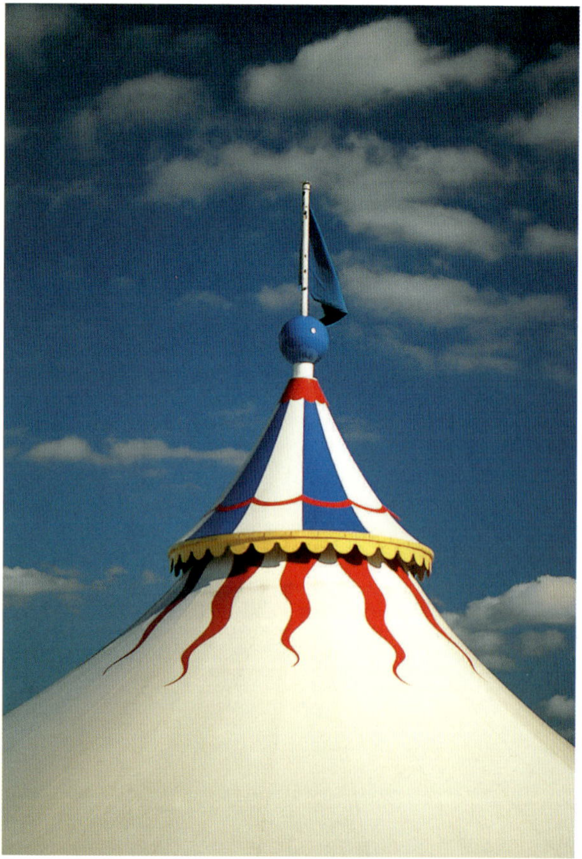

STRONG SHAPES

Once your eyes become attuned you'll notice all sorts of naturally occurring shapes. The top of this marquee describes a strong triangular shape.

VIEWPOINT

Perhaps the most effective compositional accessory you have at your disposal is your legs. When you come across a photogenic subject, don't start snapping away immediately. Instead, spend a few minutes wandering around it first, considering what the best angle might be. There's nothing more frustrating than eagerly rattling off several shots, only to walk on and find a far better viewpoint.

One of the best ways to improve many compositions is simply to step closer to the subject; tightly framed images have impact and immediacy. Shooting from a viewpoint that's higher or lower than your eye-level will also let you see things differently and bring a whole new dimension to your picture-taking. Climb a hill or a high building for a bird's-eye view, or crouch on the floor for a worm's-eye view. Either way, you'll find experimenting with camera height will help you to take more interesting photographs.

COLOUR

Finally, if you're shooting on colour film, think about how colour can be used as a compositional tool. Some colours, such as orange and yellow, blend well together and produce restful images. But others, such as red and blue, contrast strongly, creating a bold visual clash that shouts for attention.

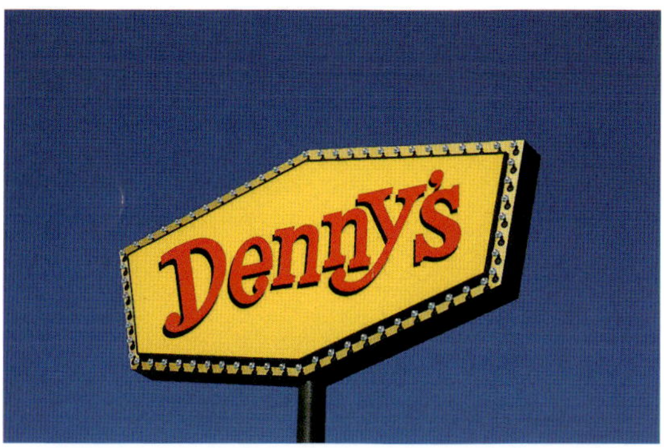

STRONG COLOURS

Colour can be used in a conscious way to produce vibrant or harmonious compositions. Shooting primary colours in bright sunlight results in a shot that can't be ignored.

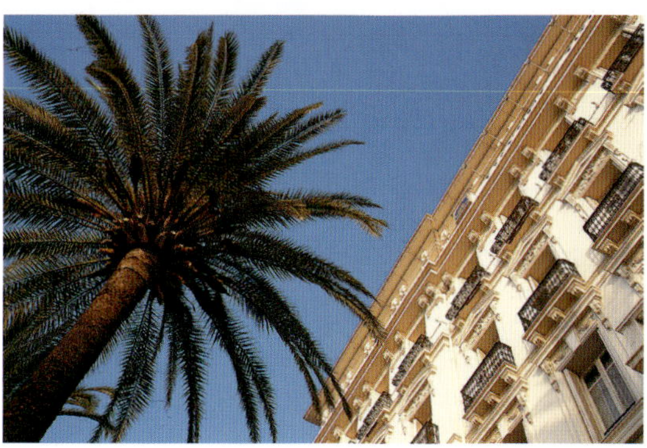

UNUSUAL ANGLES

To stop your architectural pictures getting boring, experiment with different compositions and unusual angles.

PATTERN AND TEXTURE

If you're looking for a new challenge, you could set yourself a project shooting textures and patterns. This exercise will give you a whole new way of thinking about potential subjects. Instead of paying attention to what things are, you need to concentrate on how they look. Content and identity become less important because you're shooting an abstract picture whose appeal lies in its visual strength, composition, and colour.

Choose a theme to help focus your attention. This could be a very general idea, such as textures in nature or buildings, or it might be something very specific, such as walls or tree bark.

To get started, set a timescale and stick to it, or you'll keep putting it off. For instance, you might decide to photograph 20 textures and patterns within two weeks. Don't be too ambitious; most photographers have to fit their picture-taking around other things, and never have as much time as they'd like – so aim to keep your plan achievable.

ABSTRACT PATTERNS

Can you guess what these are? It's not obvious – which is part of the fun of spotting subjects that create patterns. In fact, they're tip-up seats on a tourist boat, photographed with a 300mm lens.

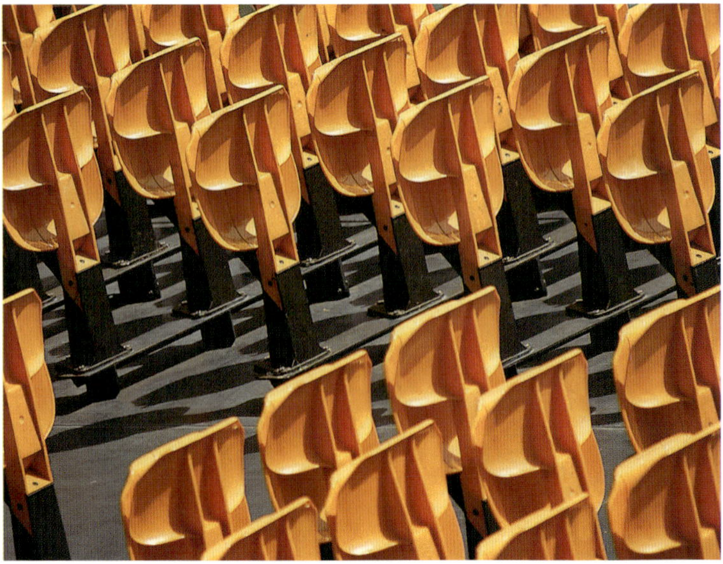

SEEING PATTERNS

Patterns can be found anywhere and everywhere, but at first you may find it hard to see them, even though they're right in front of your eyes.

A pattern is nothing more than a repetition of some visual element – such as a shape, line, or colour. But because we're so used to looking at things in terms of what they are, rather than in terms of their visual content, it can be hard to recognise the patterns around us. You can't break the habit of a lifetime in just five minutes, but with a little perseverance you'll find you suddenly start tuning in to patterns, and then you won't even need to look for them actively.

The shapes that make up a satisfying pattern can be real – such as squares, triangles, circles, or a succession of lines, or they can be implied by the position of key elements within the frame. Subjects that work very effectively in this way are rows of similar things, either side by side, such as cars in a car park, or stretching out into the distance, such as a succession of electricity pylons. Any subject with a strong vanishing point, such as a spiral staircase winding down into nothingness, also works well.

The most effective way to emphasise pattern is to crop out all unnecessary detail and create a clear visual relationship between the key elements in the picture.

Your lens choice is crucial, because with pattern pictures, you make them as much as take them, according to the focal length you choose. A wide-angle lens will let you create a relationship between the foreground and background of a picture, while a telephoto will compress perspective and make objects seem closer together than they really are. Rows of trees or a succession of mountain peaks can be stacked together in this way to create a very satisfying picture.

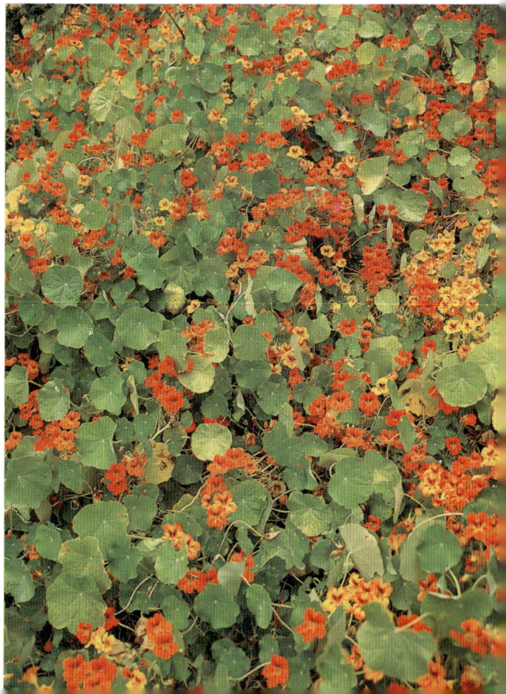

SMALL SCALE

Cropping tightly on these flowers emphasises the natural repeating pattern of green leaves and yellow, orange, and red flowers.

SHOOTING TEXTURE

The two key factors in shooting successful texture pictures are going in close and lighting the subject effectively. As a general rule, the closer you get to a subject the more its texture becomes visible.

At first sight, for instance, the average brick wall may look about as photogenic as a caravan site. But if you go in close it suddenly ceases to be a wall and becomes a criss-cross of lines. Go in closer still, with just a handful of bricks in the frame, and you'll see the rough surface texture start to emerge.

The best way to focus on texture is with a telephoto lens, as these are great for isolating parts of a subject and usually give a good degree of enlargement.

But why stop there? If you really want to bring textures to life why not consider a macro lens or an inexpensive close-up accessory, such as a screw-in close-up lens or, for the more serious enthusiast, a set of extension tubes or bellows. Seen close-up, quite ordinary objects can be revealed as a mass of intricate surface texture.

Oblique lighting

To see texture at its best you need each tiny feature of a surface to cast a shadow, and to produce shadows you need the light in the right place. The worst kind of illumination for textures is a frontal light; to bring textures to life you need light to rake down at an angle. As the light glances across the surface, it creates photogenic shadows. So when you're hunting for texture shots outdoors, aim to be out early in the morning, soon after the sun has risen, or late in the day, just before it sets.

Indoors you can create oblique lighting situations by placing a table in front of a small window, giving you the perfect conditions for throwing texture into sharp relief. After dark, use a desk lamp or the torch on your phone from the side of your subject, or maybe use off-camera flash set at an angle of around 30° to your subject.

FLOWER POWER

Whether they're individual heads or arranged in groups, flowers provide excellent raw material for images concentrating on texture and pattern.

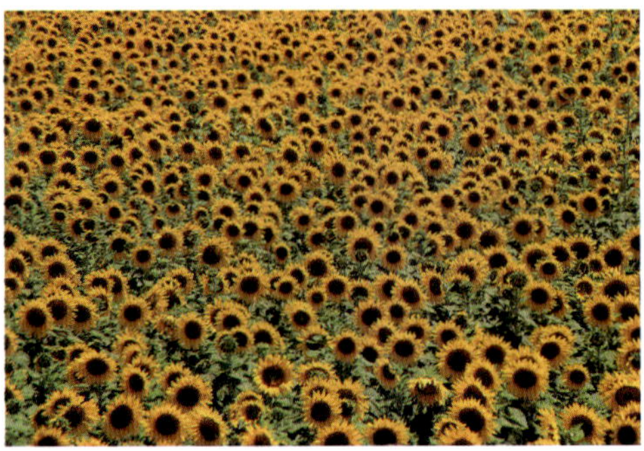

ISOLATION

Cropping tightly to fill the frame with this metal panel emphasises the peeling paint and rust textures.

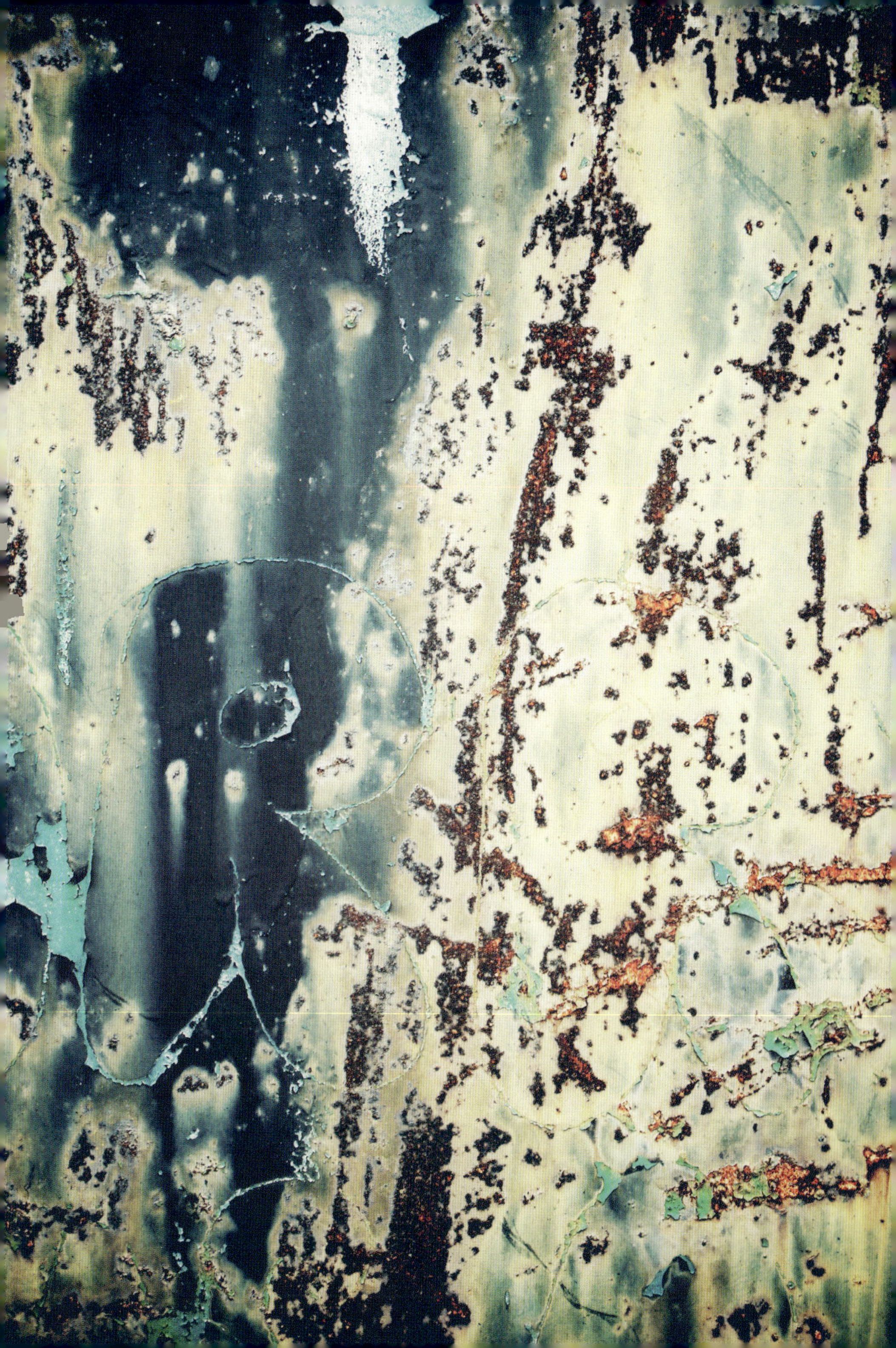

SILHOUETTES

If you want pictures with bags of impact, have a go at creating silhouettes. This couldn't be easier. All you have to do is find a scene in which the background is much brighter than the main subject. Shooting into the setting sun is a sure-fire way of achieving that – but you'll need to take care to avoid flare.

When you're aiming for a silhouette, it's important that your main subject has a strong graphic shape, such as the human body, a leafless tree, a derelict machine, or a statue – something that the viewer can identify from its basic outline. Try to avoid overlapping subjects, which could add confusion – that said, overlapping two people to create some kind of silhouetted 'monster' might be interesting!

EXPOSURE

Exposure is key to creating a strong silhouette. If the shot is too bright, detail will start to creep into your subject or, worse, it will appear washed out rather than as a strong black shape. If the shot is too dark, there's a risk that your silhouetted subject can overlap with equally dark background elements, creating a less obvious shape.

The aim is to set an exposure that is suitable for the background, not your backlit subject. The good news is that when you aim your camera at a subject set against a bright background, or towards a light source, it will underexpose slightly, giving a darker picture. In normal conditions you would correct this, but not with silhouettes.

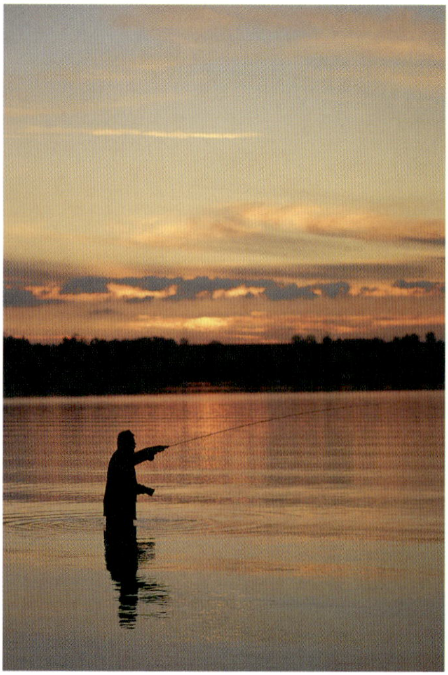

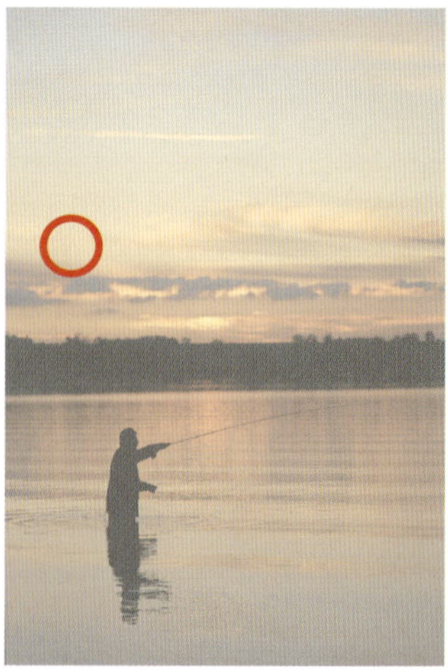

METERING

Taking a spot meter reading from a small patch of bright sky can help ensure a strong silhouette. If you're using centre-weighted metering, tilt your camera upwards and set the exposure for the bright sky, before reframing and taking your shot.

Instead, you want to lean into the camera's tendency towards underexposure by using the exposure reading given by your camera's centre-weighted metering pattern (or multi-area metering on an electronic SLR). Use that reading as your start point and take a shot. Then, reduce the exposure by 1 stop (½ stop if you're using slide film) using either manual mode or exposure compensation and shoot again to get a second darker shot. You could reduce the exposure again and take a third shot, just to be sure.

Alternatively, if your camera has a spot metering option, you can use that to take an exposure reading from a bright part of the background. Remember, your camera will always try and render the area you're metering from as mid-grey, so if you pick a bright (but not white) point to read from it will appear darker in your shot, as will your backlit subject, which should create a strong, black silhouette. Again, you might want to shoot a couple of extra frames with a darker exposure to be sure.

SHAPE

The strongest silhouettes rely on a subject that the viewer can recognise from its shape. You don't need detail to 'read' this as a ski lift.

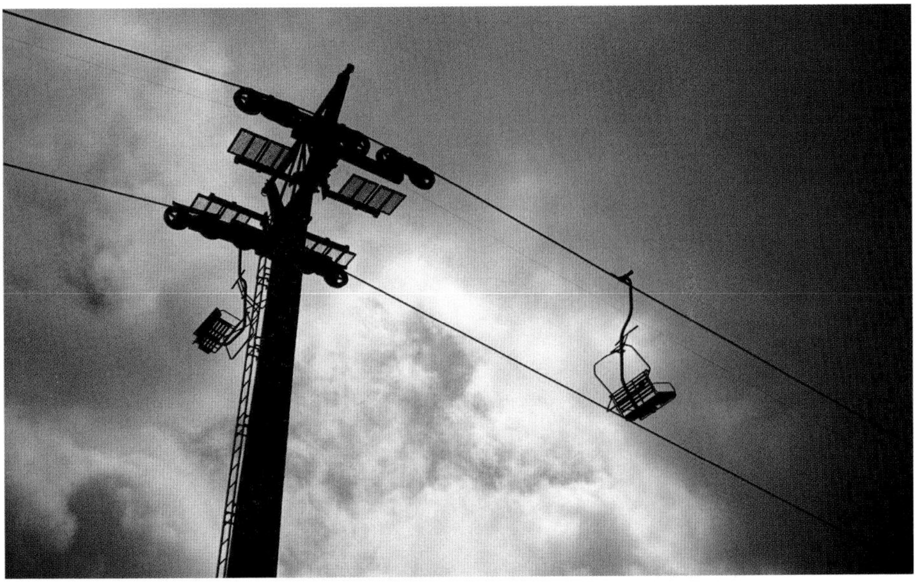

CREATIVE BLUR

Photographers spend a lot of money on lenses that give them the sharpest results, and carefully choose an exposure that will ensure their images are pin-sharp. This isn't a bad thing, but it can sometimes lead to photographs that are unnecessarily lifeless.

The fact is, not everything in a photograph has to be pin-sharp and frozen in time. Whether it's the suggestion of movement in a flowing river or the flick of someone's hair as they turn their head in an otherwise still image, or a more extreme camera movement, introducing a sense of motion through creative blur is a great way of adding life to your photographs.

MOTION BLUR

Motion blur records a moving subject with a shutter speed that's slow enough to reveal that it's moving. The camera remains in a fixed position (possibly on a tripod to avoid camera shake) as the subject moves in the frame during the exposure.

The real challenge is deciding on the shutter speed, as there is no fixed rule and plenty of subject-based variables:

- **Speed:** The slower the subject is moving, the longer the exposure needs to be to record any movement.
- **Size:** Smaller and more distant subjects need a longer exposure time to record motion blur than subjects that are larger in the frame and/or closer to the camera.
- **Direction:** A subject moving towards or away from the camera requires a longer exposure than a subject moving across the frame.

Unfortunately, there is only one approach here – trial and error and the experience gained from it. As a rough guide, a shutter speed of 1/8–1/30 sec will blur people walking, running, and cycling, while 1/8 sec or longer will blur water, depending on its speed and the level of blur you are after.

Using shutter priority or manual mode, select the shutter speed, then make a number of exposures at faster and slower settings to try to achieve the level of blur you want.

MOTION BLUR

A deliberately slow shutter speed was used to reduce this shark to a simple, fluid shape.

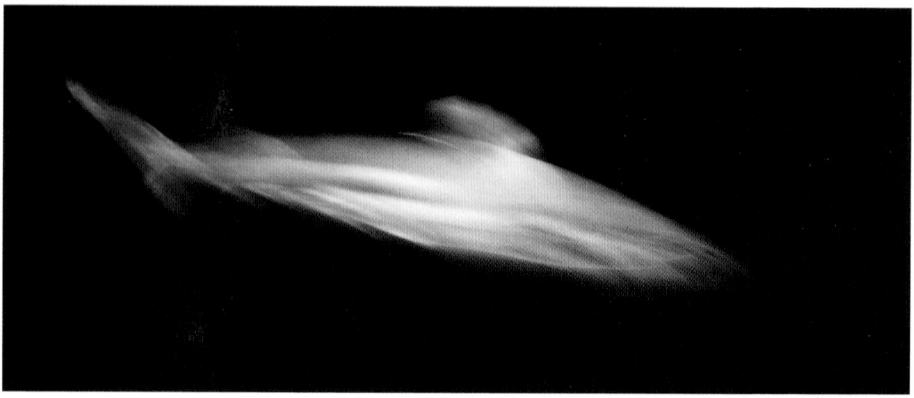

PANNING

In contrast to motion blur, where the subject moves and the camera remains still, panning involves swinging the camera horizontally in the same direction as your moving subject – and firing the shutter while both are moving. This will produce a picture in which the subject is (relatively) sharp, while the background has a distinct direction blur. Here's how it's done:

1. Choose a position in which your subject will go straight by you and which gives you a clear view.
2. Pre-focus on a point that you know the subject will pass. If you have an autofocus camera, switch over to manual focus.
3. Choose a shutter speed that matches the speed of your subject. For fast subjects, such as cars, skiers, and motorbikes, experiment with speeds from 1/125–1/30 sec. For slower action, such as running or cycling, try speeds from 1/60–1/15 sec.
4. Tuck your arms in tight to your body and prepare for the subject to appear. As it comes into sight, follow its movement with the camera, swinging the top half of your body round in a smooth and steady arc. Don't change focus.
5. As the subject passes the point you are focused on, fire the shutter release.
6. Continue to follow the subject with your panning movement – as you'd follow through a swing in golf or a stroke in tennis.
7. Repeat. And repeat again. Panning is unpredictable, and you never know whether you've got the result you are after until you get your pictures back from processing. The more shots you take, the more winners you're likely to end up with.

PANNING

Panning produces a motion-blurred background and a relatively sharp subject. The secret of success lies in matching the shutter speed with a smooth panning action.

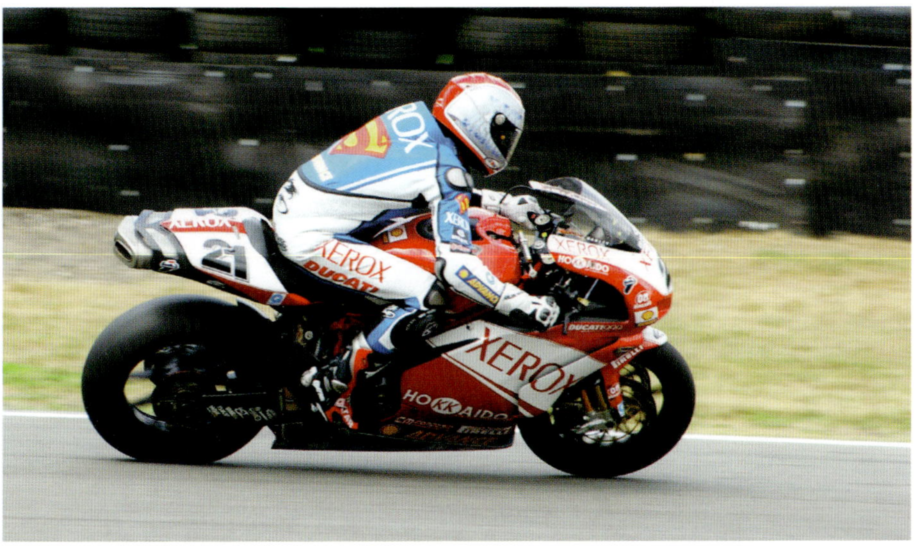

NIGHT AND LOW LIGHT

As daylight fades and lights go on, a whole different landscape of light appears. This has its own challenges when it comes to photography – and the potential to create fascinating studies after dark.

All but the simplest 35mm cameras have a wide range of shutter speeds and apertures that make it possible to take pictures at night and in low-light situations. Most SLRs offer a 'B' (Bulb) setting that allows you to select exposures running into seconds or even minutes.

Some buildings that you wouldn't look at twice during the day – and certainly wouldn't consider photographing – are completely transformed when night falls, floodlighting comes on, and neon signs light up. Ideal subjects include historic buildings such as cathedrals and neon-signed nightlife such as clubs and bars.

The term 'night photography' is a little bit misleading, though, as the best time to take photographs of street scenes and buildings is actually at dusk, just after the sun's gone down and there's still some blue in the sky. If you leave it any later, the sky will be recorded as a dense black with the lights as burnt-out highlights. As a rule of thumb, an hour before it gets dark is when you should start shooting for the best results.

NIGHT CITYSCAPE

Try to find a vantage point that gives you a commanding view. This picture was taken from the 14th floor of a skyscraper.

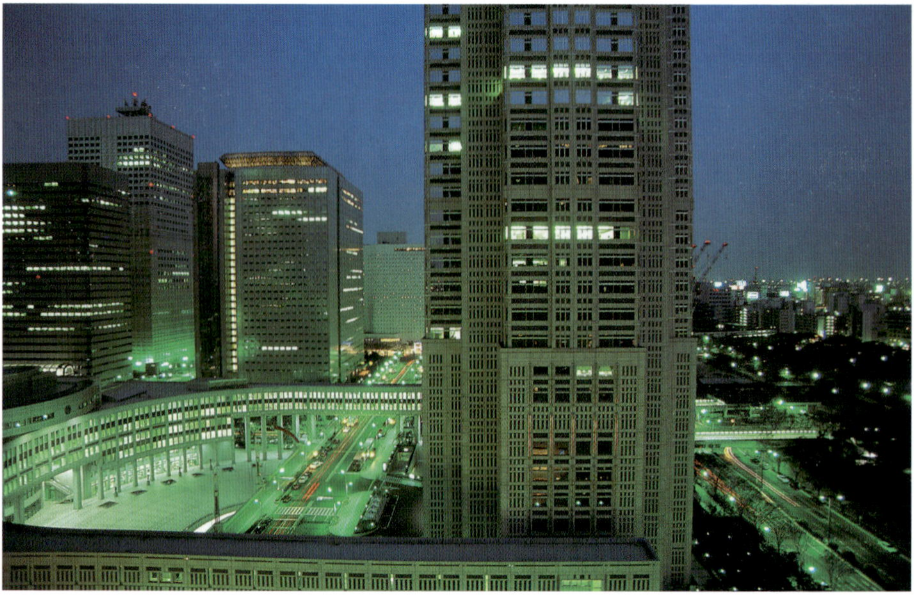

THE RIGHT EXPOSURE

When you're shooting on film, night photography can be a challenge. The enormous contrast range means getting the exposure right, and it's not until you look at your processed film that you know if you've been successful or not.

What makes night photography appealing is the bright, vivid lights. While you can use filters to compensate for them, the resulting pictures will be flat and uninspiring. You want to capture the vibrant warmth that mercury vapour and tungsten illumination give to these subjects, as well as the greens in fluorescent lighting and coloured neon.

In bright street lighting, you might just get away with hand-holding your camera, especially if you load up with a faster film, but the risk of camera shake is always present. Bracing yourself against a lampost or resting the camera on a wall can help, but if you're serious about night-time shooting a tripod is essential. Once the camera is firmly anchored, you can take pictures in conditions where there's very little light at all, and with no fear of them coming out blurred. A cable release avoids the need to touch the camera when firing the shutter, but a good alternative is to use the self-timer.

If you want to add animation to low-light shots try including moving cars, whose lights will streak across the picture during long exposures. In fact, you can make this the whole point of a wonderful special effects picture by finding a good vantage point on a bridge looking down on a busy road and shooting as traffic passes below. Wait until a burst of traffic comes along, and then fire the shutter for a period of around 15 seconds. Once again, twilight is the best time to shoot. Funfairs can also make wonderful hunting grounds for special effects at night.

NIGHT EXPOSURE GUIDE

The main challenge with taking pictures at night is calculating the exposure. Below are exposure settings for a range of common subjects, based on ISO 100 film. However, treat these as a starting point. It is sensible to bracket widely when taking pictures at night.

Subject	Exposure
Buildings with blue still in the sky	1/15 sec at f/5.6
Buildings against dark sky	4 sec at f/5.6
Funfairs/amusement parks	1/4 sec at f/5.6
Brightly lit buildings	1/4–1/15 sec at f/4
Floodlit buildings and monuments	1 sec at f/4
Neon signs	1/4 sec f/4
Illuminations	1 sec f/5.6
Traffic trails	15 sec at f/11
Fireworks/lightning	15 sec at f/16

RECIPROCITY FAILURE

Reciprocity failure doesn't occur in digital photography, but it is something that you need to be aware of if you're shooting film at night.

Under normal conditions, an exposure is directly proportional to light intensity and exposure time, so if you increase the aperture by 1 stop you will need to decrease the shutter speed by 1 stop (and vice versa) to maintain the same overall exposure.

However, at very long (and very short) exposure times, this rule breaks down. This is particularly pertinent in low-light situations, such as night photography, as film becomes less sensitive to light than expected. The chemical reactions in the emulsion slow down, meaning that additional exposure time is required to achieve the same image density. Film manufacturers provide reciprocity charts that you can use to determine precisely how much additional exposure is needed.

It is also worth noting that reciprocity failure can affect colour balance and contrast, particularly in colour film, leading to unwanted colour shifts. Although you can use colour-correction filters to compensate, most photographers will simply accept any colour shift as part of the night photography 'look'.

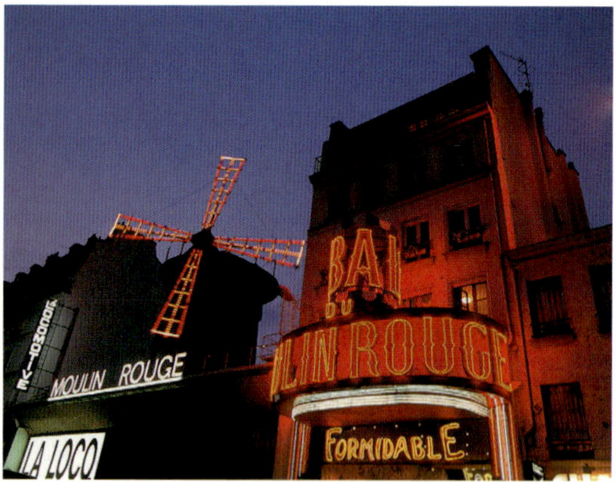

THE MAGIC HOUR

The best time to take night pictures is about an hour before it gets dark, so there is still some colour in the sky, not just black.

TWILIGHT

At twilight, the sky is often a clear, pure blue. However, the low light levels mean you'll need fast film or a tripod to be sure of shake-free results.

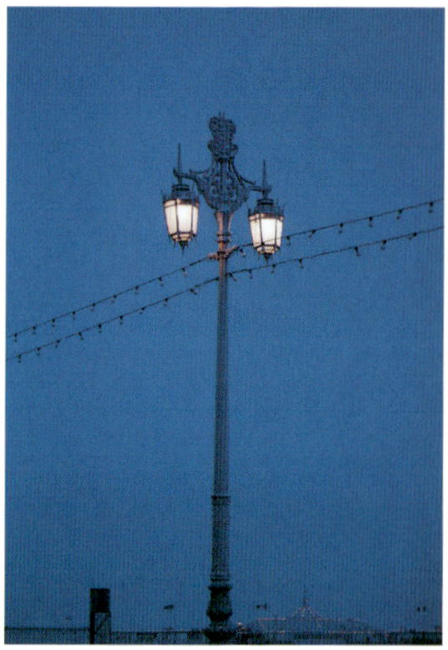

RECIPROCITY FAILURE CHART

The main challenge with taking pictures at night is calculating the exposure. Below are exposure settings for a range of common subjects, based on ISO 100 film. However, treat these as a starting point. It is sensible to bracket widely when taking pictures at night.

Metered exposure	Colour slide film (corrected)	Colour negative (corrected)	Black-and-white negative (corrected)
1 sec	1 sec	1 sec	1 sec
2 sec	2 sec	2 sec	2–3 sec
4 sec	5 sec	5 sec	6 sec
8 sec	10 sec	9–10 sec	12 sec
15 sec	20–25 sec	18–20 sec	25 sec
30 sec	40–45 sec	38–45 sec	50–60 sec
60 sec	80–90 sec	75–90 sec	90–120 sec
2 min	3 min	2.5–3 min	3.5–4 min
4 min	6 min	6–7 min	7–8 min
8 min	12–14 min	12–14 min	15–18 min

ILLUMINATED STREETS

Photographing at night completely transforms a scene, as shown far right.

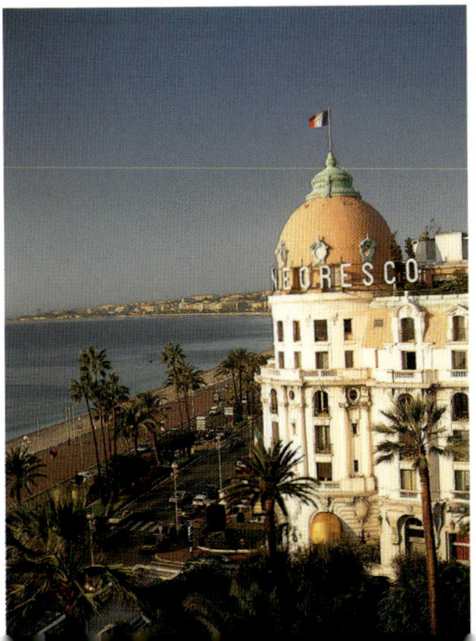

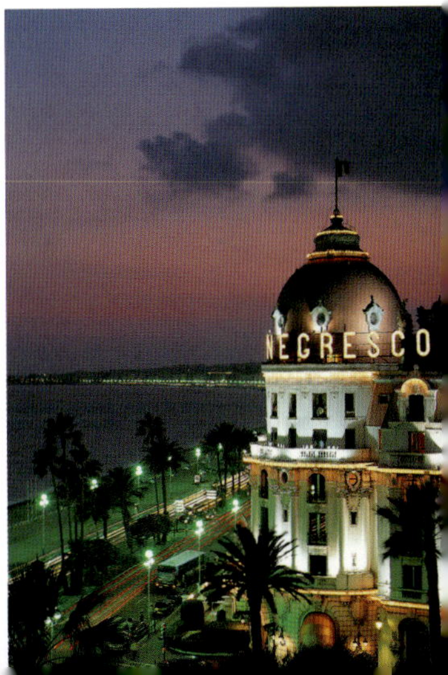

FLASH TECHNIQUES

There's no denying that using flash for film photography is more challenging than it is with a digital camera, simply because you don't get any immediate feedback. You won't know if the exposure is right or the light from the flash is falling as you want it to until you get your film back, at which point it might be too late. However, the following guide should help point you in the direction of consistent success.

FLASH CONTROL

When it comes to controlling flash, the options depend entirely on your camera and the flash. Some electronic cameras offer all of the following options, while a mechanical camera or basic flash unit (including studio strobes) may demand that you work manually.

TTL flash

TTL (Through-The-Lens) flash metering can offer incredible exposure accuracy. Found on later electronic SLRs (and their modern digital counterparts), TTL flash control uses a sensor inside the camera to measures the light reflected back from the subject.

The advantage with this system is that the exposure is based on what the lens sees, so if you bounce the flash or fire it through a diffuser, this is automatically taken into account. Similarly, if you change the aperture on the lens, the flash exposure takes this into account. However, as with regular exposure metering, it can be affected by excessively light or dark subjects.

A forerunner to TTL flash metering is off-the-film (OTF) metering, which can be found in a number of older, advanced SLRs, such as the Canon T90, Minolta X-700, Nikon F4, Olympus OM2, and Pentax LX.

SHUTTER SPEED MATCHES FLASH SYNC SPEED

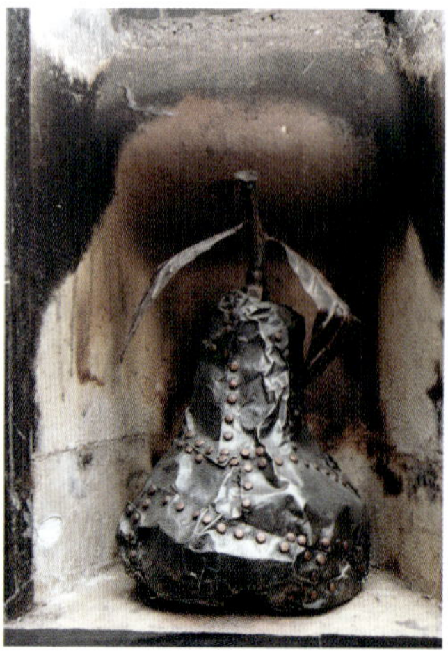

SHUTTER SPEED TOO FAST

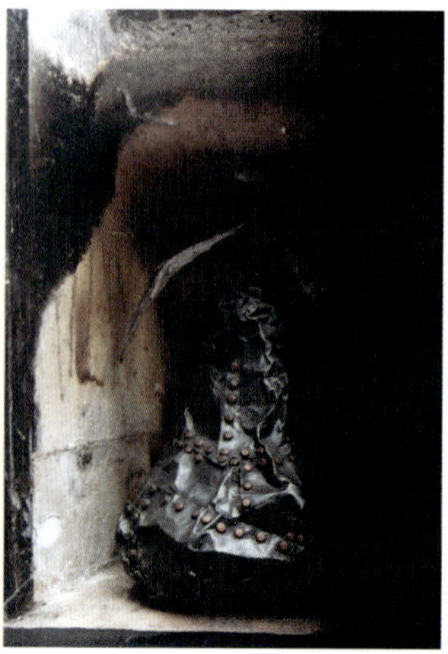

SYNC SPEED

If you use a shutter speed that is faster than the camera's flash sync speed, your film won't be exposed in its entirety, resulting in a black, unexposed bar across (or down) the image.

Automatic flash

Automatic flash uses a sensor on the front of the flash unit to measure the light reflected back from the subject. As with TTL flash control, when it determines that enough light has been given out, it cuts off the output.

All you have to do when you use automatic flash is set the aperture indicated on the back of the flash unit and make sure your subject is within the distance range shown. Simple flash units offer a single auto setting, while others boast multiple automatic options covering a variety of power settings.

Although automatic flash is generally reliable, you need to make sure you set the aperture correctly. It's also possible to get 'bad' exposures if the sensor on the flash is covered in any way – adding a softbox diffuser to the flash may partially obscure the sensor, for example.

Manual flash

Manual flash is as simple as it gets. It gives out the same amount of light every time, regardless of your camera settings or subject distance.

When it comes to determining the exposure, you either need to use a hand-held flash meter or the guide number (GN) of the flash and a bit of basic maths.

To calculate the aperture you need for your exposure, divide the GN by the flash-to-subject distance. So, if the flash has a GN of 36m (118ft)/ISO 100 and the flash-to-subject distance is 3m (10ft), the aperture you need with ISO 100 film will be f/11 (36/3 = 12, but the closest aperture is f/11).

You can also work it out the other way around. If you want to use a particular aperture (f/8, for example), divide it into the GN to get the flash-to-subject distance – in this case 4.5m (14.5ft) equals 36/8.

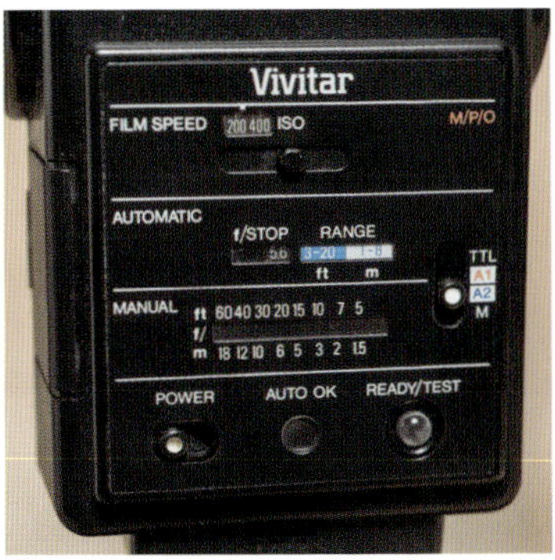

AUTO

This old Vivitar flash offers TTL, automatic, and manual control. Set to automatic, the analogue display shows the f/stop (aperture) you should use and the distance range – here it's f/5.6 and 1–6m (3–20ft).

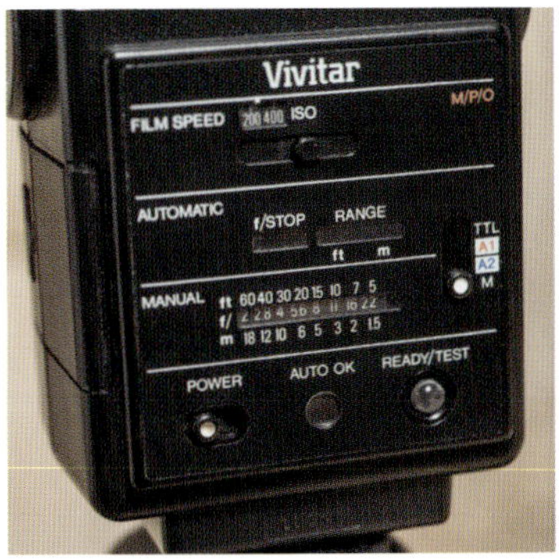

MANUAL

Set to manual, the analogue display aligns flash-to-subject distances with aperture settings. It's up to the photographer to choose their preferred combination.

MODIFYING THE LIGHT

Whether you use TTL flash control or manual, your camera's built-in flash (if it has one) or the direct flash in the hotshoe on top of the camera delivers flat, frontal lighting and harsh shadows. There is also the risk of red-eye when photographing people. However, with a little imagination you can produce much better results.

Flash diffusion

The first problem with direct flash is that it is a small, 'hard' light source, which is why it creates dark, hard-edged shadows.

A simple, low-cost way of softening the light is to attach some tracing paper or soft tissue over the flash. If you're using a hotshoe flash, there are numerous commercial diffusers available that perform a similar role. These range from hard plastic diffusers that slide onto the front of the flash, to larger 'softbox' style diffusers.

In each case, the diffuser (or diffusion material) will spread the light and make it slightly softer, taking the edge off those dark shadows. Although putting something in front of the flash will reduce its power output slightly, automatic and TTL flash – including a built-in flash – will automatically compensate for this.

Bounce flash

Hotshoe flashes that feature a bounce-and-tilt head provide another way of softening the light. Rather than aim the flash directly at your subject, you can aim it at a convenient ceiling (or wall) and bounce the light off it. This spreads the light before it reaches your subject, which softens it in the process.

Check that the surface you're intending to use is white (or at least a neutral tone), as coloured ceilings and walls can add an unpleasant colour cast to your pictures. You also don't want to get too close to your subject, either – you need sufficient space for the light to bounce up and down at an angle so it still illuminates the subject fully.

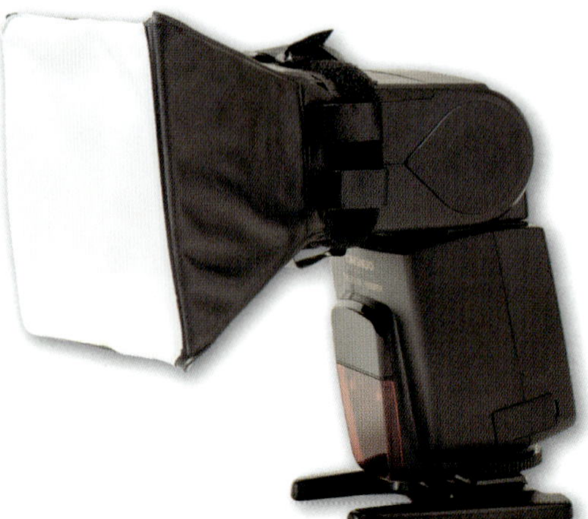

FLASH DIFFUSER

There are numerous diffusers available for hotshoe flashes, including universal-fitting softboxes of various sizes.

An alternative to relying on a ceiling or wall, is to use one of the many types of flash reflector that are on the market. Most fit above the flash head and are held in place by Velcro® or an elastic band, providing you with a small 'bounce board' that you can reflect the flash off, no matter where you are shooting. The light is not as soft as flash bounced from a ceiling, as these reflectors have a smaller surface area and are closer to the flash, but this is still a big improvement over direct flash, especially if you're shooting outdoors.

Off-camera flash

Another major problem with on-camera flash is that it's directly in line with the subject, creating flat lighting that kills any shadows that might otherwise add form and texture to the subject.

If you're using a hotshoe flash, simply taking the flash off the camera can transform lighting by allowing you to light your subject from the side, above, below, or from behind.

You will need a cable to connect the flash to the camera to do this, and some SLR systems have dedicated leads that let you retain TTL (or OTF) flash metering. If yours doesn't, use manual flash control instead – just bear in mind that exposure should be based on the flash-to-subject distance, *not* the camera-to-subject distance.

BOUNCE FLASH

Bouncing the light from a flash off a wall or ceiling creates a softer, more uniform light with reduced 'hotspots' and less dense shadows.

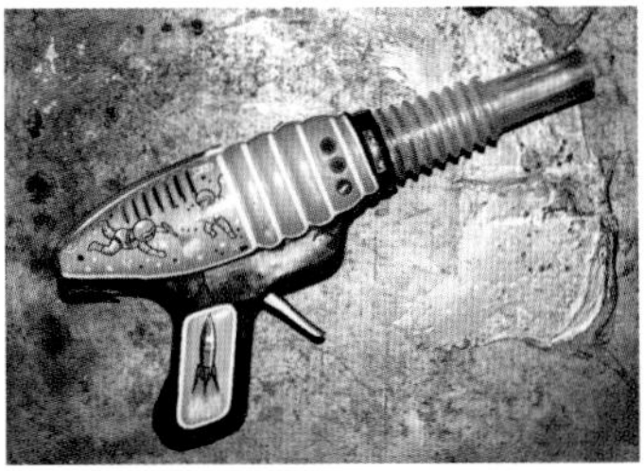

Direct flash

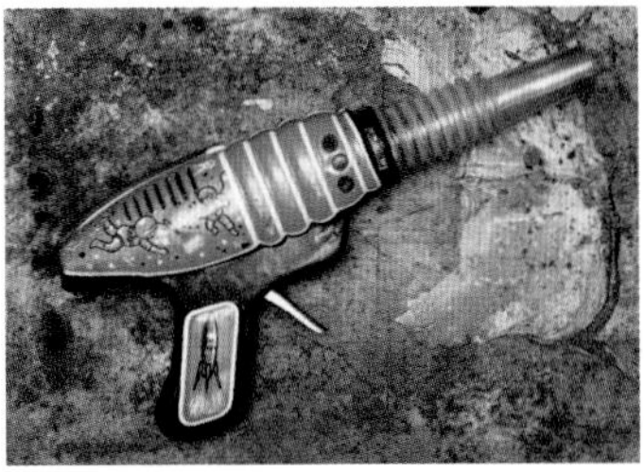

Bounce flash

RED-EYE REDUCTION

Photographing people in low light using direct flash can easily result in pictures where their eyes glow red – a fault generally called 'red-eye'. This common problem is caused by the flash reflecting off the blood vessels at the back of the eye.

Most cameras with a built-in flash feature a red-eye reduction setting that fires a pre-flash to close down the subjects' pupils just before the picture is taken. This generally reduces the risk of red-eye, but it takes a small amount of time for the pre-flash to fire, so you could miss the moment in fast-changing situations.

FILL-IN FLASH

One of the essential techniques of flash photography is fill-in flash. Master it, and the quality of your pictures will improve enormously. In the simplest sense, it involves using the flash in daylight to provide a controlled burst of low-powered flash to illuminate, or 'fill in', areas of shadow on the subject and soften harsh contrasts.

The aim is to maintain a natural-looking effect, so getting the balance right between the flash and ambient light is essential. If there's too little flash, the effect won't be visible. If there's too much, the flash will be overpowering and obvious.

Fill-in flash is particularly valuable when photographing people on a sunny day, when lighting is harsh and casting unpleasant shadows. In this situation, put the sun behind your subject to produce a halo of light around their hair, while the flash illuminates their face.

Fill-in flash also works well on overcast days when the light is flat, as it lifts the colours slightly and helps your subject stand out.

Some SLRs and compacts with a built-in flash provide fill-in flash automatically when you activate the flash in daylight, so if your camera does this, give it a try. However, with many cameras, the effect is too strong. For the best results, take control yourself.

A lighting ratio of 1:4 – one-quarter as much flash as daylight – generally works well for fill-in flash. However, flash is normally set to be the only light source, so to use it for fill-in you need to trick it into giving out less light.

Using automatic flash (the most universal control option), take an exposure reading from your subject based on your camera's flash sync speed. This is typically 1/60 sec or 1/125 sec, and on a sunny day this will give you an aperture of about f/8. Then set your automatic flash at an aperture 2 stops greater than the metered reading. So, if the camera reading is f/8, set the flash to f/4.

When you take the picture, the daylight exposure will be correct, but the flash exposure will be 2 stops underexposed, giving the attractive 1:4 fill-in required.

If you're using TTL flash, things become easier still; simply set the flash exposure compensation (on the flash unit) to -2 stops.

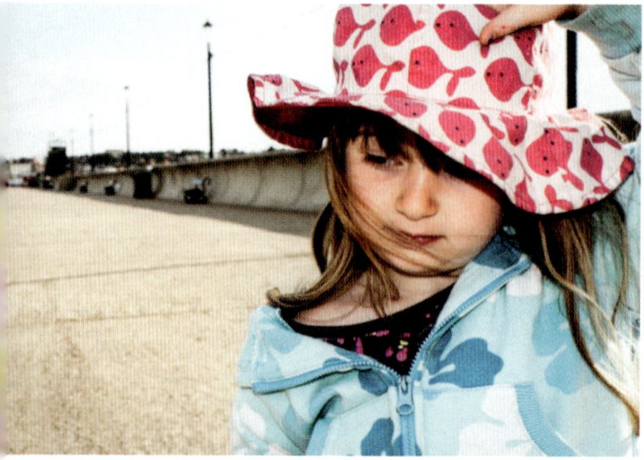

FILL-IN FLASH

As the name suggests, fill-in flash is designed to 'fill' the shadows, rather than dominate the shot. Here, the flash was balanced equally with the ambient light to illuminate the subject's face.

ADVANCED FLASH TECHNIQUES

- **Slow sync flash:** This combines a long shutter speed with flash to capture both ambient light and motion. While the flash freezes the main subject, the slower shutter speed records background detail or motion blur, adding a sense of movement. For dramatic results, try panning with the subject to produce a sharp, flash-lit figure against a streaked background – ideal for close action and creative portraits.
- **Rear curtain flash:** Most cameras fire the flash at the start of the exposure (first curtain flash). However, when used with slow shutter speeds, this makes motion trails appear in front of the subject, reversing the sense of movement. Rear curtain sync solves this by firing the flash at the end of the exposure, so motion blur appears behind the subject and creates a natural, forward-moving effect.
- **Multiple flash:** This captures several images of a moving subject within a single frame. In a dark room, set the camera on a tripod, open the shutter on B (Bulb), and manually trigger the flash multiple times as the subject changes position. For subjects that don't overlap, use the flash's normal exposure settings, but when images overlap, reduce the exposure by 1 stop for each repetition to avoid overexposure. This technique is great for creative motion studies, showing stages of movement across a single image.
- **Stroboscopic flash:** Stroboscopic photography automates the multiple flash technique by using the 'strobe' mode on a flash (typically found on high-end flashes with TTL control). This fires a rapid series of low-power bursts that capture a sequence of motion – a golf swing or a dancer's movement, for example – in a single frame. You can control the number and frequency of flashes to suit the subject. As with multiple flash, a dark background and tripod produce the clearest results.
- **Open flash:** Also known as 'painting with light', open flash involves manually firing one or more flashes during a long exposure to illuminate different parts of a scene. Mount the camera on a tripod, and trigger the shutter in B (Bulb) mode so it is held open. Move around your subject, firing the flash to light specific areas – your movement won't register if you keep moving. Auto and TTL flash units make exposure easier, and using coloured gels can add atmosphere. This technique originated in architectural photography, and is ideally suited to large subjects, low-light situations, and creative lighting for still-life compositions.

DOMINANT FLASH

Taken without flash, this scene was pretty underwhelming. The lighting was flat and the sky washed out. However, using a powerful hammerhead flash transformed the scene into something far more atmospheric. Just make sure the flash is stronger than the ambient light so it becomes the dominant light source. This is most easily done when the ambient light levels are low (at dusk or at night, for example) and your flash is powerful.

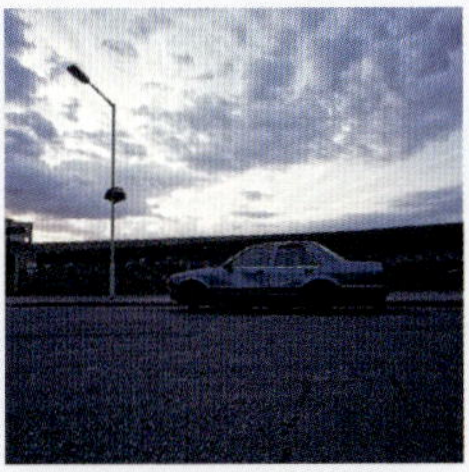

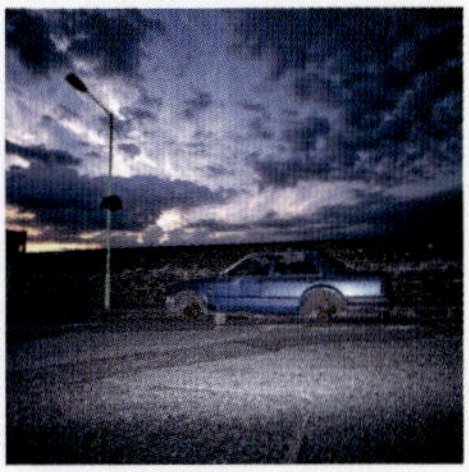

MULTIPLE EXPOSURES

A lot of electronic SLRs have a multiple-exposure facility and it can be fun to combine two or more images in a single frame. However, don't expect it to be easy – unlike digital cameras, which let you overlay multiple images and preview how they will look before you take your shot, on film you are largely shooting blind.

There are two approaches you can take to multiple exposures on film. The first is where two or more exposures are made on the same frame, one after the other, with the subject of each exposure chosen deliberately. The second involves the same film being run through a camera from start to finish, two or more times, which delivers results that are generally more reliant on luck than judgement, but are no less impactful when they work.

FRAME-BY-FRAME

This technique can be applied in numerous ways, from the kitsch 'trick' photographs of the 1970s and 80s (think girl in a Martini glass), to two or more disparate overlaid images, or the same subject photographed repeatedly to give a 'jittery' look. In each case, the approach is the same; you are building up an overall exposure.

OVERLAY

This shot was taken on a Nikon F100, which has a multiple exposure setting. In this instance, two exposures of the same subject were overlayed to create a layered effect.

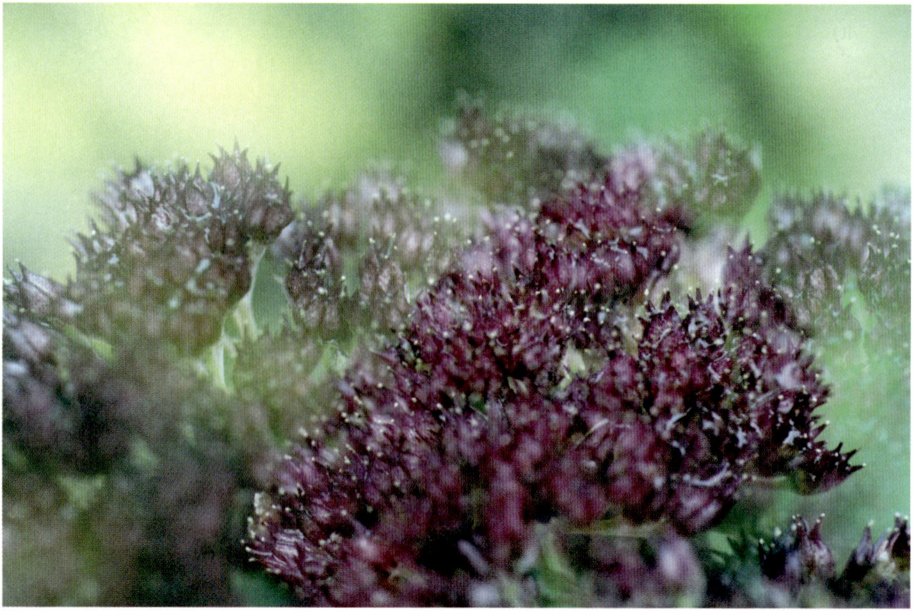

The simple way of thinking of multiple exposures is that you're adding light to what starts as a black frame. Your first exposure can lighten any part of this frame, but subsequent exposures will only affect areas that are darker. If the first exposure adds a bright white highlight, the second exposure won't be able to add to that – you can only add light and make an area brighter, not make it darker.

If you want your multiple images to combine equally, you need to adjust the exposure for each shot. As shown in the grid (right), the exposure adjustment needed depends on the number of images you plan to combine. If you want to combine four images, for example, each one should be shot at -2 stops to build up the overall exposure. If your camera has a multiple exposure mode, it may automatically do this; if not, you will have to override the exposure manually.

Having taken your first shot, you will need to 'wind on' to reset the shutter, but without actually transporting the film. Again, if your camera has a multiple exposure mode, this will be done for you. If you're using a manual SLR, the process is a little more involved, as you will need to hold down the film rewind button as you wind on. This will release the take-up spool so the shutter resets when you wind on, but the film doesn't move. You can then make your second exposure.

EXPOSURE ADJUSTMENT

When you shoot multiple exposures, each shot builds up the overall brightness. Depending on how many exposures you are looking to combine, use the grid below to determine how much darker each image needs to be. You can do this by deliberately rating the film at a higher ISO – by dialling in negative (-) exposure compensation, by closing the aperture, or by setting a faster shutter speed.

Number of exposures	Exposure/ISO adjustment (stops)
1	0
2	-1
3	-1½
4	-2
6	-2½
8	-3
12	-3½
16	-4

DOUBLE-LOADED FILM

Running film through a camera more than once guarantees unpredictable results, because you'll never be entirely sure what's in each frame until you get your film processed. This is something you can do yourself or just as easily try with a friend (or two), with each of you using the same film on different occasions.

The process is simple:

1. Load the film as normal, but set the ISO faster than its nominal rating. If you plan on exposing the film twice, rate it 1 stop faster than normal (so set ISO 200 for an ISO 100 film). If you want to expose it more than twice, refer to the table on the previous page and adjust the ISO accordingly. This will mean the film is deliberately underexposed each time it goes through the camera, but each run-through will build up to the correct exposure overall.
2. When you get to the end of the roll, rewind it. So it can be easily reloaded, it helps if you leave the 'tongue' or leader of the film out of the cassette. Some electronic SLRs with auto-rewind have a setting for this, but if you manually rewind your film just listen for a distinct 'click' as the film comes off the spool – at that point you can open the back of the camera and the leader will be out.
3. Load the film and shoot again. It doesn't have to be loaded in the same camera, but remember to increase the ISO rating as you did in step 1. When you get to the end of the roll for the second time, either get it processed and see what you've got, or run it through the camera again.
4. The more times you expose a film, the more abstract and disjointed your images are likely to be, but the fun of this technique is you never really know what you're going to get!

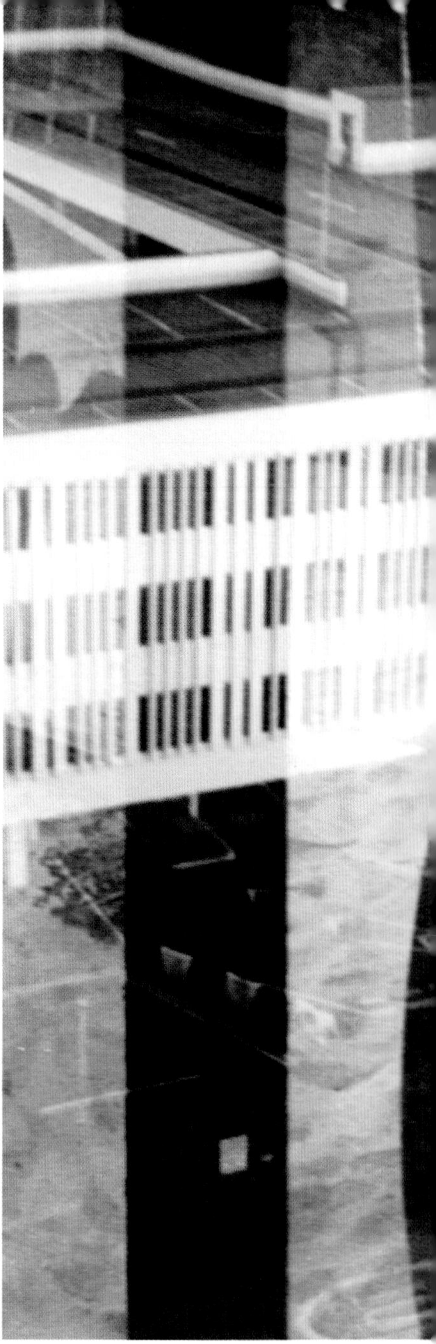

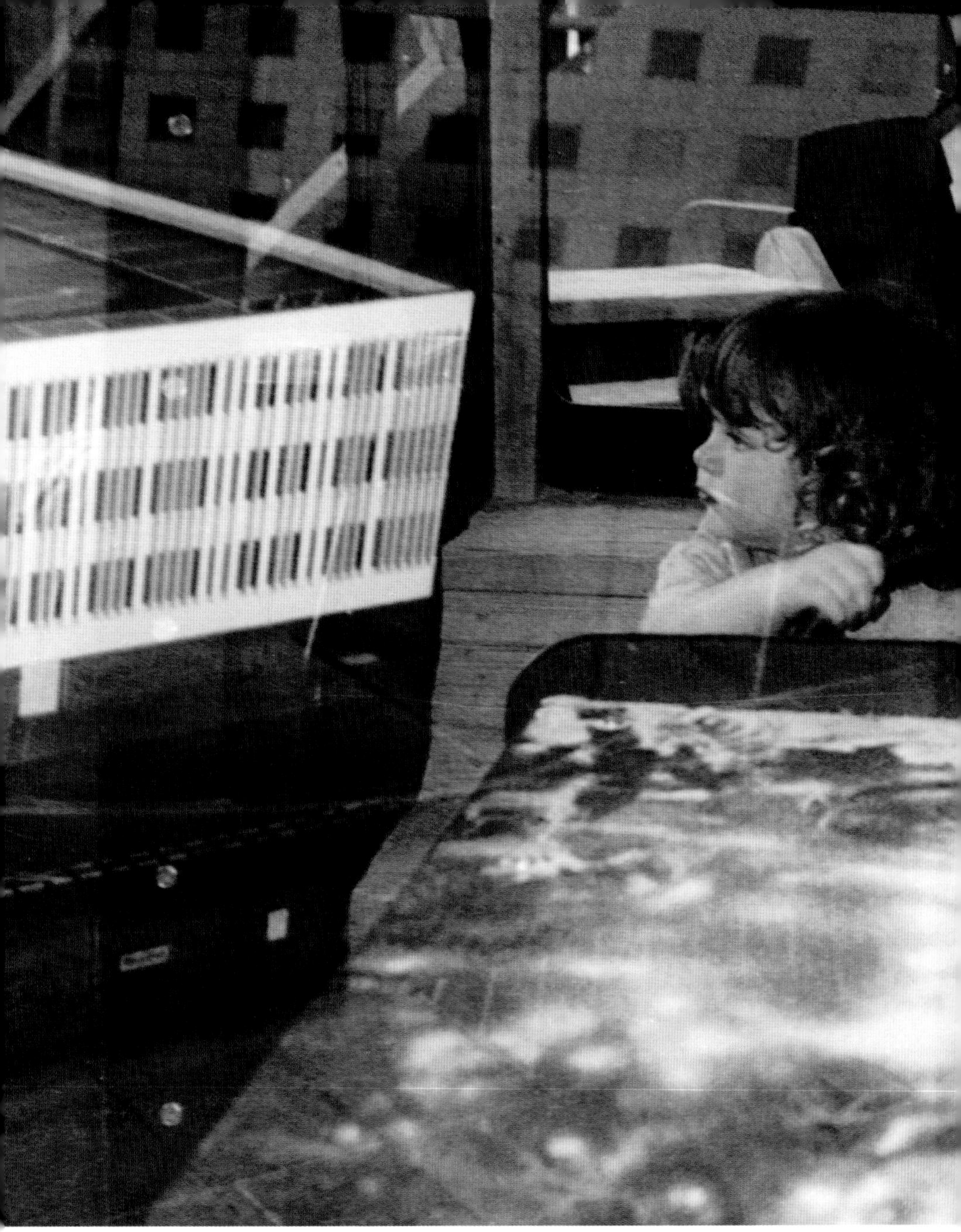

SERENDIPITY

By pure chance, this frame contained a child driving a toy tractor and a shot of a road and car park. It was the only combined exposure on the film worth keeping.

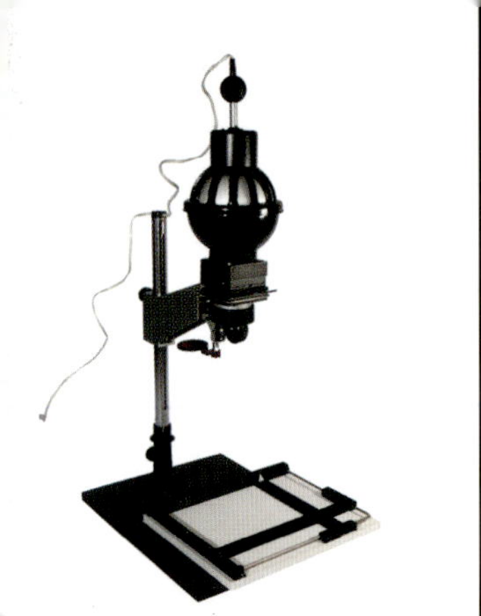

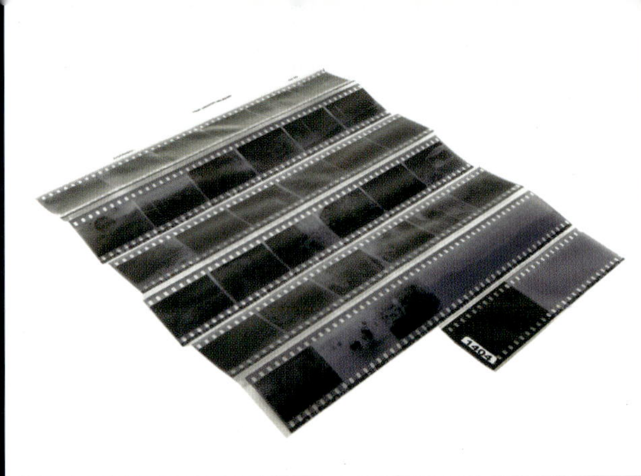
1404

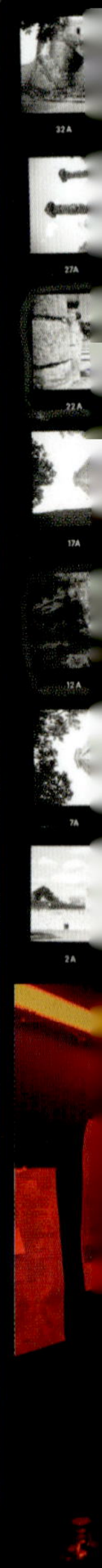
32 A
27A
22 A
17A
12 A
7A
2A

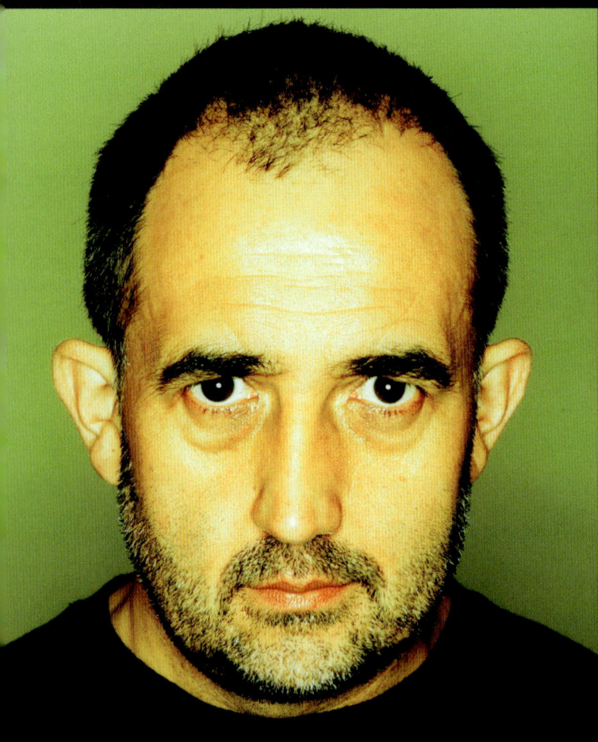

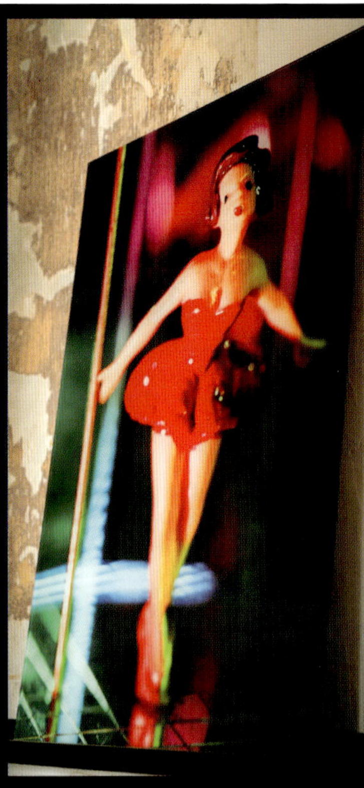

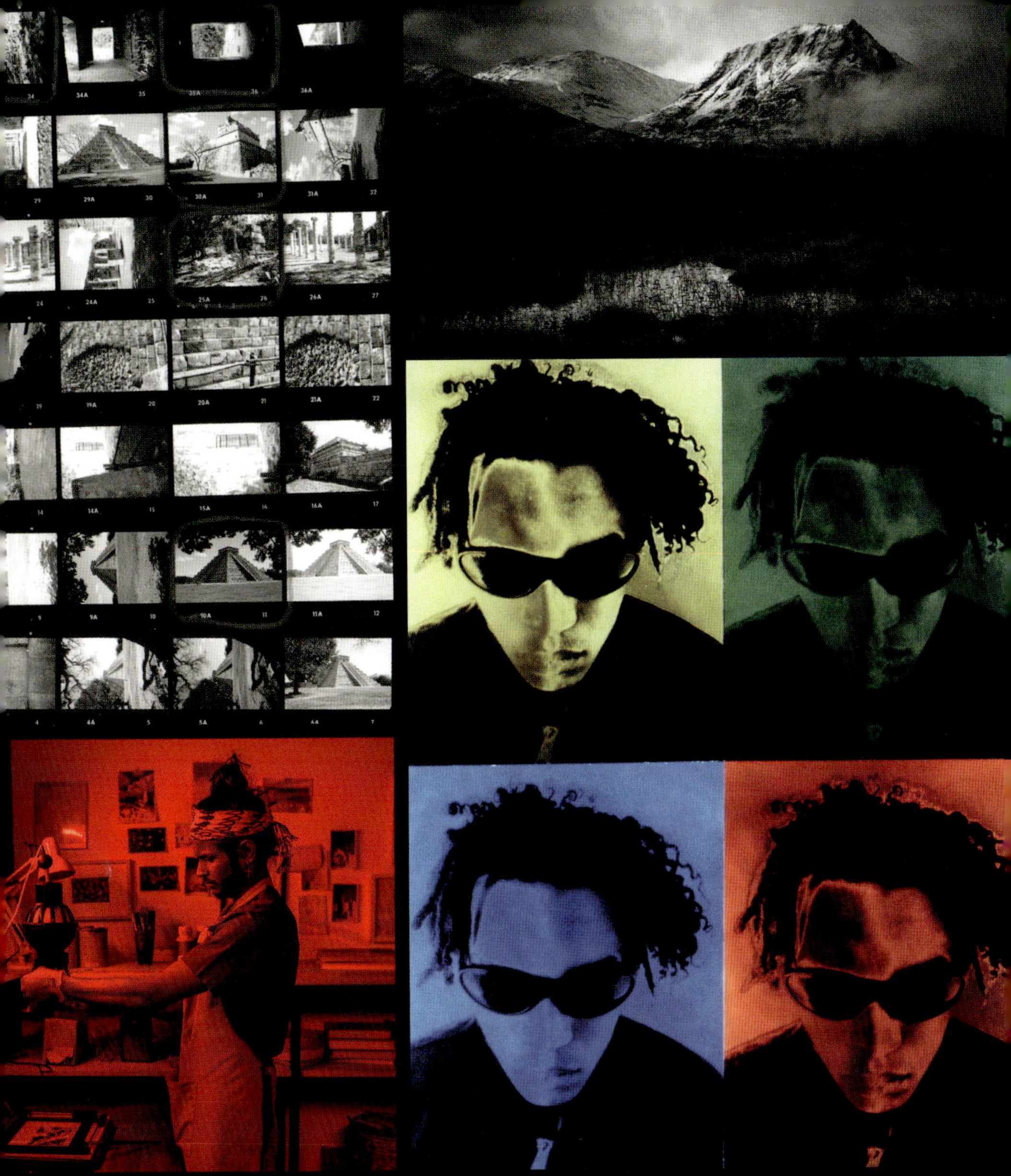

PROCESSING AND PRINTING

THE DARKROOM

If you like the idea of having complete control over your photography, then doing your own processing and printing may be for you. While darkroom work is no longer as popular as it once was, it's still worth considering so that you can have the satisfaction of being able to produce a print and say, 'This is all my own work.'

Many photographers fancy the idea of processing their films and making prints at home, but don't pursue the thought any further because they don't think they have anywhere to put a darkroom. That problem arises because of a fundamental misunderstanding of the term 'darkroom'. In many minds it conjures up images of a specially designed room, perfectly blacked out, with worktops immaculately laid out with 'dry' and 'wet' areas.

Most of the time it's not like that, and many photographers have produced masterpieces in makeshift darkrooms. And no matter how humble your abode, there's bound to be a corner of it that can be converted, even if on a temporary basis.

If all you want to do is process film, then you don't actually need a darkroom at all. The only part of film processing that requires absolute darkness is when you take the film out of its cassette, and that can be done in a changing bag.

However, if you want to go further and make your own prints, it's true that you're going to need somewhere to do it, and this is where things can become more involved.

The space needs to be big enough to house an enlarger and either a set of trays or some kind of processor. It also needs electricity to power the enlarger, safelight, and electronic timer (if you have one). Although water is essential, running water is not, as processed prints can be kept in a tray of water, and then transferred later to be thoroughly washed with tap water.

By definition, you need to be able to black out the space completely, although you don't need to go as far as painting the walls and ceiling black – just make sure no daylight can get in. Generally speaking, a spare bedroom or study that can be temporarily blacked out is ideal.

If you don't have suitable space at home, you may be able to hire the use of a darkroom at a local college, or through a photographic club or arts centre.

BLACKING OUT

Your darkroom must be completely light-tight, but with a little bit of do-it-yourself, you can probably get by. Blacking out is needed at the doors and windows, and thick card together with black insulation tape is a quick and effective fix.

If you're going to use the room reasonably often, it's worth spending a bit of money to save yourself a lot of time – if it's going to take you ages to black out the room, you're less likely to do it.

You can buy special blackout material, sold by the metre, which you can attach using Velcro®, or you could make some plywood covers, paint them black, and then lock them securely in place. However, the best solution – if funds allow – is to have a set of blackout blinds made for your space.

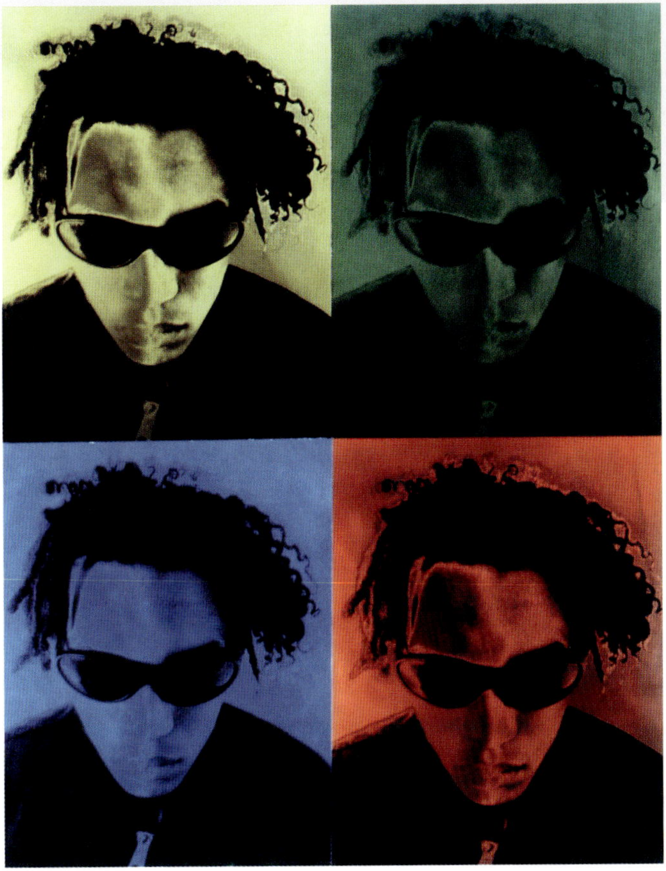

EXPERIMENTATION

When you start processing and printing your own film you can also start experimenting with your photographs. These black-and-white prints were 'flashed' during development to introduce a partially solarised look, and then toned using fabric dyes. No lab is going to do that for you.

PROCESSING BLACK-AND-WHITE FILM

There's very little reason not to process your own black-and-white film. For a start, it doesn't require a lot of specialist equipment, and the kit you do need can be bought relatively cheaply second-hand.

In addition to a dedicated film-developing tank and some measuring cylinders, you will need a measuring jug or two, a thermometer, a bottle opener, and a timer, plus a room that you can black out while you load your film.

You will also need two chemicals for the actual process itself: a developing agent to bring out the latent image on your film, and a fixing agent to make it permanent. A chemical 'stop bath' can be used between these steps, but this is entirely optional, as you can simply use water instead.

CHEMICAL CHOICES

When it comes to chemicals, the most important one is the developer, because that is the one that will have the most impact on your negatives. Some developers produce higher contrast than others, some keep grain to a minimum, some maximise film speed, and others are general all-rounders.

By comparison, the fixing agent is more perfunctory. It performs an important role, but it won't fundamentally impact your negatives unless the developing process goes very wrong.

Despite their differences, most developers will develop most films, so from the outset there are creative choices to make. Perhaps the safest place to start is with a good all-round developer, and numerous manufacturers offer starter kits containing all the chemicals you need.

It's worth noting that some developers come as a concentrated liquid while others are supplied as a powder (and some are available in both forms). Liquid developers are the easiest type to use as they simply need diluting with water rather than mixing, but powdered developers tend to be less expensive and have a longer shelf life once mixed, so remain usable for longer.

LOADING FILM

Before processing your film, you need to load it into a developing tank, which must be done in complete darkness. You can purchase dedicated film-changing bags for this, or work in a blacked-out room, which has the advantage of giving you more space. If you opt for the latter, make sure it is completely dark before you begin – if you can see anything in your blacked-out room, it isn't dark enough. LED standby lights are particularly easy to overlook – yet bright enough to fog your film while you load it.

The most common type of developing tanks require you to load the film into what is known as a 'spirals'. Although some tanks use stainless steel spirals, the most common type are plastic self-loading spirals with a pair of tiny ball bearings that help draw the film into a spiral track. This is the type we use here.

If you're new to developing film, it's a good idea to practise loading a spiral a few times with an old piece of film with the lights on, just to get the hang of it before you try it in the dark. It's also worth keeping a spare spiral to hand when loading your film, just in case the first spiral won't load smoothly (which can happen occasionally).

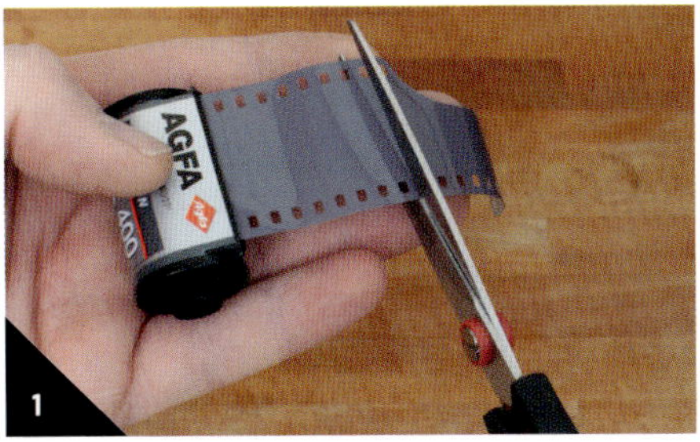

Trim the narrow leader off the end of your film, so it's square. Do this with the lights on if the film hasn't been wound back into the cassette. If the film has been wound back in, do this in the dark, after step 2.

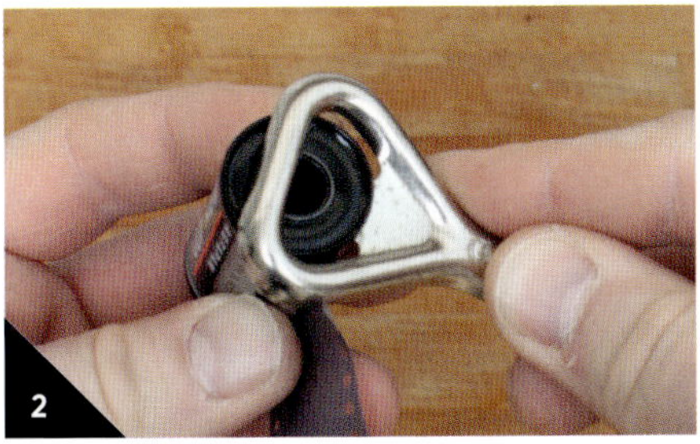

IN THE DARK: Use a bottle opener (or film cannister opener) to lift the flat end off the film cassette and remove the film. If you didn't do it in step 1, cut the end of the film square to remove the narrow leader.

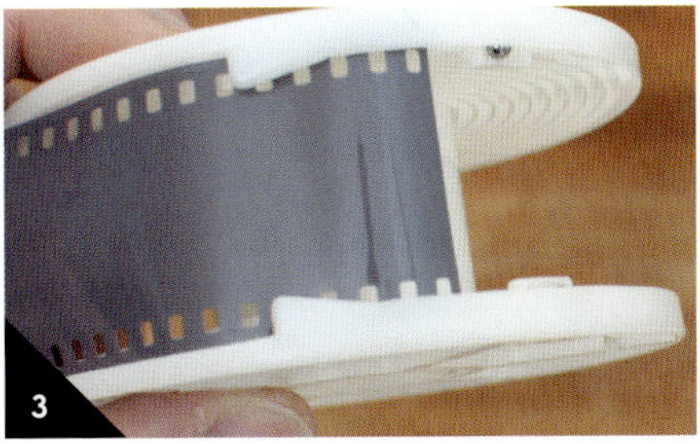

There are two locating tabs on the spiral, which indicate the start of the film track. Slide the end of the film under the tabs and pull it gently across the ball bearings further along.

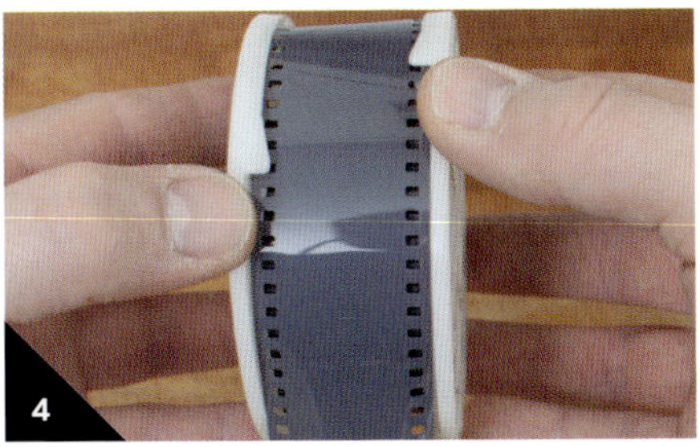

Rotate the sides of the spiral in opposing directions to wind the film onto the spiral. When you reach the end of the film, cut off the plastic spool it's attached to.

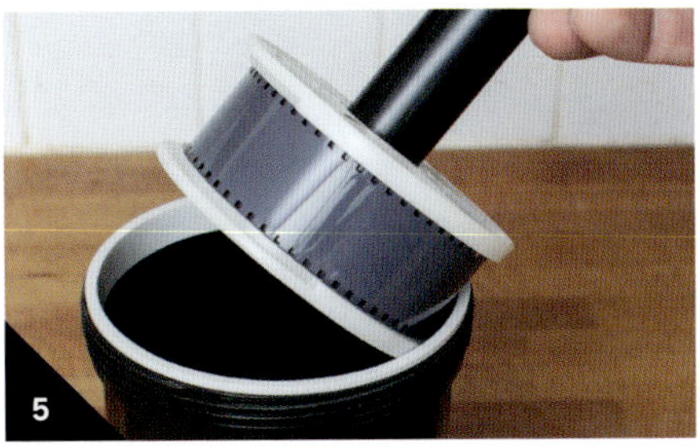

Still in the dark, slide the spiral onto the centre column of the developing tank and place it in the developing tank. You can now fit the tank's light-tight lid and switch the lights back on.

MIXING CHEMISTRY

The process of developing a film can be broken down into three key stages: develop, stop, and fix. Unless you use water for your stop bath, each stage requires its own chemistry. It is generally easiest to mix all of these at the same time, before you start processing the film.

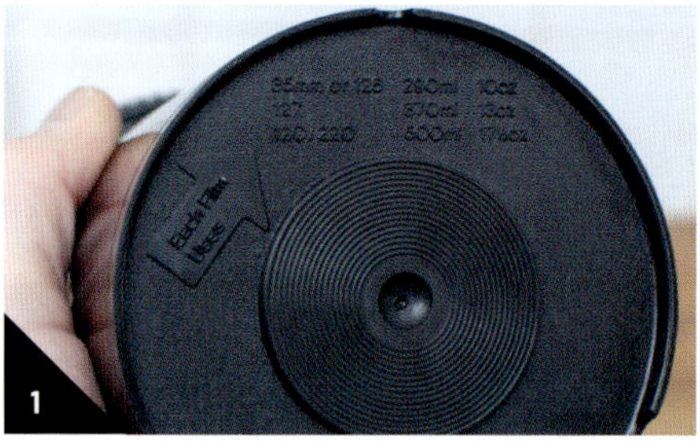

1

The volume of chemistry needed to cover a film, and therefore process it fully, is usually stamped on the bottom of the development tank. If you're processing more than one film, multiply the volume accordingly.

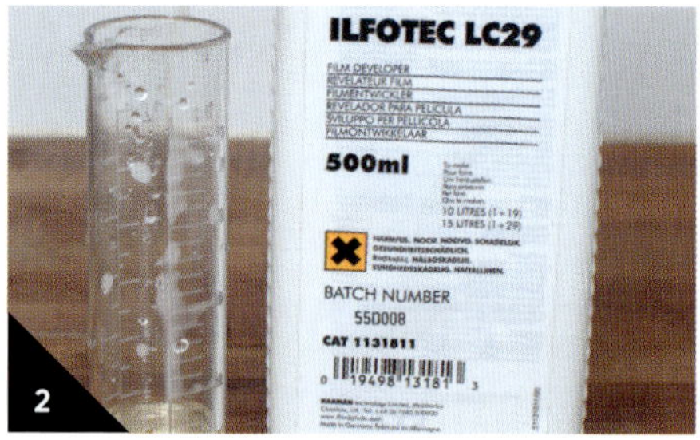

2

The dilution for your chemicals will be printed on the bottle or label, telling you how many parts chemical to mix with how many parts water (1:4, 1:9, 1:19, for example). You'll need to do some maths to work out the relative volumes required, based on the number of films you are processing.

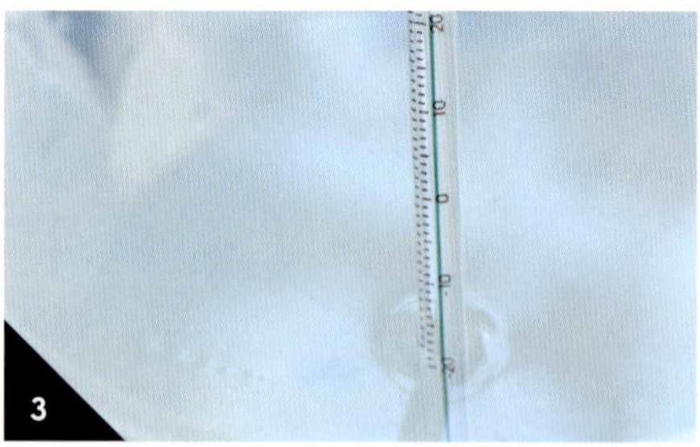

3

Black-and-white film processing is usually done at 20°C (68°F), but always check the manufacturer's recommendation. If the temperature is higher than the target, stand the mixed chemistry in cold water to cool it; if it is lower, place the chemistry in hot water to raise the temperature.

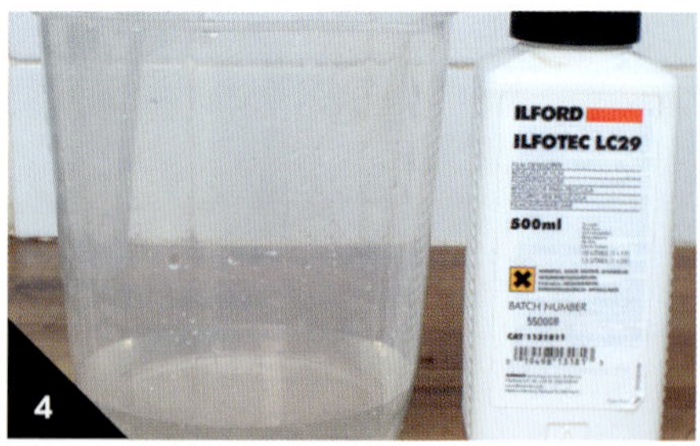

4

Mix all the chemicals at the same time and stand the relevant bottle next to each jug of chemistry so you know which is the developer, the stop, or the fix. As temperature is most critical for the developer, mix this last (as you will use it first) before it can cool.

PROCESSING

With your chemicals mixed you can start to process your film, following the steps outlined below. If you're struggling to find the development time, The Massive Dev Chart is a great online resource, or you can check the chemical manufacturer's website.

The key thing here is consistency. The more consistent – and accurate – you are with your temperatures and timings, the more consistent your negatives will be. This will ensure you're getting the best results with every film you shoot and process.

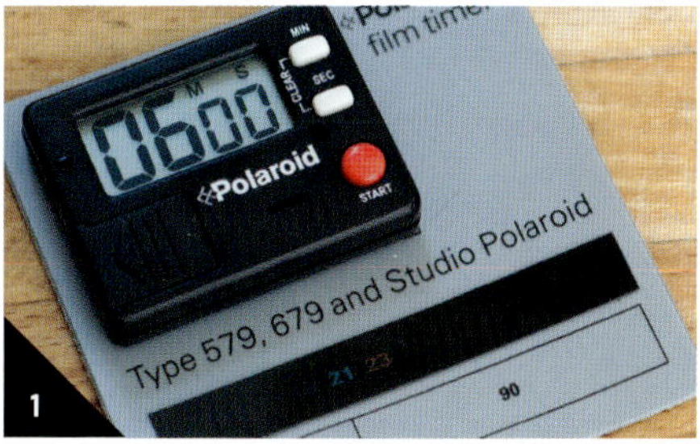

1

Set a timer for the development stage. There are plenty of apps that let you set the time for each stage before running through them automatically. Or use a simple timer and reset it for each stage.

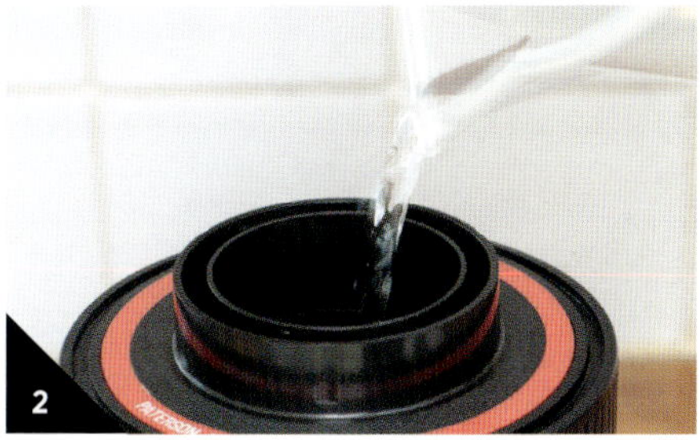

2

As you pour in the developer, start the timer. Pour the developer in quickly and smoothly to prevent air bubbles forming on the film.

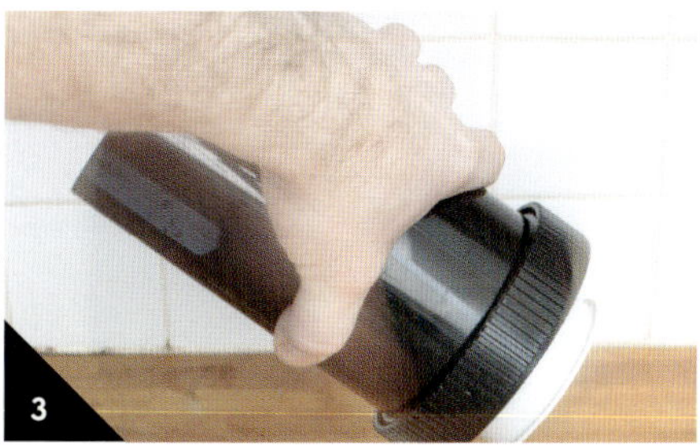

3

Invert your developing tank a couple of times every minute during the development process to ensure fresh developer reaches the film. After the inversions, give the tank a tap on your work surface to dislodge any air bubbles on the film.

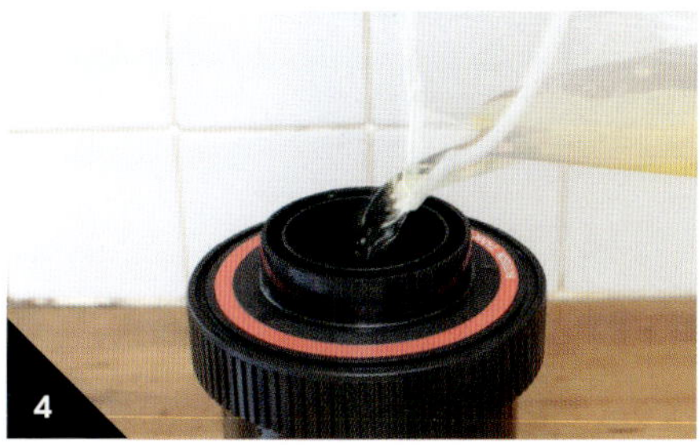

4

A few seconds before the development time is up, begin to pour out the developer. Immediately pour in the stop bath to halt the process. The stop bath stage is quick – about 30–60 seconds – at which point you can pour out the stop, and add the fixer.

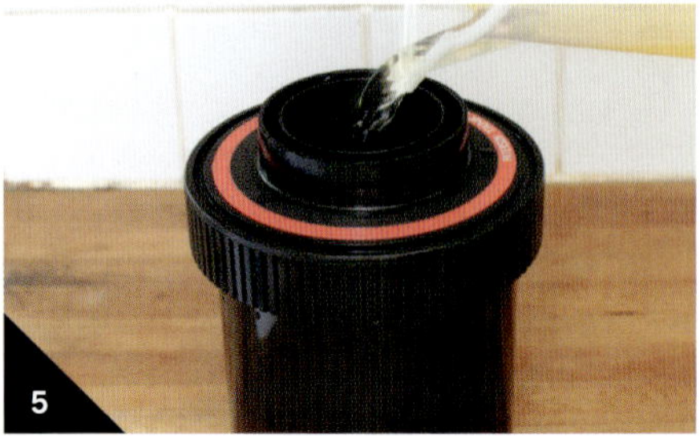

The fixer stage can take up to 10 minutes, depending on the fixer type and its dilution. Regardless of time, the fixer should be agitated intermittently throughout. Don't be tempted to cut the time, as insufficiently fixed negatives will gradually fade.

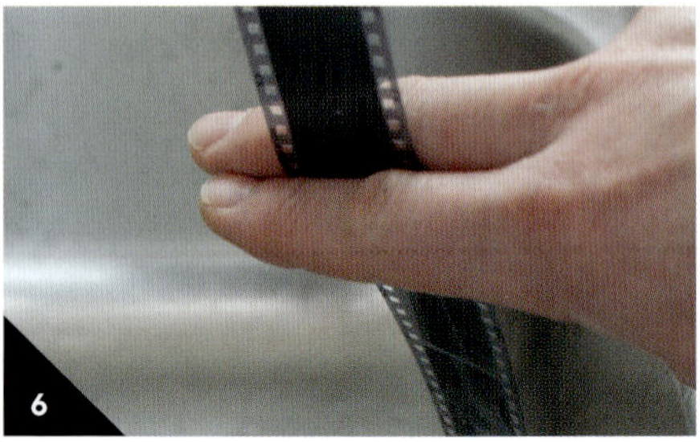

Before emptying the water from the tank, add a couple of drops of wetting agent to reduce the surface tension and help prevent drying marks. Remove the film from the spiral and wipe off any excess water using a dedicated film squeegee, or your fingers.

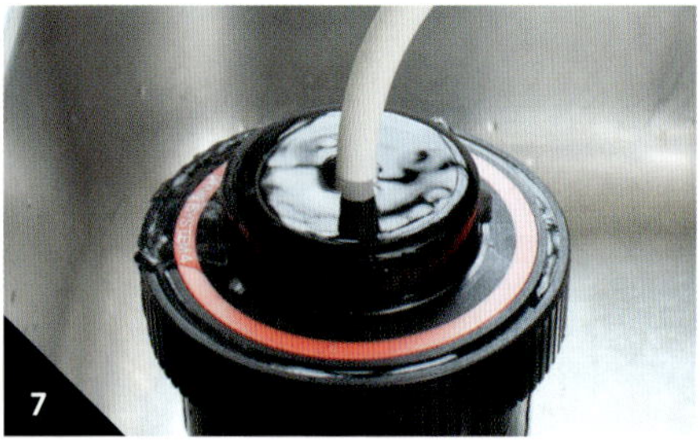

Once it's fixed, the film needs to be washed. The easiest way to do this is to put the developing tank under a tap and let the water run for 15–20 minutes.

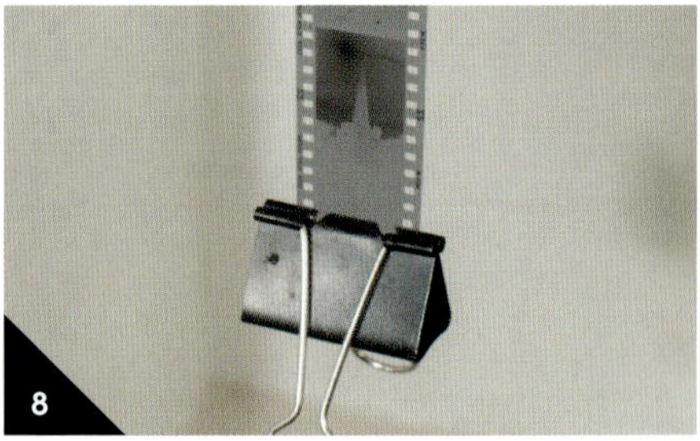

Finally, hang the film up to dry. You can invest in a specialist drying cabinet and use film clips to hold it straight, or hang it from a shower rail with a coat-hanger and metal bulldog clips on each end. Keep the drying area as dust-free as possible.

SAFETY FIRST

- When working with chemicals, wear gloves and safety goggles. If any chemistry gets in your eyes wash them immediately with water for several minutes. Follow the manufacturer's guidelines for other health and safety details.
- Discard chemicals according to your local regulations. Fixer is the most hazardous, due to its dissolved silver content. Your local photo lab may help you dispose of it safely.

PUSH AND PULL PROCESSING

Although black-and-white film has an ISO rating indicating its sensitivity, it also has a wide exposure latitude that means you can under and overexpose it by quite some margin and still get a usable result.

Often, these wayward exposures will be accidental, but you can also under and overexpose film *deliberately*, and then adjust the development time to compensate.

For example, imagine you head out with a roll of ISO 400 black-and-white film, but find yourself indoors or in darker conditions than expected, with shutter speeds that are going to cause camera shake. In this situation you could 'uprate' your film, which tells your camera the film is more sensitive than it actually is.

You might set the film speed to ISO 1600, so the camera acts as if the film is more sensitive, and determines exposures accordingly. In this case, because ISO 1600 is 2 stops faster than ISO 400, your shutter speeds would also be 2 stops faster – hopefully enough to avoid camera shake.

However, although the camera is acting as if the film is faster, it is still ISO 400 film. The film is being underexposed by 2 stops, which is where the processing comes in. If you extend the development time, this compensates for the underexposure and 'rebalances' your negatives: underexposure makes images darker, while over-development makes them lighter – one can be used to cancel out the other.

Uprating film in this way, and extending the development time, is known as 'push processing'. Manufacturers give different development times for different ISO settings when a film is well-suited to pushing.

There is a slight trade-off, though; pushing film increases contrast and grain. It is also worth noting that you must apply this to the whole roll of film – it doesn't work on a frame-to-frame basis like digital photography!

You can also 'pull' black-and-white film by down-rating the ISO (rating an ISO 400 film at ISO 100, for example) and then reducing the development time. This can lead to low-contrast, 'flat' images, which is less desirable.

CREATIVE CONTROL

Uprating film can be a creative choice. Here, the film was pushed 3 stops to deliberately increase the grain and contrast, to add to the mood.

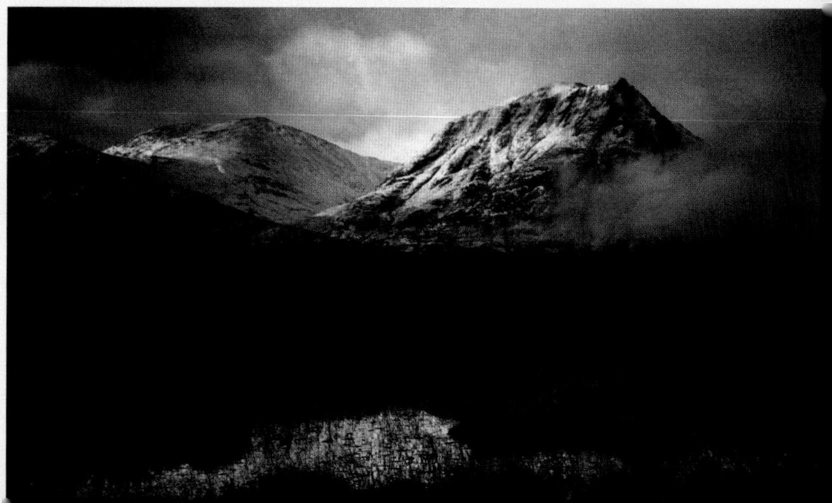

PROCESSING COLOUR FILM

Processing colour film is not much more complicated than processing black-and-white film. However, while you can pick your black-and-white developer to alter the look of your film, colour processing is all about following the necessary steps as accurately as possible to get the job done; there isn't the same level of creativity. It also isn't much cheaper than taking your film to a lab, yet it carries a potentially greater risk of things going wrong. Perhaps this explains why so few photographers process their own colour film.

NEGATIVE FILM

Producing colour negatives that are consistent is imperative if you intend to print directly from them. If your negatives vary from film to film, it can be difficult, which is why it's a good idea to standardise on a single film type and one set of chemicals.

The C41 process uses higher temperatures than black-and-white processing. A thermostatically controlled processor is recommended, especially when the ambient temperature is low.

SLIDE FILM

The E6 process used for colour slide film is a relatively easy three-bath process, and the chemicals are sold in kits. The higher processing temperature – 38°C (100°F) – for colour slide films means that a thermostatically controlled processor is almost essential. Without one, you need to to ensure the temperature of the processing solutions doesn't drop.

TO PROCESS A COLOUR NEGATIVE FILM

ESSENTIAL

- Accurate thermometer
- Bowl or bucket of water for waterbath
- Darkroom clock
- Developing tank
- Film squeegee
- Force film washer
- Kit of chemicals
- Rubber gloves
- Set of measuring cylinders
- Wetting agent

USEFUL

- Drying cabinet
- Process timer
- Thermostatically controlled processor
- Waterbath

TO PROCESS A COLOUR SLIDE FILM

ESSENTIAL

- Accurate thermometer
- Darkroom clock
- Developing tank
- Film squeegee
- Force film washer
- Kit of chemicals
- Rubber gloves
- Set of measuring cylinders
- Wetting agent

USEFUL

- Drying cabinet
- Process timer
- Thermostatically controlled processor
- Waterbath

CROSS PROCESSING

We now know there are two main colour film processes. Colour negative films go through C41 chemistry and colour slide films are bathed in E6 chemistry. In each case, the time and temperature parameters are reasonably fixed, but one creative option is to break all the rules and put films through the wrong process: E6 for a colour negative film and C41 for a colour transparency film.

For obvious reasons this is called 'cross processing' and the results can be extremely dramatic, if rather difficult to predict. Contrast increases and colours change, producing an often hyper-realistic image that's really unusual.

To start your experimentation, it's a good idea to shoot a test film at various ISO ratings above and below that suggested by the manufacturer, to find out which setting gives you the best results, then use that in future – although you will still find bracketing the exposures is worthwhile.

Most pro labs will cross-process film, but expect to be charged more. This is perhaps one instance when it might be worth processing colour film yourself.

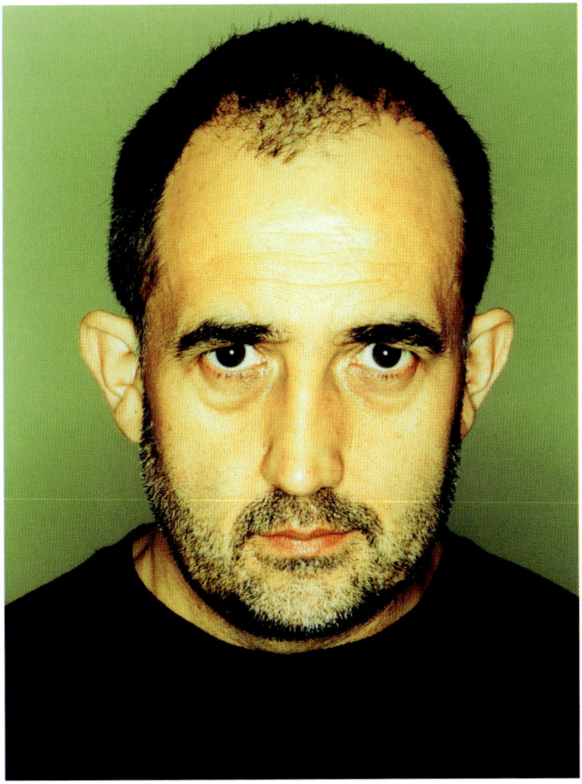

EXPERIMENTATION

The startling colours and vivid contrasts of this image were created by cross processing transparency film in the C41 chemistry designed for colour negative film, and then making a print from the negative.

MAKING PRINTS IN THE DARKROOM

Once you get used to working under the dim and slightly eerie glow of a safelight, you'll find knocking out prints a doddle.

The key points to follow are: start with a clean negative, do a test strip to ascertain optimum exposure, and develop and fix for the recommended times. Always think creatively when making an enlargement; ask yourself if you can improve the picture by cropping it differently. Beyond that, you can make a print to fulfil your own vision. By varying exposure and the type of paper, you can print light or dark, contrasty or soft in tone. By 'dodging' and 'burning' some areas you can lighten and darken specific parts of the print.

MAKING A BLACK-AND-WHITE PRINT

The equipment required for printing is relatively modest. Simple, open dishes allow you to see the image emerge on the paper under the safelighting, and processing is carried out at 20°C (68°F).

The main area of expense is the enlarger. If you can afford it, buy a model with a colour head. This may sound strange if you only plan to make black-and-white prints, but having a colour light source means you can work with variable-contrast 'multigrade' printing papers. This makes it easy to boost or soften the contrast in your images. It also means you don't have to buy multiple boxes of papers of different grades.

Remember to replace the lid on your paper before you switch the lights back on, or you'll fog all the sheets and ruin them. It's a mistake that everyone makes once, but rarely twice! Here's the whole process described step-by-step. The first two stages can be carried out in daylight or under safelight conditions.

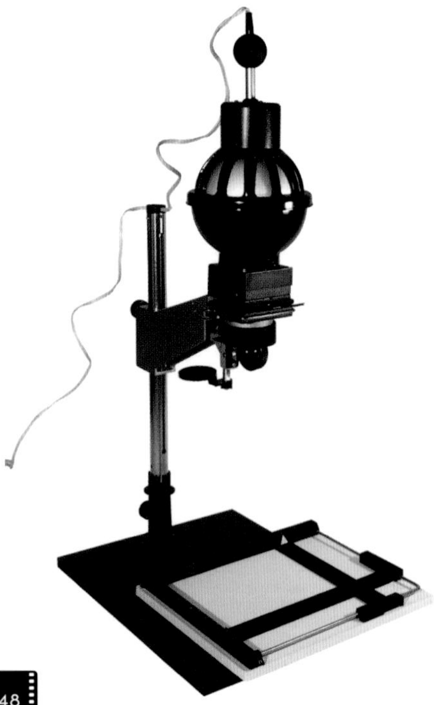

ENLARGER

An enlarger is the biggest darkroom investment you will make. As with choosing a camera, it pays to do some research before making a purchase.

1. **Preparing the enlarger**
   Place your negative in the negative carrier of the enlarger, making sure it's clean and dust-free. Switch on the enlarger and adjust the height of the column until the image on the baseboard is the size you want, with the image roughly focused.

2. **Framing and focusing**
   Set up your enlarging easel so the picture is framed and cropped as you want it. Then focus precisely, preferably with the aid of a special magnifying 'focus-finder' that allows you to focus on the individual grains in the image.

SWITCH OFF ANY ROOM LIGHTS THAT MAY BE ON: FROM NOW ON, WORK ONLY UNDER SAFELIGHT CONDITIONS

3. **Putting paper in place**
   Remove a single sheet of paper from its pack, remembering to reseal the pack. Place the paper in the easel, if you have one, or on the baseboard. Position the red filter under the enlarger head, select an aperture of f/8 or f/11, and switch on the enlarger.

4. **Making a test exposure**
   To make a test strip to determine the correct exposure time, swing the red filter aside, but use a sheet of black card to block the light. Then move the black card at 3-second intervals to expose more of the paper, producing eight strips with exposures from 3–24 seconds.

5. **Developing the test print**
   Put the exposed print in the first of your three trays of chemicals – the developer. Agitate continuously for the first 20 seconds by tipping the tray up and down, and thereafter occasionally to ensure that it's always covered by developer. Keep agitating the tray; typically 1–2 minutes for resin-coated papers and 3–4 minutes for fibre-based papers.

6. **Fixing the test print**
   Using print tongs, place the print in the second tray – the stop-bath. After 30 seconds, move it to the third tray – the fixer. Follow the manufacturer's recommendation for fixing time, then transfer the print to a tray of wash water.

7. **Inspecting the print**
   Switch the light on and inspect the print. Which of the exposures gives the best density? Repeat the process, using that single exposure time for the whole print.

8. **Washing**
   For prints to last, the fixer has to be completely removed by effective washing. This means changing the wash water frequently, or, ideally, using a custom-made print-washing unit for at least 30 minutes (longer if archival permanence is required).

9. **Drying**
   Resin-coated paper can then be stood on its edge on a sheet of kitchen paper to drain. Fibre-based papers can be dried on their back on photographic blotting paper. Both types are best dried in hot-air or hot-bed dryers.

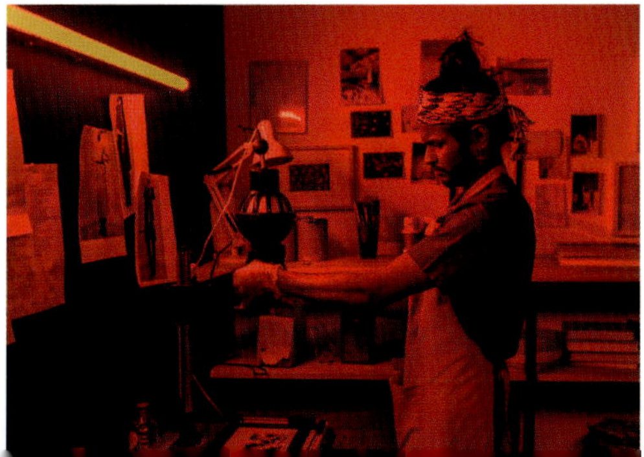

SAFE

Most darkroom work is conducted under a red safelight. You soon adapt to working under this light.

MAKING A CONTACT SHEET

Even experienced photographers find it hard to 'read' negatives – to see by looking at them exactly what the finished print will look like. Facial expressions can be particularly difficult, and it's often hard to see whether someone is smiling or frowning when you examine the negative. For that reason, many photographers like to make a contact sheet of the entire film before they start to make enlargements from it.

Contact sheets are so-called because they're produced by putting negatives in direct contact with the paper they're printed on, so they show actual-size positive images of each frame.

Usually, 10 x 8in paper is used, as it will accommodate a 36-exposure 35mm film in six rows of six negatives per row. Developed and fixed in the normal way, these sheets allow you to assess the viability of each shot and help stop you wasting paper. Filed alongside the negatives, a contact sheet provides a useful quick reference when you're looking for a shot in the future.

ALL STAGES MUST BE CARRIED OUT UNDER SAFELIGHT CONDITIONS

1. **Using a contact printer**
   If you have a contact printing frame, slip your negatives into it – the right way round and in order when viewed from the top. Place a sheet of 10 x 8in paper behind the negatives, with the emulsion side facing them. Close the lid and clip it firmly in place.
2. **No contact printer**
   If you don't have a contact printer, place a sheet of 10 x 8in paper on the enlarger baseboard with the negative strips on top of it – the right way round and in order – and a plain, clean sheet of glass on top. Some negative filing sheets are transparent enough for you to print directly through them.
3. **Setting up the enlarger**
   Switch on the enlarger, having first put in position the red filter that shields the paper from exposure. Set the enlarger column to a height at which the light covers an area slightly larger than your printing paper. Select an aperture of f/8 or f/11.
4. **Making and evaluating a test exposure**
   Follow the instructions on the previous page for making a print, starting with the test exposure. If you have a set of negatives of varying density (which is often the case), some will inevitably be too light or too dark on the contact sheet, so choosing the right printing exposure will be a juggling act.

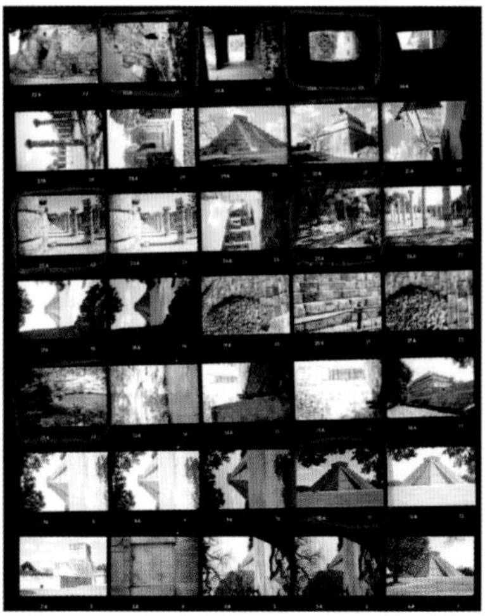

CONTACT SHEET

The quickest way of identifying which negatives to enlarge is to produce a contact sheet by printing actual size onto a sheet of 10 x 8in paper. This can then be stored in a binder along with the negatives for easy reference.

PRINTING FROM COLOUR SLIDES

If you are new to colour work, printing from colour slides is the easiest option for several reasons. Any colour cast on your prints can be eliminated by removing the same colour from the filters set in the colour head of the enlarger. If, for example, there is a magenta colour cast, you simply need to reduce the level of magenta. Once a filter pack has been set for a particular type of film, little correction is required when printing different slides.

However, as with processing, printing from slides is more about getting it right in terms of matching the original transparency, and less about creative interpretation. Unlike printing from a black-and-white negative, there are fewer creative options in terms of dodging, burning, or altering the contrast of the print.

PRINTING FROM COLOUR NEGATIVES

Making your own prints from colour negatives requires more equipment than printing from slides or black-and-white negatives. It's also technically more demanding and time-consuming. However, great quality prints are possible if you work patiently, carefully, and deliberately.

Determining the correct enlarger exposure is accomplished in the same way as when printing from a black-and-white negative, but with the added problem of getting the colour balance right. However, once you get used to dealing with colours in a way that's the reverse of the usual principles – a colour cast is removed by dialling *more* of that colour into the enlarger – things become much easier.

TO PRINT COLOUR SLIDES

ESSENTIAL

Accurate thermometer

Blower brush

Chemical kit

Darkroom clock

Enlarger

Enlarger easel

Focus finder

Measuring cylinders

Processor: simple drum, deep tank, or dishes

USEFUL

Colour safelight

Dodging tools

Print dryer

Process timer

Thermostatically controlled processor

TO PRINT COLOUR NEGATIVES

ESSENTIAL

Blower brush

Darkroom clock

Enlarger

Enlarger easel

Measuring cylinders

Processor kit

Thermostatically controlled processor

USEFUL

Colour safelight

Enlarger timer

Focus finder

Print dryer

FILM AND PRINT STORAGE

You will be investing a lot of time, effort, and money into taking great pictures, so it's important that you not only show them off to the best advantage, but also make sure they're safely stored for posterity.

It's easy to be so excited about getting out and taking new photographs that the ones you already have are left in the envelopes and boxes in which they came back from the lab. What a waste! It doesn't have to be that way, though.

PRESENTATION

When you take a picture that's really special, have an enlargement made. Don't just get a 10 x 8in print, but go for something with impact – 12 x 16in or even a 20 x 16in enlargement if it's pin-sharp and shot on a fine-grained film.

But don't just leave it at that. If you want to maximise the impact of your pictures it's worth getting them properly mounted and possibly framed. You could hand this job over to a framing company, but you'll find it a lot more satisfying – not to mention cheaper – to do it yourself.

Alternatively, you could opt for a less traditional print; canvas, acrylic, and aluminium are all popular alternative print surfaces to paper. If you'd rather not put your pictures on show, you could put them in a portfolio instead, in which case some kind of transparent sleeve will be essential.

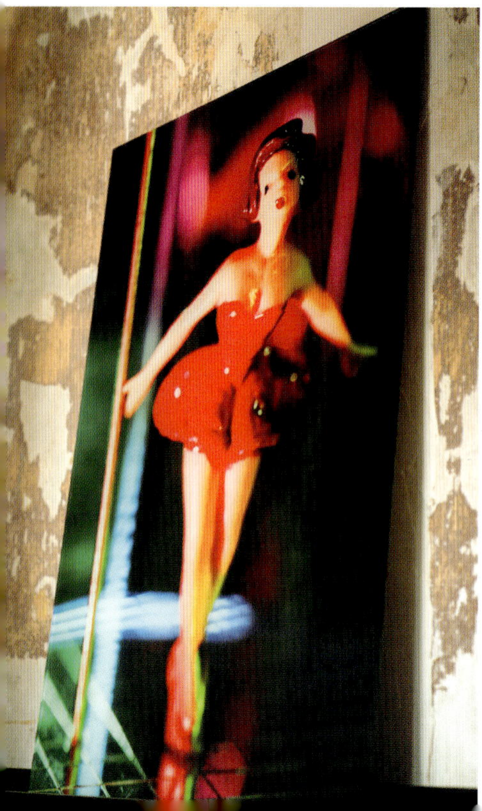

ALTERNATIVE PRINTS

Prints made on acrylic or aluminium don't need a frame, giving them a clean, contemporary look. However, their high-gloss finish means they work better with bold, graphic images than with soft monochrome shots.

STORAGE

Let's face it: storage isn't exciting. But it is important. If you don't look after your images they can easily get damaged, you won't be able to find them when you want them, and they may not be around for future generations to appreciate. But if you protect them from harmful chemicals, excessive heat and humidity, strong daylight, and physical damage, they'll be around for a long time to come.

Slides

Keeping slides in the plastic boxes supplied by the processing lab may be convenient, but as your collection grows it can become difficult to keep track of which box a particular picture was in, and where that box is now.

A decent transparency filing system solves this. Transparent filing pages are widely available that will enable you to store 20 or 24 slides per page, which can then be put in a ring binder or hung in a filing cabinet on suspension bars, depending on the pages you choose. All you have to do to view them is hold them up to the light or place them on a lightbox.

However, don't cram too many slide storage sheets into a filing cabinet – if air can't circulate they can easily develop mould. It's also important to check that the pages you buy are archivally safe and don't contain any chemicals that could damage the slides.

Negatives

It's a similar story with negatives (both colour and black and white). These are normally cut into strips of six or seven frames, and are best filed in special A4 sheets, each designed to accommodate one 36-exposure or 24-exposure film. Keep them in an A4 ring binder, together with a contact sheet for easy reference.

If you choose negative filing sheets that are completely transparent you can produce the contact sheet without having to remove the negatives. This minimises the risk of scratching and problems with dust and debris. Once again, it's really important to ascertain that the sheets you are using are chemically inert.

Prints

The main issue with print storage is light. You only need to leave a colour print exposed to sunlight for a short while to see the colour start to drain away from it and a blue cast appear. Clearly when you frame a picture and display it on a wall this means it's going to fade, but you can reduce the speed at which it fades by placing it out of direct sunlight and using a frame with UV-resistant glass.

Prints that aren't going to be on show are best stored away from light completely: in albums, portfolio cases and, yes, even the envelopes in which they came back from the lab.

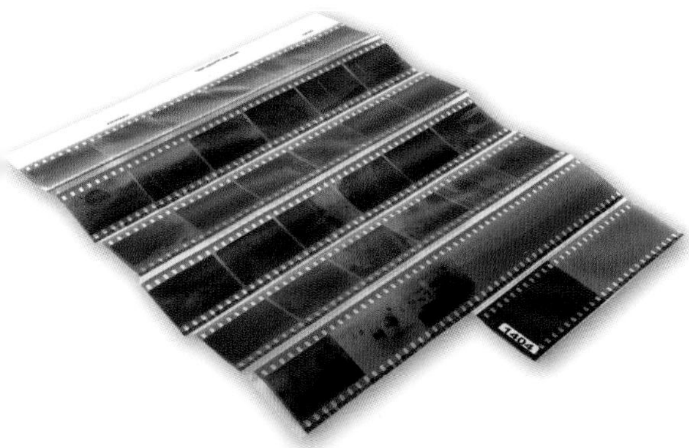

CONTACT SHEET

Transparent sleeves make it easy to see what's on your film. This is useful for viewing strips of slides without handling them, and also for making contact sheets from black-and-white negatives.

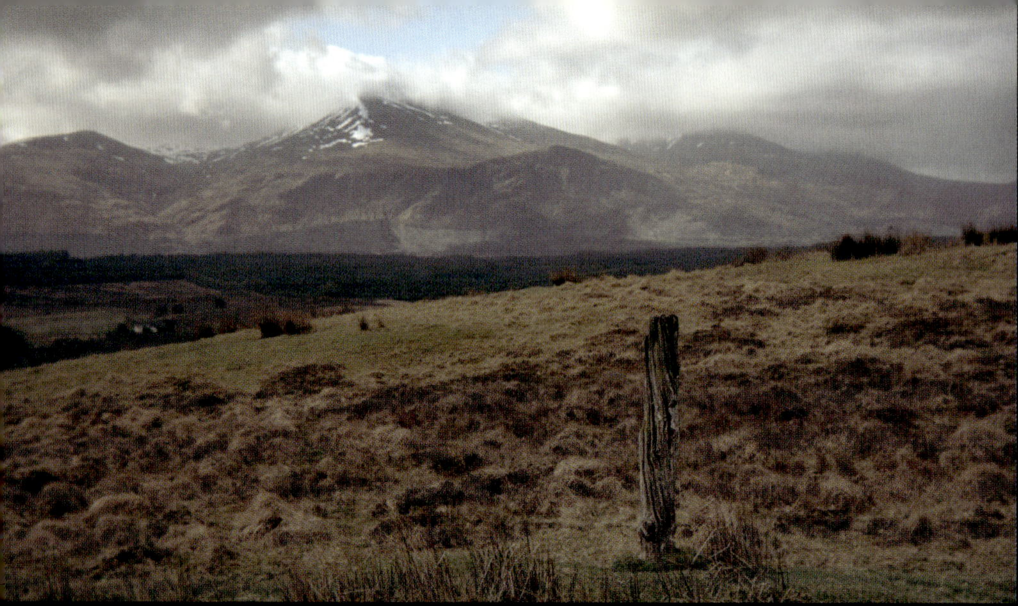

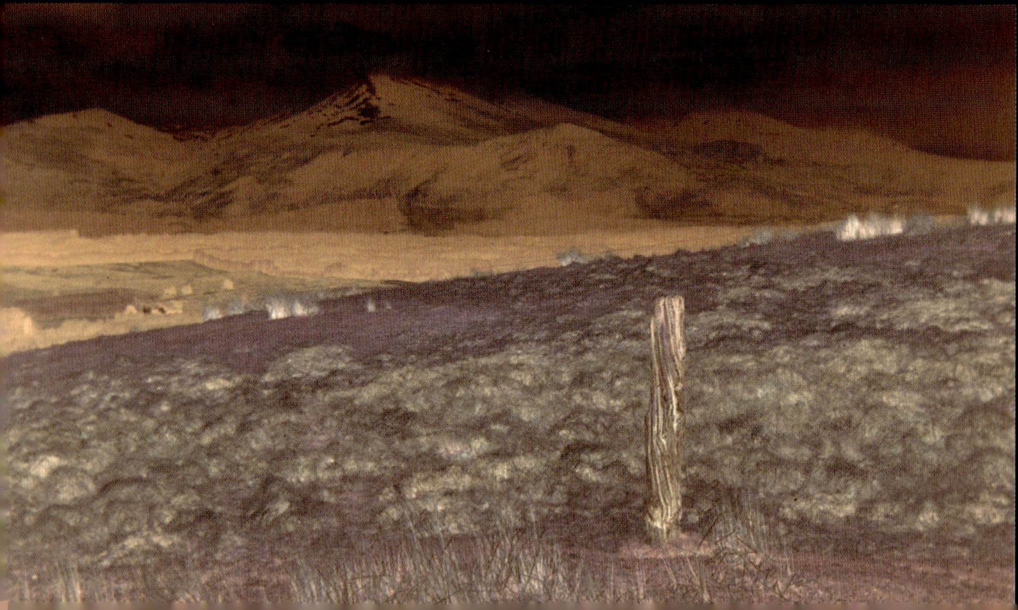

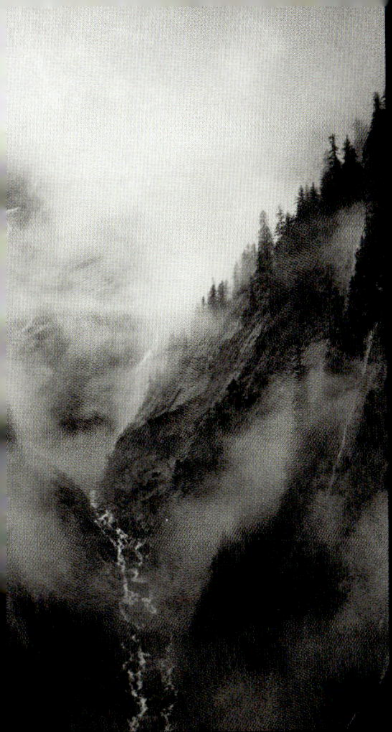
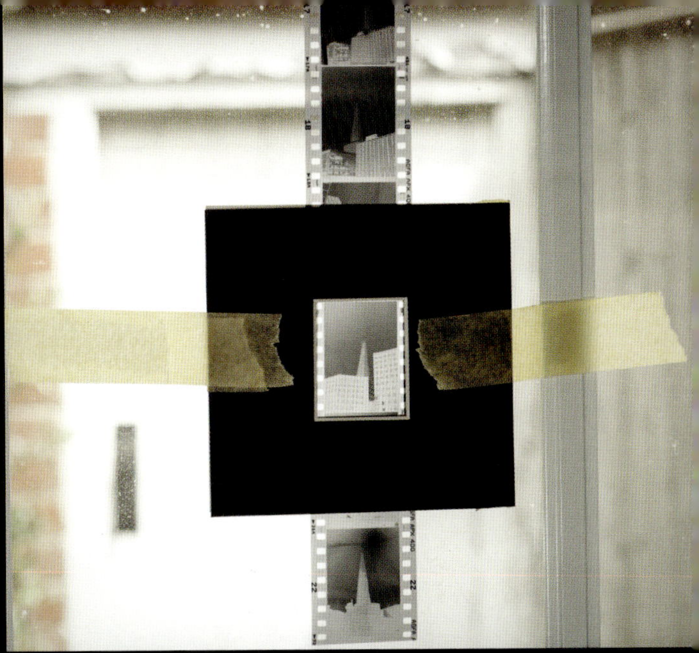
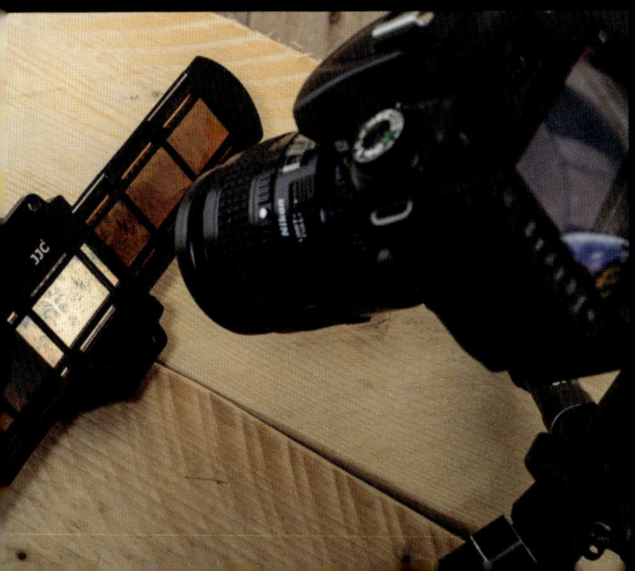
JJC
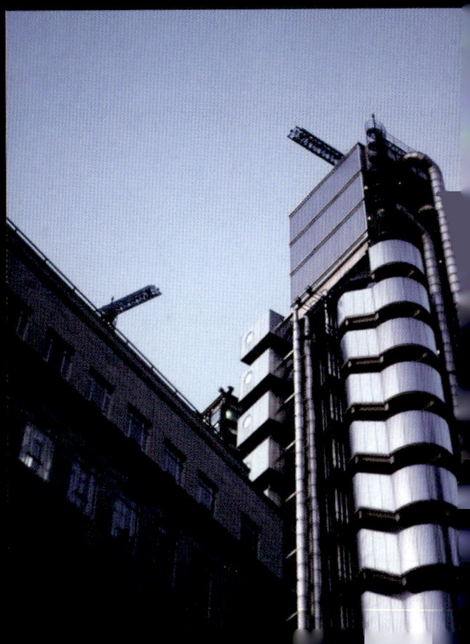

DIGITISING FILM

Let's be clear – this *isn't* a book about digital photography, so we're not going to spend any time looking at how to tweak the colours in your images, alter the exposure, or anything else that image-editing software has to offer.

Instead, we're going to explore the various steps you can take to move your film originals into the digital realm, so you can post them on social media, share them with friends and family, or send them to a lab for printing. What you (or the software's AI) do after your images are digitised is between you and your computer.

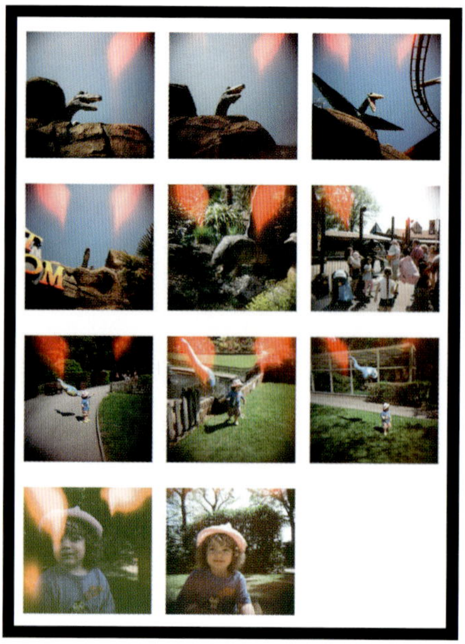

LAB SCANS

By far the easiest way to get a digital version of your negatives and slides is to have the lab scan the film when they process it. It's not too expensive for a good quality scan.

It's hard to come up with a compelling reason *not* to do this, especially if you send your film away for processing. At the very least it means you have a digital copy of your photos if the film gets lost in the post on its return to you.

It's also useful if you're shooting colour negatives, as the lab will convert your images into positives. As you will see in this chapter, negative conversions can be quite involved when you're working in colour.

You end up with a bespoke scan of every frame, but that's often not a problem. Negative film is so forgiving that most of the detail can be extracted in a simple scan. Besides, you can always work on it in the editing software.

DIGITAL CONTACT SHEET

Getting low-resolution, low-cost scans when you get your film processed will let you make digital contact sheets. These let you see what's on the film and worth pursuing further.

HOME SCANNING

When photography transitioned to the digital realm, digital cameras were incredibly expensive and their image quality was – by today's standards – mediocre. Scanning film and prints was therefore seen as a great way of getting a high-resolution digital image. The scanner market was ripe with dedicated film scanners and flatbed scanners catering to amateurs and professionals alike.

Once you have a scanner, the benefits are obvious. You can pick which frames you digitise and spend as much time as you like extracting the maximum amount of detail and sharpness. Over the following pages we will look at how this can be done.

However, just as film cameras slowly disappeared from mainstream production, so did scanners. At the time of writing, Plustek is one of the few manufacturers still committed to the film scanner market, with several models of 35mm film scanners, as well as a medium format option.

Older models of scanners haven't simply disappeared, though, and there are still some fantastic models out there. These include dedicated film scanners from Canon (CanoScan), Nikon (Coolscan), and Minolta (DiMAGE). Epson's V-series of flatbed scanners also provides professional-level film-scanning capabilities.

The main problem with these scanners today is getting hold of them at a reasonable price. Supplies are limited and second-hand prices reflect their premium status. Even then you might encounter compatibility issues, as the 'vintage' cables are not widely used today, and older driver software may not run on the latest operating systems. Cable adaptors and a universal scanner driver such as VueScan can usually resolve these issues, but adds to the cost.

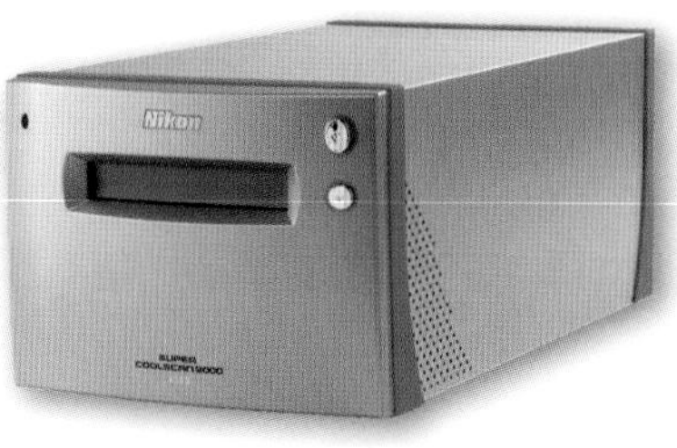

FILM SCANNER

Nikon's Coolscan 9000 does a great job at scanning film from 35mm up to 6 x 9cm medium format, but second-hand prices are eye-wateringly high.

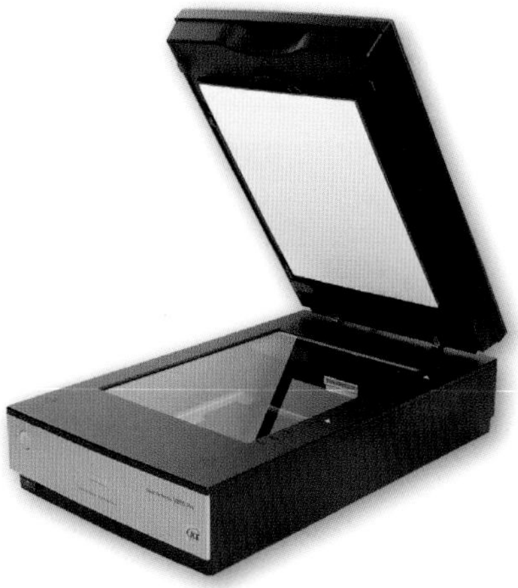

FLATBED SCANNER

The Epson V850 (and 800/750/700 before it) is a high-end flatbed scanner that scans film from 35mm up to 10 x 8in, as well as prints.

SCANNER OPTIONS

When it comes to choosing a scanner there are two options: a dedicated film scanner that will only scan film, or a flatbed scanner with film-scanning capabilities that also scans prints and other non-photographic documents.

Of the two, film scanners are the more specialist type, and generally the most sought after by keen film photographers. As noted previously, there's not a great deal of choice either new or second-hand.

Film scanners are also better at holding film flat. This is important, because the flatter a piece of film is held, the sharper it will be across the frame when it's scanned. If an edge is just a fraction of a millimetre higher or lower than the rest of the frame, it can be enough to make that area appear soft and out of focus in the final scan.

However, that's not to say that there aren't some very capable flatbed scanners available, not least Epson's V-series. In either case, there are several areas worth considering when you choose a scanner.

Format

By design, film scanners have one significant limitation; they're only designed to scan film, and most will only scan 35mm film. Although scanners are available that will take medium format film, these can be expensive – not least because they rarely come up for sale, which leads to bidding wars when they do.

The advantage of flatbed scanners is that most can accommodate film from 35mm up to large format, as well as prints, so they're incredibly versatile. If you think you'll be shooting medium or large format film at any point, a flatbed makes a lot of sense.

Resolution

Just like a digital camera, scanners have a resolution, which tells you how many pixels they can generate. This is measured in 'dpi' (dots per inch) or 'ppi' (pixels per inch) and the simple rule is the higher the resolution, the bigger your scans can be. A scanner with a 9600 dpi resolution can create bigger scans than a scanner with a 4000 dpi resolution.

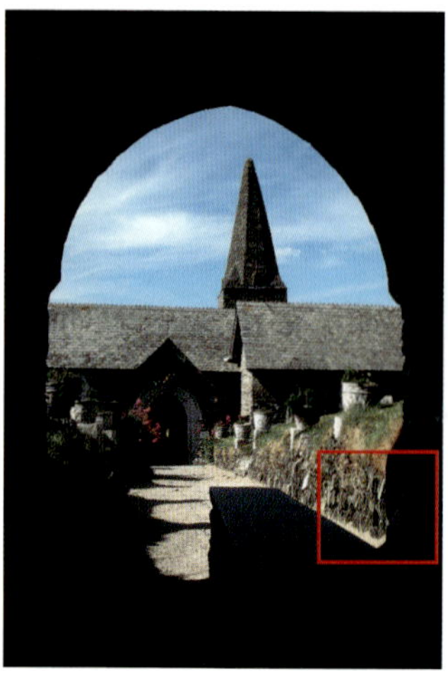

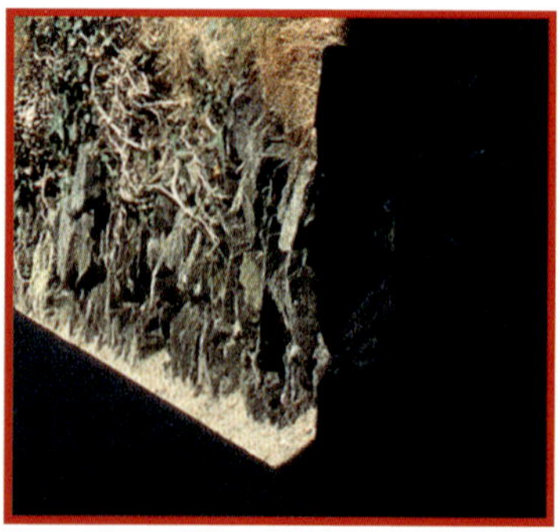

DMAX

Photographed on slide film, this scene needed careful exposure to hold the full tonal range, and a scanner with a Dmax capable of seeing into the shadows.

However, it's important to note that a higher resolution only gives *bigger* scans and not necessarily *better* ones. Some cheaper scanners use what is known as an 'interpolated' resolution figure in their spec sheet, which is a software-enhanced resolution, rather than the optical resolution of the scanner. Optical resolution is the figure to go by when making comparisons between scanner models.

It's also worth considering that you may not need a high resolution to start with. A 35mm frame scanned at 4000 dpi is enough to give you a high-quality A3 (12 x 16in) print, which is about the limit of enlargement from this film size.

Dmax

Dmax indicates the maximum density that the scanner can 'see' detail in. This figure isn't a consideration with negative film, as both black-and-white and colour negatives have a tinted film base and a relatively low Dmax (typically in the range of 2.0–2.5). As long as your scanner has a Dmax of 3.0 or more – and most flatbeds and film scanners do – you can scan the full tonal range.

However, slide film has a clear film base, so there's a much greater dynamic range between the clear, white highlights and deep shadows. The Dmax of slide film is at least 3.0, and possibly as high as 3.6. If you want to shoot and scan slides, you'll need a scanner with a Dmax of 4.0, found on higher-end dedicated film scanners.

Infrared dust removal

This feature is found in some older models of scanners, and it uses infrared light to detect dust and scratches on the film's surface. The scanner software 'intelligently' removes the defects, replacing them with detail in the final scan. It's a useful time saver, especially if you do a lot of scanning, but it's worth keeping an eye on the process to make sure the software doesn't remove fine detail alongside any defects.

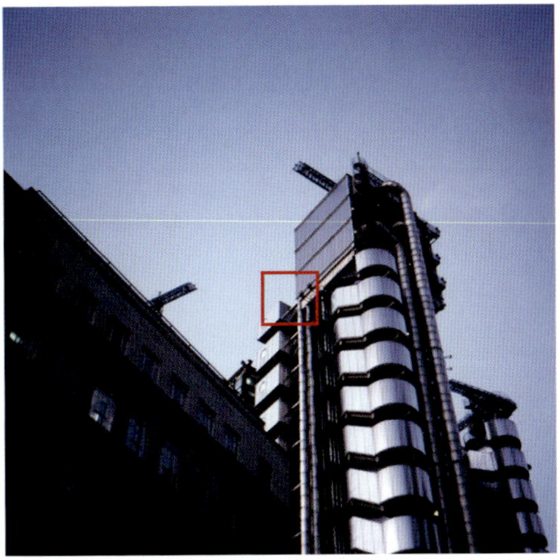

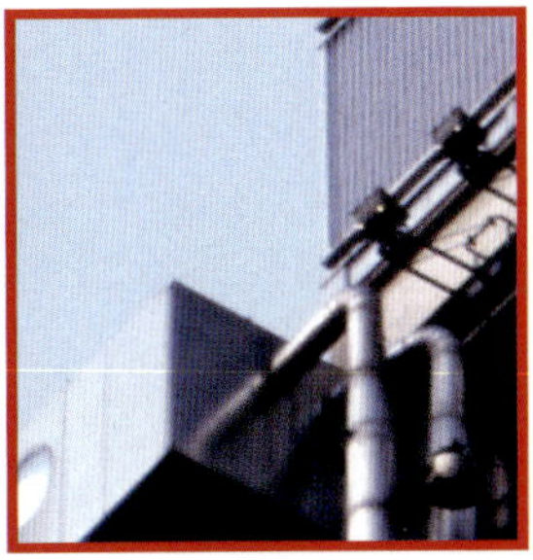

DUST AND SCRATCHES

Your scanner's dust removal tool is a double-edged sword. On one hand it is likely to make dust spots disappear; on the other, it can soften images.

SCANNING ESSENTIALS

Whether you use a flatbed scanner or a dedicated film scanner, the basic scanning process is very similar. In general, slide film is easier to scan than negatives because you're working with a positive image.

The actual software (scanner driver) you use to make your scans largely depends on the scanner. Some ship with a proprietary scanner driver, while others rely on a third-party driver, but they ultimately do the same job – tell the scanner how to convert film into a digital image. In each case, the basic scanning process is relatively straightforward:

1. Load your film in the scanner's film holder. It's important that you load the film with the emulsion (matt) side towards the scanner's sensor. The film holder will likely indicate which way round the film should be.
2. Use an air blower or compressed air to dust off your film. Most scanners and/or scanner drivers offer some sort of digital dust removal, but the process can affect fine detail in an image.
3. Load the film holder into the scanner and open the scanner driver. Choose the film type you're scanning; negative or slide, colour or black and white.
4. Set the scan resolution. As a guide, scanning a 35mm film frame at 2000 dpi (dots per inch) is enough for a high-quality A4 (12 x 8in) print. Scan at a higher resolution if you intend to crop the image or print it at a larger size.
5. Set the file format to TIFF or JPEG. Generally speaking, TIFF is preferrable if you intend to edit your images further.
6. Run a preview scan so you can see the image on screen. You can now crop and adjust the photograph – changing the brightness and colour, for example – before making your final scan.

RIGHT WAY ROUND

The scanner's film holder will tell you which way round to load the film. Here, the film needs to be loaded so the frame numbers are back to front.

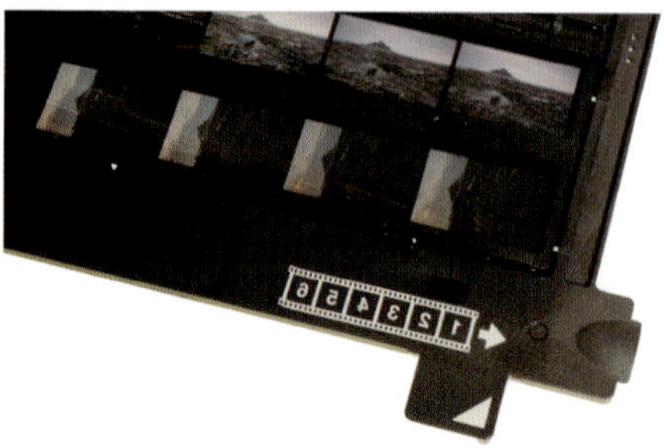

DUST FREE

An air blower is a simple way of cleaning dust from film before you scan it, saving you from doing a lot of retouching work afterwards.

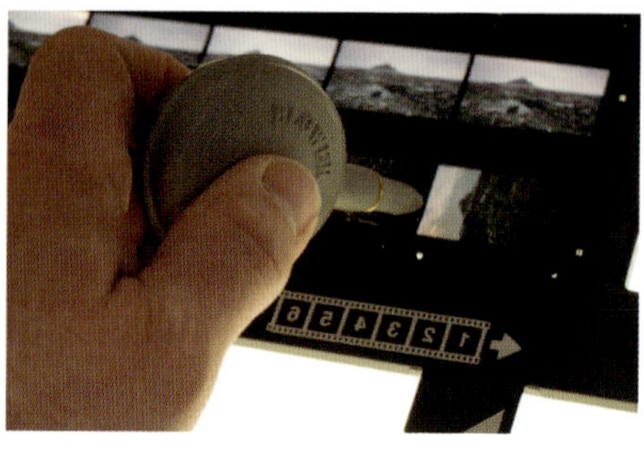

ADVANCED SCANNING

Although the basic scanning process outlined opposite can deliver a high-quality image, some scanners and scanner drivers have advanced settings that can take your scanned film to the next level.

Bit depth

Most scanners aimed at the consumer market give you a choice of making 8-bit black-and-white scans or 24-bit colour scans. In a greyscale image, this means there can be up to 256 tones, from pure black to pure white. Colour images contain up to 256 colours in each of the three colour channels (red, green, blue), giving you 16.7 million colours overall.

This might sound like a lot, but some scanner drivers let you make 16-bit greyscale scans, with 65,535 tones, and 48-bit RGB images, with just over 281 trillion colours – a huge increase! You might not see an immediate difference on screen, but if you do any editing work on your scans, having a greater bit depth ensures images won't start to break down.

Raw files

As well as saving your scans as TIFFs or JPEGs, you may also have the option to save your scans in the Raw DNG format. This type of file can be treated in the same way as a Raw file from a digital camera, allowing you to make non-destructive changes to the exposure, colour, tone, and so on. If you are making 48-bit colour (or 16-bit greyscale) scans, saving them as Raw files is the logical choice.

Multi-pass scanning

When you hit the 'scan' button, a scanner typically buzzes into life, runs the scanning head across your film to read the information, and gives you a scanned frame. However, some scanners let you scan the same frame multiple times and combine these multiple passes into a single final image.

This has a couple of benefits. Not only can it reduce noise – especially in darker areas – but it can sometimes be combined with a multiple exposure option to increase the dynamic range in a scan. The downside is that it takes longer to make multi-pass scans, and the more passes you make, the longer it takes. Increasing the number of passes can also soften your images slightly.

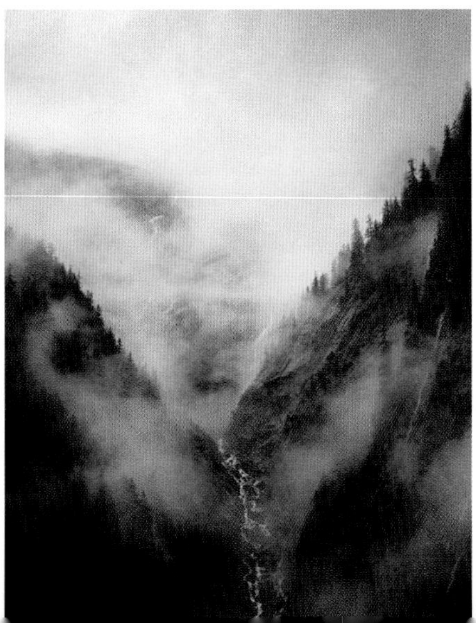

HIGH-END SCANS

Combining 16-bit greyscale scanning with a Raw DNG file meant there was plenty of leeway when it came to fine-tuning this black-and-white landscape in Photoshop.

CAMERA AS SCANNER

As good as scanners are, they're becoming harder to source, and if anything goes wrong with them it's increasingly difficult to get them repaired. If you only use your scanner occasionally there's also the chance that it will end up in a cupboard or on a shelf, so you'll have to spend time setting it up, and then try and remember how the software works.

An easier alternative – and cheaper if you already own one – is to use a digital SLR or mirrorless camera to digitise your film. There are plenty of adaptors and devices available that will help you do this, such as second-hand vintage slide copiers from the 70s and 80s that you attach instead of a lens to modern equipment. These allow you to shoot film with an existing lens. Alternatively, try a zero-cost DIY approach, and make a simple card frame to tape to a window – see what works best for you.

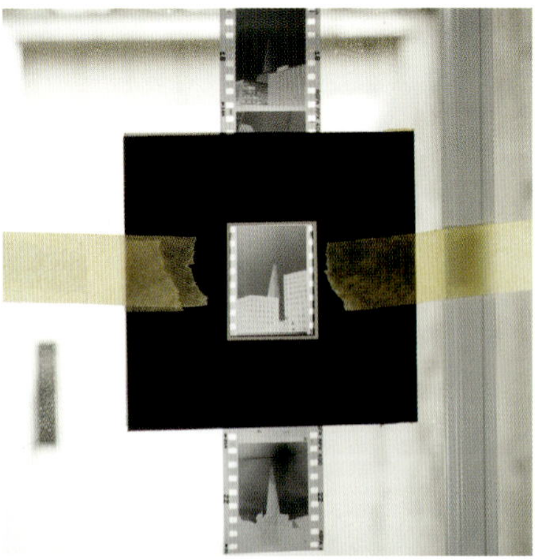

DIY FRAME

A card frame taped to a window is a simple, yet effective, way of shooting negatives.

SETTINGS

Whichever option you choose, you need to optimise the settings on your digital camera to get the best 'scans'.

- **Format:** Set your digital camera to shoot Raw files, as this will give you the most image data to work with. If you prefer to shoot JPEGs, choose a neutral preset (picture mode) so you're not increasing the saturation or contrast.
- **White balance:** Set the white balance manually to match the colour temperature of the light source you're using to backlight your film. Don't rely on auto white balance – especially if you're shooting colour negatives – as any dominant colour in the image could fool the camera into adding a false colour shift to compensate.
- **Lens:** Unless you're using a copier that has a built-in lens, you need a lens on your digital camera. The best type for this purpose is a prime macro lens. Not only does it allow you to focus closely, but a macro lens exhibits minimal distortion – ideal for photographing flat film.
- **Focus:** If your camera will focus automatically on your film, go for it. If not, switch to manual focus. Either way, it's a good idea to mount the camera on a tripod so the camera-to-film distance is locked down and there's no chance of the distance (and focus) shifting.
- **Exposure:** Most lenses perform best at a mid-range aperture of around f/8, and you should set the ISO at 100 for optimum quality. If your camera is on a tripod, shutter speed is largely irrelevant.

SHOOTING FILM

The film scanning adaptor shown below combines a film-scanner-style film holder with a USB-powered LED light source. It's not the most sophisticated piece of kit, but it's not the most primitive, either – nor is it the most expensive. Here's how it works:

1. Fit a macro lens to your digital camera and mount the camera on a tripod. You can shoot hand-held, but it's best if everything is locked down on a tripod.
2. Load the 35mm film strip into the adaptor and use the built-in stand to position the adaptor on a table. Alternatively, mount it on a tripod.
3. Switch on the adapter's LEDs and line your camera up with the film. Take your time. Fill the frame as much as possible with the film, and have your camera parallel to the film – the more square-on the camera is to the film, the sharper the scan will be from edge-to-edge.
4. Set the focus and white balance manually; the adaptor below uses LEDs with a colour temperature of 6500K. This is the best setting to ensure there is no colour cast in the scan.
5. Set the exposure using aperture priority mode. Use ISO 100 to keep noise to a minimum, and set the aperture at f/8. The camera will choose the shutter speed, but use Live View to make sure the exposure isn't too light or too dark.
6. Make a test exposure, triggering the camera with an electronic release or the self-timer to avoid movement as it's fired.
7. Check the exposure on the camera's LCD, using the histogram to guide you. If necessary, use exposure compensation to lighten/darken the exposure, then shoot again.
8. Download the images to your computer for processing. How much processing you do will largely come down to the original film format and personal preference. If you're scanning negatives these will need converting to positive images; if it's slides, you might not need to change anything.

ALIGNMENT

Make sure that the camera and film are parallel. The more closely aligned the sensor and film are, the better the result will be.

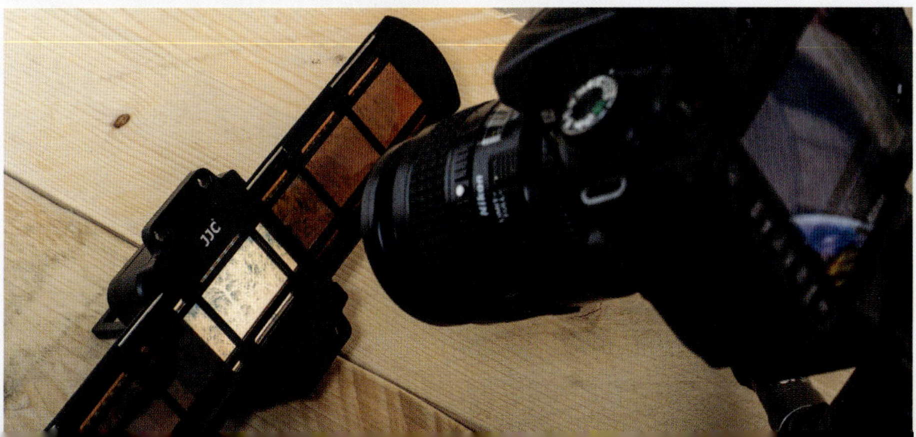

NEGATIVE SCANS

While slides are relatively easy to scan – providing your scanner has a good Dmax – the same can't be said of negatives. Black-and-white negatives are tonally inverted, which makes them tricky to 'read', but it's not impossible. However, the heavy orange/brown film base and reversed colours of a colour negative make them almost impenetrable when viewed in Raw form.

A scanner has the same problem. It not only needs to reverse the tones in the image to create a positive version, but in the case of colour negatives it also needs to reverse the colour *and* remove the orange colour film base. If this weren't enough to deal with, the colour of the film base on different colour negative emulsions varies between manufacturers and individual films, so there's no single correct conversion.

Faced with all these variables, most scanner drivers resort to an automatic colour negative scanning option to deal with a myriad of films. It's not surprising that most scanners struggle to get the best result.

However, if you're serious about getting the best scans from your negatives, dedicated negative conversion software may be the answer. There are various options available, from premium-priced apps, to plug-ins that work with existing image-editing software.

They are designed to tackle the tricky process of converting colour negative scans to positive images, regardless of whether you use a conventional scanner or a digital camera to digitise film.

Some do this through preset conversion options, some use sophisticated algorithms, and others take the individual characteristics of specific emulsions into account to ensure your scanned image is as true to the original film as possible.

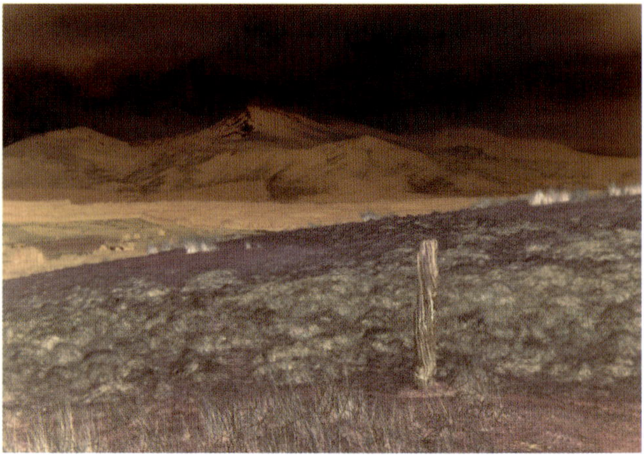

READING NEGATIVES

Trying to work out what the picture on a colour negative is can be tricky. Not only is the image reversed tonally, but it also has a strong orange colouration.

CONVERSION OPTIONS

The are numerous negative conversion apps and plug-ins, many of which offer a trial version so you can 'try before you buy'. Here are a few to get you started:

- **CS Negative+ Convert Tools (CineStill):** This plug-in provides multiple presets to convert your colour negatives through Adobe Creative Cloud products.
- **ColorNeg (ColorPerfect):** Not the prettiest-looking Photoshop extension, but conversions are based on the characteristics of individual emulsions, rather than automated algorithms.
- **FilmLab:** A stand-alone app with both desktop and mobile versions, the latter enabling you to use your phone to digitise your film.
- **SmartConvert (Filmomat):** This app was inspired by industrial scanners to provide simple and powerful negative conversions.
- **Negative Lab Pro:** An Adobe Lightroom plug-in that claims to provide lab-quality conversions from Raw files.

COLOUR CONVERSION

If you regularly shoot and scan colour negatives, a dedicated conversion app is worth considering, as it takes a lot of the guesswork out of the colour conversion process.

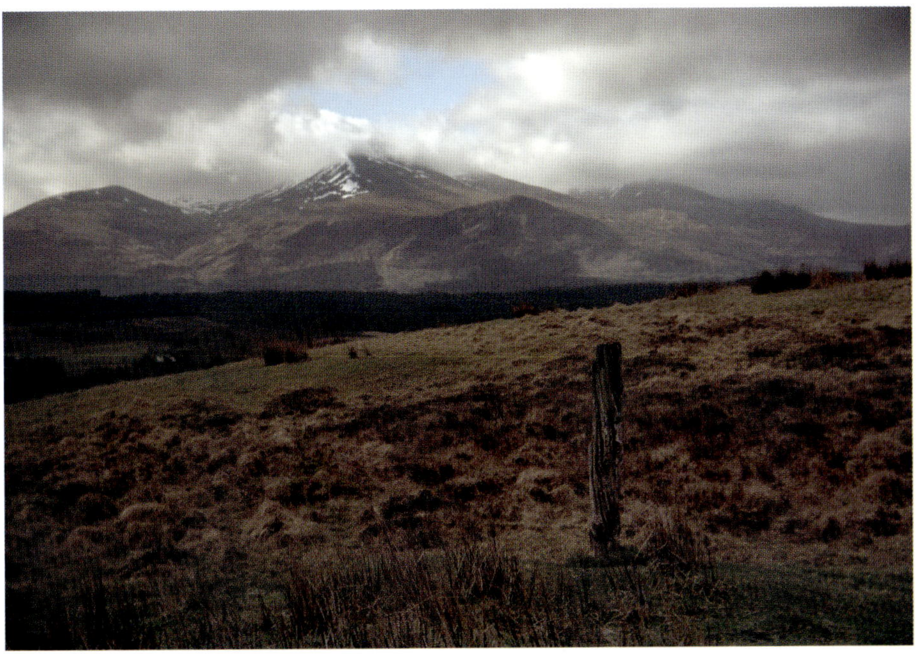

FAULT FINDER

Whether you're using a manual, mechanical SLR, or an electronic model with a high level of automation, things can sometimes go wrong. It's not always easy to understand the reason, as some faults have similar effects, but the most common problems you're likely to encounter are described here – along with advice on how to avoid them in the future.

FOCUS

Subject out of focus

Problem: The most important part of the picture is fuzzy and indistinct, while other areas are sharp.

Cause: This is a focusing problem; the camera has focused somewhere other than the subject. Exactly what type of problem it is will depend on the kind of camera used. If it's an autofocus camera, the chances are that the focusing sensor at the centre of the viewfinder area has missed the main subject, perhaps focusing on the background instead. If it's a manual focus camera, then the focus has not been set accurately.

Cure: With an autofocus camera, make sure the main subject falls under the central focusing window, or use focus lock to ensure that an off-centre subject is correctly focused. With a manual focus camera, use the microprism/split-image aid at the centre of the viewfinder to ensure critical focus. If problems persist, it may be worth having your vision tested.

Picture blurred

Problem: The whole picture is blurred.

Cause: Camera shake; the camera moved while the shutter was open.

Cure: When hand-holding your camera, aim to set a shutter speed that is the reciprocal of the focal length of the lens in use. If it's a 50mm lens, use at least 1/60 sec; for 200mm, use 1/250 sec; for 600mm, use 1/1000 sec. If those speeds are not possible with the film you're using and/or the aperture you want, use a tripod and a cable release to avoid jarring the camera when the shutter is triggered.

EXPOSURE

Picture too dark

Problem: The picture is too dark.

Cause: The shot is underexposed – not enough light has fallen on it. The exact problem depends on the camera used and the picture-taking situation. If the subject was extremely light in tone, or you were shooting into the light, it's likely that the camera's meter was fooled by the excess brightness. If you were using manual mode, it is more likely to be user error.

Cure: Use exposure compensation when dealing with light/bright subjects. If you suspect a metering fault, have the camera checked at a repair centre.

Picture too light

Problem: The picture is too light.

Cause: The film has suffered overexposure – too much light has fallen on it. As with pictures that are too dark, the exact problem depends on the camera and the picture-taking situation. If the subject was extremely dark, the camera's meter may have been fooled by excessive darkness. If you were using manual mode, it is more likely to be user error.

If the problem affects the entire roll of film, the ISO may have been set incorrectly. Alternatively, exposure compensation may be set to a positive (+) value.

Cure: Use exposure compensation when dealing with dark subjects. If you suspect a metering fault, the camera may need to be checked and repaired.

Entire film too dark (or too light)

Problem: All of the photographs on a roll of film are too dark (or too light).

Cause: If the exposure is 'off' on an entire roll of film, the ISO may be have been set incorrectly for the type of film, or the exposure compensation dial wasn't set to '0' – or it wasn't reset after a previous exposure.

Cure: Check the film speed was set correctly and exposure compensation isn't dialled in. If either one is wrong, make a note to double-check them next time.

If the film speed was set correctly and exposure compensation is at '0', it may be a metering fault. Take a look at the film – particularly if the entire roll of film is too light. Check the density of the 'gaps' between the frames and film edges (rebate).

On slide film, these areas should be black; if they are lighter (and the entire film is too light), the film has been fogged, possibly by brief exposure to light when it was being loaded for processing. On negatives, the rebate would appear darker. This is harder to gauge, but can be checked visually against another, correctly exposed film.

Black band

Problem: There's a black band across part of a photograph.

Cause: The most likely, the picture was taken using flash, but the wrong flash sync speed was set. When this happens, the camera's shutter starts to close before the entire frame has been exposed, creating a dark band; the faster the shutter speed, the wider the band.

Another possibility – although less likely – is that the film did not travel correctly through the lab's automated processing machinery.

Cure: When using electronic flash, make sure that the shutter speed is never faster than the manufacturer's recommended sync speed. This tends to be between 1/60 sec and 1/125 sec on amateur cameras, and 1/200 sec to 1/250 sec for professional models (if in doubt, use 1/60 sec). There is no problem if you use a longer (slower) shutter speed.

If flash wasn't used, contact the processing lab for their opinion.

Bleached-out face

Problem: On a portrait taken with flash, the face is white and harshly lit.

Cause: The flash was too close to the subject, resulting in overexposure.

Cure: If you're using a built-in flash, keep at least 1–1.5m (3–5ft) between you and your subject; for a hotshoe flash, turn the power down or use a different auto setting.

Fitting a diffuser or bouncing the light from a wall or ceiling will also soften the flash and weaken its intensity.

Double-exposed film

Problem: There are two sets of images all the way down the film, with images overlapping each other.

Cause: The film has been put through the camera twice.

Cure: If you don't want to unintentionally experiment with multiple exposures, you need to know when a film has been exposed. The easiest way to do this is to make sure the leader is fully wound back into the cassette when you finish a roll. Some electronic SLRs let you choose between 'leader in' and 'leader out' settings (choose 'in'), while you can simply rewind the film a few times more on a manual camera. If the leader does remain sticking out slightly, manually rotate the top part of the film cassette to draw it in.

Obscured corner

Problem: A strange, round, orange shape appears at the corner of the picture or along the edge.

Cause: Your finger was partly over the lens when the picture was taken.

Cure: Hold the camera at both sides so that your fingers can't stray over the lens.

Flare

Problem: Loss of contrast and sharpness when shooting towards the light, possibly with obvious bright shapes in the frame.

Cause: Flare is caused by non-image-forming light being scattered by reflections within a lens or the inside of the camera. This light can reduce the overall image contrast and detail in a shot, or reveal itself as obvious bright polygons (the shape of which tends to echo the shape of the lens aperture).

Cure: Avoid light falling directly onto the front element of the lens by changing position so you're in shade, fitting an effective lens hood, or holding your hand above the lens (just out of shot) to block out the sunlight.

COLOUR

Orange cast

Problem: The picture has an overall orange colour or cast.

Cause: Common when pictures are taken indoors/under tungsten or halogen lighting, using daylight-balanced film. Although our eyes may not see it, these light sources give out light that is extremely orange in colour.

Cure: One option is to use flash to override the tungsten lighting, although that may alter the mood of the shot. Alternatively, you could fit a blue (80A) colour-correction filter or load up with a film specifically designed for use under tungsten lighting. Finally, you could shoot in black and white, as the colour of the light would be irrelevant.

Orange patches

Problem: Some parts of the picture look fine, but other parts have bright orange patches on them.

Cause: The film has been partially fogged. That is, stray light fell on it before it was processed. The most likely explanation is that the camera back was opened accidentally as the film was being loaded, or that the back itself has a light leak (most often due to failed light seals). Occasionally, the problem can be caused by a faulty felt light trap on the film cassette, and rarely the damage can occur at the lab.

Cure: Check the light traps in the back of the camera – are there any areas that are obviously perished? If so, they will need replacing. If not, shoot another film to see if the problem repeats itself; use the cheapest film you can find. If it happens again, suspect a leak in the camera and recheck the light seals.

If the film looks fine, the problem may have been a one-off. Always ensure the film back is never opened while a film is loaded.

Red-eye

Problem: People have glowing red eyes in pictures taken with electronic flash.

Cause: The flash was reflected back from the blood vessels at the back of the eyes.

Cure: If you have an external flash with a bounce head, use it to bounce the light off the ceiling or wall. Alternatively, take the flash off the camera and hold it to one side. Try not to aim the flash directly at your subject from the camera position, especially if you want them looking into the lens.

If that's not possible, use the camera's red-eye reduction facility (if it has one). If not, switch on the lights so the pupils of your subjects' eyes shrink, minimising the risk.

MECHANICAL

Overlapping frames

Problem: All the images on the film overlap and run into each other.

Cause: The film didn't advance correctly through the camera. The first frame was not fully wound on, with the result that part of the next frame was exposed on top of it.

Cure: On most cameras this is not a user-error – it is a mechanical (or electronic) failure in the camera that needs repairing.

Mirror stuck

Problem: Camera fired, but the mirror didn't flip back down.

Cause: The battery just ran out or your camera is in need of repair/replacement.

Cure: Replace the battery with a fresh one that you know is 'good' (not that rogue cell that's been out of the packet in the bottom of a drawer for the past year or so). Has it fixed the problem? If not, it may be time to have your camera repaired and/or look for a replacement.

No images

Problem: There's nothing on the film.

Cause: If you're lucky, you've processed an unexposed film (we've all been there). If you're unlucky, your camera and/or lens has malfunctioned.

Cure: Set your camera to manual mode, open the back (without film in it), and hold it out in front of you, pointing at a light source. Look through the back of the camera and fire the shutter at a variety of shutter speeds and aperture settings. If everything's working as it should, you should see light coming through the lens. The shutter duration should also change, as should the aperture size. It should be easy to tell if either the lens aperture or camera shutter isn't opening, in which case you will know what needs to be repaired or replaced.

PROCESSING

Light band

Problem: A light band of undeveloped emulsion along the entire edge of a home-processed black-and-white film.

Cause: Not enough developer in the processing tank.

Cure: If you use an insufficient amount of chemistry during processing, the film won't be fully submerged in it, so only part of it will be developed and/or fixed. Always check the volume of chemicals needed for your film, especially if you are developing multiple films in the same tank – the information is usually stamped on the bottom of the processing tank.

Low-contrast negatives

Problem: The negatives are flat with weak highlights.

Cause: Under-development.

Cure: Make sure the film is developed for the full amount of time and at the correct temperature. Reducing the development time and/or developer temperature will mean the film is not developed sufficiently. If the time and temperature are correct, check the developer dilution isn't too weak; if you're reusing developer, it could be exhausted.

High-contrast negatives

Problem: The negatives have high contrast, with blocked highlights.

Cause: Over-development.

Cure: Excessive development time, high temperature, and overly strong developer solution can all lead to over-development that results in contrasty negatives.

Fogging

Problem: The negatives have an overall grey veil across both the image frame and the rebate (edges).

Cause: Film has been exposed to light.

Cure: This typically happens when the film is being loaded into the developing tank, because the room you are working in isn't completely light tight. LED standby lights on electronic devices are often culprits, as are light leaks around doors or blackout window blinds. If you're using a changing bag to load your film, it may have a tear in it or a faulty zipper.

Bubbles

Problem: Round circles appear when you enlarge your negatives.

Cause: Air bubbles attached to film during development.

Cure: When you pour in the developer you can introduce tiny air bubbles into the solution that can attach themselves to your film. Regular (but not continuous) agitation of the film should remove these, but it is also good practice to give the developing tank a tap on your workspace after your agitate it, to knock any bubbles free.

Film fading over time

Problem: Your negatives start to darken over time.

Cause: Film is insufficiently fixed.

Cure: Ensure you fix your film for the recommended duration. If you spot your negatives fading early enough, you can re-fix the film with minimal loss, but leave it too late and your images will be lost.

Water spots

Problem: There's a 'crusty' residue on your film and/or circular marks.

Cause: Film washed in 'hard' water.

Cure: If you live in a hard-water area (you'll know this if limescale regularly builds up in your kettle) it's important to use a wetting agent after washing the film. This helps to stop residue in the water sticking to the film.

Colour shifts

Problem: Your colour film (negative or slide) exhibits a universal colour bias.

Cause: Old film or incorrect processing.

Cure: If you've loaded up with out-of-date film, or left your camera in a warm place for for a few months with a film in it, chances are the film was past its best before it was processed, resulting in a colour shift. If the film was fresh and processed promptly, it's more likely that the processing was 'off' – the temperature was incorrect or the chemicals were past their best.

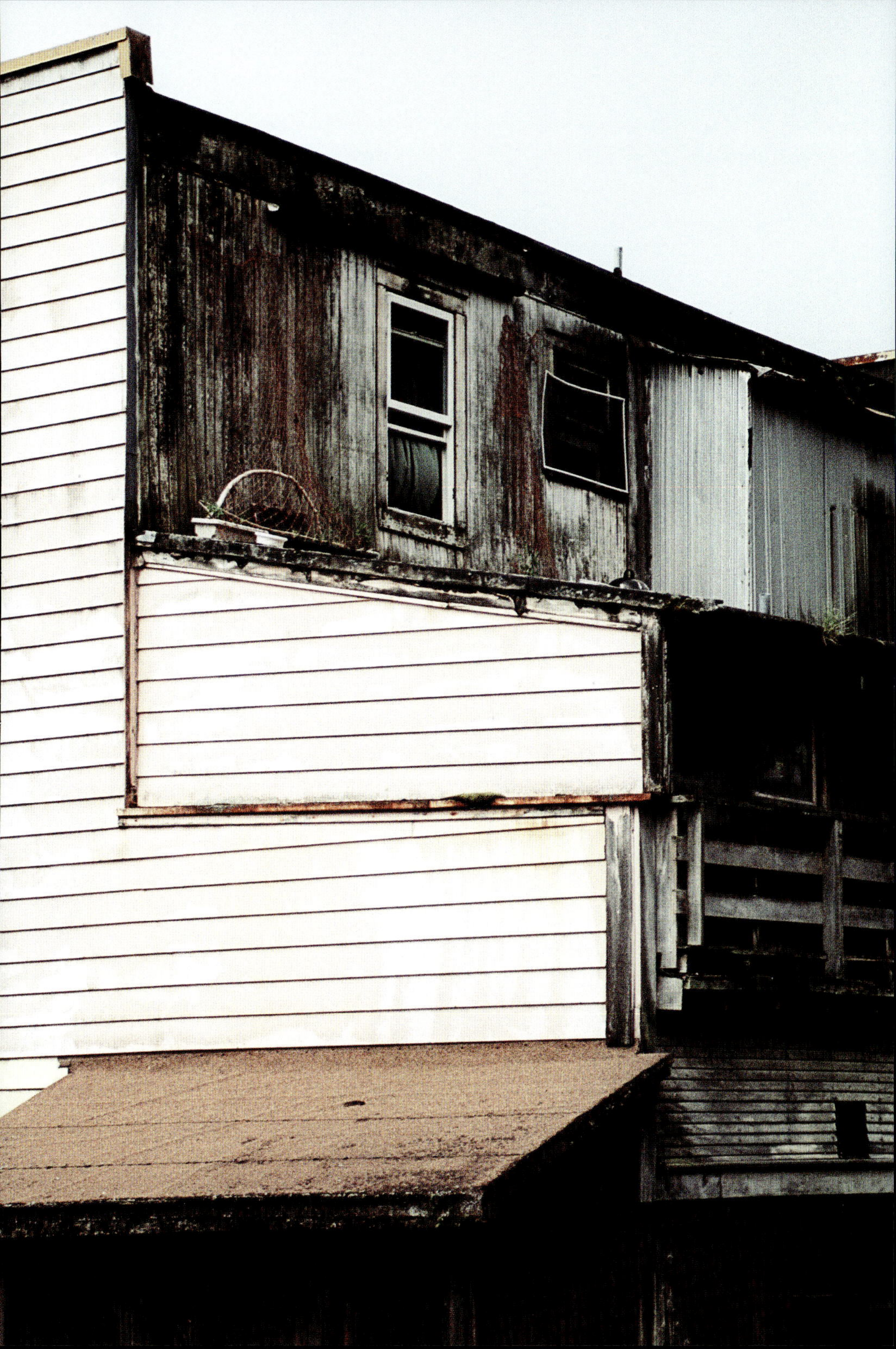

GLOSSARY

Angle of view: The area of a scene that a lens takes in, measured in degrees. Also referred to as the 'field of view'.

Aperture: A variable opening in a lens, measured in f/stops, which determines the amount of light passing through to the film.

Aperture priority: A shooting mode whereby the photographer selects the aperture, and the camera chooses an appropriate shutter speed to deliver the correct exposure. Typically used when controlling the depth of field in a photograph is of most importance, as in landscape photography.

C41: The standard process for colour negative film, involving developer, bleach, fixer, and stabiliser steps.

Colour temperature: The colour of a light source, measured in degrees Kelvin (K). Most colour film has a daylight white balance of 5500K; filters may be needed when photographing under different light sources to avoid colour casts.

Depth of Field (DOF): The area in front of and behind the point of focus that also appears acceptably sharp in a photograph. Its extent is determined by the aperture, camera-to-subject distance, and focal length.

Dmax: Short for maximum density; the darkest tone that a film can produce detail in, or that a scanner can record detail in.

E6: The standard process for colour transparency film, typically involving developer, colour/reversal, bleach/fix ('blix'), and stabiliser steps.

Emulsion: The suspension of light-sensitive halides in gelatin, which can be coated onto a flexible base to make photographic film, or onto glass or metal to create photographic plates.

f/stop: The fractional representation of the size of the aperture, determined by the focal length of the lens and diameter of the iris.

Focal length: The distance from the optical centre of a lens to the surface of the film, usually expressed in millimetres.

Incident light reading: A light reading based on the light falling onto the subject.

ISO: The unit of measurement used to indicate the sensitivity of film to light; the higher the ISO, the more sensitive it is. In the past, other units have been used, including ASA, DIN, and GOST.

Large format: A film and camera format, including 5 x 4in, 5 x7in, and 10 x 8in image formats, which use individual sheets of film.

Latent image: When an exposure is made on film, the image is 'invisible' – or latent – until it is revealed through the developing process.

Lens flare: An aberration caused when non-image-forming light reflects and refracts in the lens before reaching the film. It can show as distinct polygons or an overall lack of contrast, and is common with old, uncoated lenses.

Light leak: A camera fault whereby light 'leaks' into the camera rather than passing through the lens. Often a sign that the light seals in a camera need replacing.

Miniature film: Historic name for 35mm film, now more frequently used to refer to sub-35mm-sized film formats, such as 110 and Minox film.

Multi-area metering: A sophisticated metering pattern that breaks a scene down into distinct areas (or zones), which are analysed individually and then averaged out to give a single exposure reading.

OTF (Off-The-Film): An exposure metering system that uses a sensor to measure the light reaching the surface of the film. Can be used to measure ambient light or – with a compatible flash unit – to gauge flash exposures, functioning as a precursor to TTL flash control.

Overexposure: Caused when too much light reaches the film during an exposure. The image is overly bright, with burnt-out highlights and light shadow areas.

Parallax: When the camera viewfinder doesn't see what the lens sees. This problem most commonly occurs with rangefinder and TLR cameras, when the subject is close to the camera.

Rangefinder: A camera design that utilises two views of the same scene to achieve focus – most often executed manually. Focus is achieved when the two images align perfectly.

Reciprocity failure: The breakdown in film's response to light as exposure times become very long (or, less commonly, very short).

Roll film: A photographic film that is wound onto a spool, as opposed to single sheets. Common sizes include 120, 220, 620, and 127, of which 120 is the most common today, as used in medium format film cameras. Strictly speaking, 35mm film is also a roll film, although it tends to be treated separately as it comes in a metal cartridge.

Shutter priority: A shooting mode whereby the photographer selects the shutter speed, and the camera chooses an appropriate aperture to deliver the correct exposure. Typically used when controlling the appearance of movement in a photograph is of most importance, as in sports photography.

SLR (Single Lens Reflex): A camera design that uses a pentaprism and mirror to direct the image projected through the lens to the viewfinder. This provides the photographer with the same view as the lens, allowing accurate framing.

Spot metering: An exposure metering pattern that measures the light from a small (usually central) area of the scene. Useful for taking manual exposure readings in tricky lighting conditions but requires experience to identify an appropriate tone to meter from.

TLR (Twin Lens Reflex): A camera design that has two lenses: one for viewing the image, and one for making an exposure. The advantage is that the viewfinder doesn't 'black out' when the shutter fires, allowing for a continuous view of the subject.

TTL (Through-The-Lens): A metering system that measures the light passing through the lens at the time of shooting. Can be used to measure ambient light and/or flash with a compatible flash unit.

Underexposure: Caused when not enough light reaches the film to make the correct exposure. The image is darkened overall, with muddy highlights and dense, featureless shadows.

Viewfinder: An optical system used for framing the subject. Can be eye-level, as found in SLR and rangefinder cameras, or waist-level, as in TLR cameras and some medium format SLRs, such as Hasselblads.

Vignetting darkening: Seen at the corners of an image. It can be caused by something partially obstructing the lens, such as an incorrect lens hood or stacked filters, in which case it is 'mechanical' vignetting, or can be caused by the design of the lens, in which case it is 'optical' vignetting.

Zone System: A system developed in the 1930s by Ansel Adams and Fred Archer for controlling the tones in a black-and-white image. It uses a combination of exposure and film development techniques to create the optimum black-and-white negative for printing on fixed-grade photographic paper.

INDEX

A DAVID AND CHARLES BOOK

David and Charles is an imprint of David and Charles, Ltd, Suite A, Tourism House, Pynes Hill, Exeter, EX2 5WS

EU GPSR Authorised Representative:
Logos Europe, 9 rue Nicolas Poussin, 17000, La Rochelle, France
Email: contact@logoseurope.eu

Some content originally published as *35mm Photography: The Complete Guide* in 2004
This edition first published in the UK and USA in 2026

A catalogue record for this book is available from the British Library.

ISBN-13: 9781446317853 flexiback
ISBN-13: 9781446317860 EPUB

This book has been printed on paper from approved suppliers and made from pulp from sustainable sources.

FSC
www.fsc.org
MIX
Paper | Supporting responsible forestry
FSC® C020056

Printed in China by Leo Paper Products Ltd for: David and Charles, Ltd, Suite A, Tourism House, Pynes Hill, Exeter, EX2 5WS

10 9 8 7 6 5 4 3 2 1

Publishing Director: Ame Verso
Senior Commissioning Editor: Nigel Browning
Publishing Manager: Jeni Chown
Editorial Assistant: Jenna McGill
Copy Editor: Belinda Gallagher
Lead Designer: Sam Staddon
Designers: Giulia Sandri and Kirsty Kaye
Pre-press Designer: Susan Reansbury
Production Manager: Beverley Richardson

David and Charles publishes high-quality books on a wide range of subjects. For more information visit www.davidandcharles.com.

Share your images with us on social media using #dandcbooks and follow us on Facebook and Instagram by searching for @dandcbooks.

Layout of the digital edition of this book may vary depending on reader hardware and display settings.